The Likeness

ETHNOGRAPHIC STUDIES IN SUBJECTIVITY

Tanya Luhrmann, Editor

The Likeness

SEMBLANCE AND SELF
IN SLOVENE SOCIETY

Gretchen Bakke

UNIVERSITY OF CALIFORNIA PRESS

University of California Press
Oakland, California

Cataloging-in-Publication Data is on file at the Library of Congress.

ISBN 9780520320031 (cloth : alk. paper)
ISBN 9780520320048 (pbk. : alk. paper)
ISBN 9780520974173 (ebook)

29 28 27 26 25 24 23 22 21 20
10 9 8 7 6 5 4 3 2 1

With thanks, to Georges Bataille

Time and again for more than two millennia the people we call "Western" have been haunted by the specter of their own inner being: an apparition of human nature so avaricious and contentious that, unless it is somehow governed it will reduce society to anarchy.

Marshall Sahlins, 2008

Couples are wholes and not wholes, what agrees disagrees, the concordant is discordant

Heraclitus, -535 (give or take)

Contents

Illustrations

Preface

Andandpersand

There is a fictive marker of punctuation called the *andorpersand*. It's a joke, a sort of swirly doubled ampersand in which one bit stands upright in the normal way (&) and the other is caught lying down (⅋). It is described as "one simple symbol for 'and/or'" and included on a short list of punctuation marks that should exist but do not. This list also includes the *Morgan Freemark*—a kind of quotation mark that intimates one should read what is written in the voice of Morgan Freeman—and the *sinceroid,* which lets the reader know that what comes next no matter how sarcastic-seeming should in fact be taken as truth (its opposite, the *sarcastises,* also makes the list—all from themuse.com). Graphically, the andorpersand has a pivot point, such that one could build a mandala of them—or a compass rose—an ampersand for each of the cardinal directions (four, eight, sixteen), one layered upon the next until it looks like a crappy picture of a flower.[1] ❀ Still a punctuation mark, this odd floret—now an *andandpersand*—would be used to signal moments of "aesthetic thickening" (Lewis 2019). When adding the flower to the soup, one gets not a deeper or more flavorful outcome, but a denser, more complex one,

1. Andandpersand design by Stinson Lenz.

marked by layers of meaning and interpretation (four, eight, sixteen) that are also relatively easy to overlook.

This is after all part of the fun, not seeing the trees for the forest they constitute, yet nevertheless feeling them there (oak *and* oak *and* pine *and* linden *and* ferns *and* badgers *and* blackflies *and* a wind that blows through it all). One can call it by the name *forest* but in so doing the nuance is lost— the infinite *and and and* of interrelated constituents that makes a forest what it is. The andandpersand does not name every element that could possibly constitute a thing—this would be dizzying—rather it points only to those that can be simultaneously perceived just by stopping, taking a breath, pivoting, and noticing. In this, it is the anthropologist's punctuation mark; a method in ink. The andandpersand is minimally artful— which will matter to this story—and it is surprisingly uneasy, because it marks a sentence, an utterance, a claim with an emphatic partiality. "The whole," to quote Adorno, "is the untrue" (1978, 50). "Indicating," Slovene curator and theorist Igor Zabel continues, "that the effect of completeness and wholeness is essentially ideological. If this is so, then that which is incomplete, unordered, and heterogeneous might, in fact, point a way to the true" (Zabel, n.d.).

All that is a long way from here. It comes into full flower around page 105; this is only the second page, incomplete and heterogeneous by its nature (slightly unordered by my own). Let us begin, rather, in a proper and scholarly way with a parable and a trap.

The philosopher Mladen Dolar in a short book published in English with MIT Press in 2006 presents on page 77 the story of Zeuxis and Parrhasius, two Roman painters engaged in a not entirely friendly competition. Dolar attributes his version of this story to Lacan, who told the tale in his eleventh seminar, published first in 1964, and later included in the 1979 Penguin volume entitled *Four Fundamental Concepts of Psychoanalysis* edited by J.-A. Miller. Lacan, for his part states that he borrowed the story (via what intermediary I do not know) from Pliny the Elder who recounted it in his *Naturalis Historia,* written some time around the year 78 AD. Where Pliny got it from is unclear, but by the time he put it to paper the story had been around at least five hundred years (rumor has it that Aristotle really did loathe Zeuxis back in the fourth century BC). The point of relaying this flow of attribution is that, as I string this parable (which is also a trap), it would be wise to consider your-self warned that borrowings, in this book as a whole, will be rampant. The origin stories of likenesses, which fall everywhere and all about with a gentle patter like rain, can be traced, as I have done here, but this is often the least interesting thing one can do with them.[2]

The story Dolar (and all the rest) tells goes like this: Zeuxis and Parrhasius were both remarkable painters, the best of their generation. Their brilliance at their art, however, did not translate into friendly rela-tions, as both wanted the matter of who was the best painter definitively settled. They decided to enter into a competition in which each would attempt to out-paint the other. Their theme was deception.

Zeuxis painted some lovely grapes hanging heavy upon the vine and Parrhasius set himself to the decoration of a wall. Here is Dolar quoting Lacan, himself paraphrasing Pliny the Elder:

> In the classical tale . . . Zeuxis has the advantage of having made grapes that attracted the birds. The stress is not placed on the fact that these grapes were in any way perfect grapes, but on the fact that even the eye of the birds was taken in by them . . . his friend Parrhasius [however] triumphs over him for having painted on the wall a veil, a veil so lifelike that Zeuxis, turning toward him said, Well, and now show us what you have painted behind it. (Lacan 1979: 103). (Dolar 2006, 77)

Dolar, without Lacan, continues:

> There are two opposed strategies of deception: the birds are duped by looks, the animals are deceived by the appearance of reality; while the humans are deceived by the veil which does not merely imitate reality but conceals it. The properly human way of deception is the lure: the deception lies in the fact that the gaze has been enticed to penetrate behind the veil of

2. Of the similar tendency of Kuna grammar to "not readily make a distinction between direct and indirect quotations," Michael Taussig (1993) writes (quoting Sherzer 1983), "'it becomes very difficult at each moment in the narration to decode exactly who is speaking.' This difficulty holds for outside analysts (such as himself [Sherzer]) as well as for native members of the community. He [Sherzer] quotes a chant in which the chanter is quoting his teacher who is quoting a mythical hero who is quoting a Chocó Indian, who is quoting a chief in the spirit world who is quoting God (and I [Taussig] am quoting him [Sherzer] quoting this chanter who . . .)." Such that "what one is listening to at a given moment is always a retelling, a rehearsing, a reviewing, or a reinterpretation of something said before'" (109–10).

appearance, [yet] there is nothing behind the curtain except the subject himself who has been lured behind. The gaze has already pierced the veil and entered what cannot be seen; it was duped into taking a step behind the appearance . . . (Dolar 2006, 77)

The trap is sprung. The human animal with its proclivities has been duped as surely as the birds. Each painter knows his audience; each has devised a temptation suited to his prey. As every trap maker knows, the psychology of the animal one seeks to catch must be reflected in the structure of the trap. If you want to catch a chimpanzee, you build a trap that appeals to his curiosity.[3] If you want to catch an eel you make a long dark tube within which she might comfortably secret herself. If you want to catch a mouse, cheese—like grapes to the birds—has long been acknowledged a formidable bait. Of this proclivity of effective trap makers—a category within which both Zeuxis and Parrhasius should be included—anthropologist Alfred Gell says, "It is not really the case that the trap is clever or deceitful, it is rather [that the hunter] knows his victim's habitual responses and is able to subvert them" (1999, 201).

Parrhasius is not, thus, the better painter because he "caught" Zeuxis in his artful trap while all Zeuxis caught was birds. Nobody in fact wins (despite Dolar's claims to the contrary): both have proven themselves equal in their skill and equal in their knowledge of what might snare their intended prey. But Parrhasius gets a point, and has lived long in history, for having caught a more interesting quarry. Gell's point is that, in revealing both something of its maker and something of its victim in its very form, a trap is much like an artwork, so much so in fact that we'd be right to put more of them in museums (203).

Dolar, following Lacan, is interested instead in the difference between what traps a bird and what traps a human. The bird is confused by appear-

3. "[The Pygmies] have a special trap for chimpanzees, because chimpanzees are like human beings: when they have a problem, they stop and think about what to do, instead of just running off and crying out. You cannot catch a chimpanzee in a snare because he does not run away. So the Pygmies have devised a special trap with a thread, which catches on the arm of the chimpanzee. The thread is very thin and the chimpanzee thinks he can get away. Instead of breaking the thread he pulls on it very gently to see what will happen then. At that moment a bundle with the poisoned arrow falls on it, because it has not run away like a stupid animal, like an antelope would" (Boyer 1988, 55–56, quoted in and translated by Gell 1999, 198).

ances (it pecks at painted grapes) while the human is trapped by the impression that appearances conceal something else and thus attempts to brush aside a painted curtain. But, there of course is no "behind" to step into, just as there is no veil to be pushed to the side; it is just a colorful bit of wall. The birds' beaks were thus bent; the humans' pride wounded. Though there is no "behind" to the veil, there is the assumption on Parrhasius's part of a rapacious human curiosity and the desire to uncover, reveal, discover, and divine what might be hidden behind or within what is given. The trap for the humans, Dolar says, is their own proclivity to search even when everything they need is already available to them on the surface of things.

If the andorpersand exists to signal that two things may, or may not, be true—one can be taken in by the curtain and/or see that it is just a pretty bit of wall—then the trick of the andandpersand is, in contrast, to hold both realities present in mind simultaneously: it is a curtain (*and* one can be taken in by it) *and* it is just a pretty bit of wall. The trap is to believe that only one reality or one facet of the story is the case. Gell's unlucky eel, for example, chooses to secret itself in the trap because it lives in a world governed by the *or*; when the choice is safety in a dark tight space *or* exposure in a wide open ocean, the path to continued well-being seems clear. It also makes a dinner of that eel.

Zeuxis is equally trapped, not simply for believing that a painted curtain is a real curtain, nor because he attempts to seek the truth behind the veil of the given, but because he fails the test of the andandpersand; he is snared as easily as any beast for he cannot see that the wall *and* the painting *and* the curtain *and* the trap all hang there together. Much as the andandpersand brings unrelated things into weird graphical interrelation, the wall, painting, curtain, seeking, and trap gain their substance and effect by virtue of being intertangled. Untangling them, much like tracing the historical providence of a two-thousand-year-old story, may yield a string of datums but it misses the point. It is the simultaneity of the incongruous, of history, of verbs and nouns, of interwoven references (some explicit, others left unremarked upon) that give this story (like any story) both its ferocity and its efficacy.[4]

4. "The word in language is half someone else's" (Bakhtin 1981, 293). This is as true of my words here as of Dolar's or Pliny's or Gell's or Taussig's or the Kunas' or what is in the newspaper or on the Internet. The likenesses are always there in the way words are interwoven

Parrhasius made all that needed knowing—the deception and the substance necessary to overcome the deception—complexly and intimately
available to the eye. It was all there. One can be taken in by the painting
and be attentive to the wall—Parrhasius's likeness marks out both paths.
The beauty Dolar holds, and I with him, is seeing the folly of Zeuxis's single
mindedness. One might learn, rather, to walk both paths simultaneously,
to live in the andandpersand, such that one might come to see the demand
for the inner as both trick and truth, so that one might see a stone surface
as both an expressive surface and a barrier, both an utterance and a
quote, both an anticipated response and a quilting of historical references
(Bakhtin 1986).

   This simultaneity of doubleness is what gives this book, *The Likeness*,
its form and its purpose. It also motivates the Slovene artists and philosophers whose work sits central herein, pulling the jokes and practices and
scalpel slices of subjectivity into consonant knots. The search for what lies
beneath what is given, this parable and trap intimates, might be a human
proclivity, a cross-cultural constant as predictable as the eel's search for
safety in the narrow and the dark. But, if true, thwarting this inclination,
as the andandpersand reminds us, is an equally viable pastime, one that
can be turned for personal profit and political efficacy and philosophical
ferocity and simple play.

---

with contexts, the ways in which they are fit together into what is told and said. They are like
puzzle pieces assembled with nary a boxtop image for guidance. As such every story is a poetic
sort of guess, a work of small art, forged from one's own expropriations and manipulations of
language as "a living, socio-ideological concrete thing." For it is language that "lies on the
borderline between oneself and the other . . . [it] becomes 'one's own' only when the speaker
populates it with his own intention, his own accent, when he appropriates the word, adapting
it to his own semantic and expressive intention. Prior to this moment of appropriation, the
word does not exist in a neutral and impersonal language (it is not, after all, out of a dictionary
that the speaker gets his words!), but rather it exists in other people's mouths, in other people's contexts, serving other people's intentions: it is from there that one must take the word,
and make it one's own. And not all words . . . submit equally easily to this appropriation, to
this seizure and transformation into private property: many words stubbornly resist, others
remain alien, sound foreign in the mouth of the one who appropriated them and who now
speaks them" (293–94; see also de Certeau 1995). This too is the story of *The Likeness*, this
wresting of references, these difficult appropriations that are made over into new stories,
stories half one's own and half belonging to the worlds from which they've come.

In *The Likeness* surfaces are accorded their power, traps are strung and sprung, and the fight is on. The fight, not so much to fool the birds, though this can be a happy side effect, but to claim provenance over the proclivities of the human.

Figure 1. Slovenia in Europe. Design by Stinson Lenz.

Introduction

I. OF SEMBLANCES AND . . .

> a copy is out in the open, obvious and blunt; once it is
> incorporated into the system it starts questioning everything.
>
> Walter Benjamin, "On Copy," 2006

Most of the months, short dry months and long wet months, between January of 2001 and October of 2003, I spent in Ljubljana, Slovenia's capital city, doing research with artists and curators whose work was—in decidedly backhanded ways—helping to build a postsocialist, post-Yugoslav version of that nation. I had chosen to study Slovenia because there was something odd, or at least unfamiliar, about the ways in which mimicry was being used there for self-expression, most especially in the last years of Yugoslavia (1980–91) and through the first few years of independence (1991–2003). Not that the oddities in this regard ceased somehow with Slovenia's entry into the European Union (2004), its startlingly quick leap into the Euro zone (2007), or even when one of its own gained the White House (albeit by marriage) in 2016.

In *The Likeness* I braid and twist these strands of resemblance through the whole of this historical period, from Josef Tito's death to Melania

1

Trump's ascendance. Proliferating incidences of the unoriginal and the difficult-to-differentiate are here laid side by side to give a glimpse of the artful complexity at work in Slovenia, where likenesses were often effective vehicles for change—whether on the intimate sphere of the individual or the much larger scale of the national. These likenesses are not all of a type. There are many forms of resemblance: one can borrow names or appearances; disrupt or make obvious a symbolic order; copy a sound, a rhythm, a walk, a taste, an institution, or a document. Likenesses can be used to increase legibility or to diminish it. Like most anthropologists, I am interested here not in the catalog of different instances (even when these are conducted in the tune of the same) but in the uses to which these instances are put socially, politically, and, in Slovenia's case, also playfully. It will be a funny book, in which power, the capacity for change, and the ability to protest what cannot be changed are given form in the idiom of repetition. Likenesses here tie geopolitical transition to the more intimate register of self-conception and self-performance as these mattered to local experiences of social, cultural, economic, and political upheaval.

These three and a half decades of transition were far from Slovenia's alone. Between 1989 and 1991 the Soviet Union slipped almost magically into history and as the literal (cement) walls and figurative (iron) curtains were brought down the whole center of Europe lurched back from "East" to "West," from communism to the free market. The roots of this shift were older than twenty short months of surprising politics (Ost 1990). There is a joke, with a nut of truth in it, that in Poland the "revolution" took ten years; in Hungary—ten months; in East Germany—ten weeks; in Czechoslovakia—ten days; and in Romania—ten hours. In Romania it seemed there was just enough time to execute the emperor Ceaușescu (a sentence carried out on film and widely distributed) before stepping blithely over the line from West to East, marked only just hours before by men with machine guns, barbed wire, and impossibility. In Berlin the last man to be killed trying to escape died just half a year before the wall was brought down by hands and hammers on both side; the people scrabbling to bring the city and, shortly thereafter, the nation together again.

In Yugoslavia the aftermath of state socialism was worse, though during socialism things had been better. The borders had not been closed, nor had the nation been under the leaden wing of Soviet protection. Yugoslavia had not been threatened by tanks, occupation, and other grave sanctions as had the nations of the Eastern Bloc. After its admittedly stressful break from the Soviet Union in the 1950s, Yugoslavia became a founding member of the movement of nonaligned states. These countries—India and Egypt, Indonesia and Ghana—sought to forge a route between capitalism and communism. Their aim was to build a future that would not be determined by an alliance with one superpower or the other. In other words, throughout the second half of the twentieth century Yugoslavia was a driving force toward a hopeful alternative. An alternative politically and economically, but also in other domains, as Tito, its erstwhile leader struggled to bring the world together under separate cover. There was a third way, a path between ideological communism and ideological capitalism, and Yugoslavia's economic as well as diplomatic successes proved it possible (Gupta 1992; Rubinstein 1970).

A conglomerate nation, Yugoslavia was a linguistically, ethnically, and religiously diverse country that worked. This too made it unusual in the twentieth century. Many of its people felt themselves to be Yugoslavs, marriages crossed lines of all sorts, there was free movement, intellectual interchange, commerce, and uplift as generation followed generation in which things got better. The rapidity with which all of this shattered in the 1990s was breathtaking even to those in the midst of it, as neighbors turned to hate neighbors and Yugoslavs turned back into Serbs, Croats, Muslims, each at the throats of the others. At the speed of a blink (it seemed) enmities turned to massacres.

I remember a friend showing me an empty field in Bosnia that had been a Muslim neighborhood, now emptied of people (some killed, most driven away); the houses had been burnt and their remnants hauled out and away. And then, hard work though it was, even the pipes had been dug out of the ground and made to disappear into the rest of the town, such that no trace remained of the people who had lived there, neighbors, friends, shop owners, and teachers to those who did the routing. There were always pockets of comradery, places and people that resisted this turn toward ethnic and religious divisiveness, where diverse communities had flourished (Baker 2015). Nevertheless, when people write the history of Yugoslavia in the 1990s as a horror story this is what they mean: mundane functionality that flipped, like a coin falling, to genocide; it happened so quickly it felt like entering a vacuum and feeling the air pulled from one's lungs, the eyes from their sockets.[1]

In Slovenia none of this happened. Yugoslavia's northernmost republic, a tiny place squeezed between Italy, Austria, Hungary, Croatia, the Alps, and the sea, with its own quirky language and relative ethnic homogeneity, Slovenia seemed from the outside to have just turned its back quietly on Yugoslavia, severing ties, keeping a bit of money in its banks that wasn't properly speaking its own, and like a greased eel, slipping away from the terrible history the rest of that nation would bear.

When confronted with this story of their escape, Slovenes protest that they too saw violence, they too suffered death. And this is true. There were ten days of war with casualties on both sides; this feels like "a peaceful transition" only in light of what would happen to the rest of Yugoslavia.[2]

The aplomb with which Slovenia accomplished its transition out of federated Yugoslavia and also out of state socialism initially caught my ear and rubbed itself down into consciousness because of the many (indeed innumerable) ways in which it proved to be the exception, not only within Yugoslavia but also among all the former postsocialist republics and countries. At gatherings of postsocialist this and postsocialist that, which were so common in the 1990s, there was always someone who, when making sweeping generalizations about the hardships attendant to the end of communism, would at some point say, "except in Slovenia." There was rampant inflation, except in Slovenia; there was a turn to right-wing ethnopolitics, except in Slovenia; there was a tendency for individuals to refuse to pay utility bills, except in Slovenia. And so on and so forth. Then, quite suddenly, the Open Society Foundation—George Soros's massively funded undertaking committed to the promotion of peace and cultural flourishing in the formerly communist center of Europe—pulled out of Slovenia in 2000.[3]

1. For a far more thoroughgoing history of Yugoslavia and its undoing, see Woodward 1995a, 1995b.

2. About 50 members of the Yugoslav Peoples' Army were killed, with three times that number wounded. On the Slovene side, 19 were killed and 182 were wounded. From www .slovenija2001.gov.si/10years/path/war/, accessed July 2019.

3. Likely a pragmatic rather than ideological decision, the Soros Foundation's withdrawal from Slovenia followed on the heels of a World Bank declaration that the country was "developed" and thus no longer eligible for aid. See www.ce-review.org/00/43/slovenianews43 .html, accessed April 2018.

It alone of the socialist East was "open" enough to merit no further funding in this regard.

After enough of this sort of off-the-cuff gesturing toward Slovenia's exceptional functionality in a situation that flummoxed (at times catastrophically) other newly independent states across the region and into Central Asia, I decided to go there. I was a student of late communism, myself transitioning to become a student of postsocialism and it struck me as curious that nobody was talking in any detail about this place that appeared to be doing the transition so right.

My curiosity was also piqued by a more pointed weirdness. At the time Slovenia's single most important exports (after refrigerators) were a seemingly neofascist punkish band and a sort of crazed Lacanian philosopher. Both Laibach (the band) and Žižek (the philosopher) commanded devoted followings—in Slovenia and beyond—but neither could really be said to be a "normal" sort of harbinger for a functional nation-state. In the end I even got Fulbright money (which is to say, money from the US government) and from the Woodrow Wilson International Center for Scholars, both of whose interest was in policy-relevant research, to jet off to Slovenia, one of the few anthropologists to have done so, to try to determine what made it such an exceptional exception.[4]

One might not immediately guess from the pages that follow that this book began with questions related to untoward geopolitical success. Largely this is because my initial questions were quickly answered and also because they were only the tip of a much larger and more interesting iceberg. The answer, just so you have it, is that Slovenes did so well in their transition from communism because they looked to systems that functioned well and copied them. Likewise, they were attentive to demands made upon them and, when not opposed to particular suggestions, they did their best to meet expectations. And when crises did occur, and they did, Slovenes also did their best to resolve things quickly and without undo fuss. A good history of the postsocialist period can lead you through the details of this (Meier 1995; Benderly and Kraft 1996; Gow and Carmichael

---

4. Slovenia has its own anthropologists, who were very kind to me as I came bumbling into their world. Rajko Muršič was particularly genteel and smart and his book, *Neubesedljive zvočne igre: Od filozofije k antropologiji glasbe* (1993) always gave me hope, in the morass of fieldwork, that I was on the right track.

2000; Plut-Pregelj 2000; Cox 2009; and the plain-spoken Prunk 1994), but suffice it to say here that in Slovenia, care was taken to determine the parameters of a good thing and then to make that good thing their own via, in most cases, institutionalization rather than political fiat or (equally dangerous) whimsy. It's not a perfect nation-state, but it does prove the point that intelligent governance is possible even in situations of extreme stress. In Slovenia's case this "intelligence" was linked explicitly to the fact that other people in other places had provided positive precedent. There were exemplars worth following and models that seemed wise to adopt.

More interesting, to me, was that similar processes of attentive concern and thoughtful copy were happening far beyond the limited realm of statecraft. And, more important to those Slovenes I came to know, was that through all of the twentieth century, within shifts of geopolitical fortune ran thick veins of artistic interest, production, and talent. The arts and their artists, the philosophers and their philosophy were not developing somehow in parallel to the state: the two domains were mutually constituting. So much so that when speaking of statecraft in Slovenia it is right to put the emphasis on the second word. The *craft* of the state was what mattered most. Or to put it otherwise, something artful—more of a maneuver than a clearly identifiable object or end form—was playing out in the slow and steady tread from state socialism to welfare state capitalism. In the end, then, I turned from political and institutional functionality toward the arts, for these public functionalities were but symptoms of a larger cultural care for resemblances and what they are good for.

Thus, while much has been written about notions of transparency in the early days of European integration, along with transparency's anxious Other, "authenticity"—both concepts relying on the notion of a hidden interior that can be revealed—in Slovenia the expressive power of exteriors, not interiors, took center stage (Shore 2013; Jarosinski 2002). There, far from making everything as transparent as possible, such that one could see "through" walls or "into" bureaucratic processes to whatever was going on "inside," the turn was toward crafting likenesses by copying the obvious and available forms of things: musicians performed covers; artists painted other people's pictures; punks, rockabillies, and skinheads looked, sounded, smelled, and acted like punks, rockabillies, and skinheads; the politicians organized themselves into an (almost) two-chambered parliament; the business newspaper was printed on salmon-colored newsprint (Erjavec and Gržinić 1991; Stankovič, Tomc, and Velikonja 1999).[5] I once saw an ideotypical Scotsman ducking into a Ljubljana cafe. Every day I saw a perfect linzer torte—or two or three—in shop windows. Once, early in fieldwork, I found myself confronted with a perfect piano bar. I'd never even been to a piano bar before and, this is the point, I still knew it was perfect. It was like a piano bar from a TV show about fancy foreign policemen who cut into a piano bar to do business. Close your eyes; you can see it too.

Despite the constant repetition of things and styles and sounds and even, as we shall see, persons, there was also always something weird going on. Copies and counterfeits were not really made to dupe people into thinking they'd just happened upon a *real* painting by Mondrian or Pink Floyd *really* performing in a converted periurban factory. Instead of a perfect fidelity to form, Slovene copies were consistently made to be recognizable *as* copies—as *not* the real thing. The most common route to accomplishing this was situational: likenesses, like that Scotsman, were often just enough out of place that it was difficult to take them for the real deal.

Take, for example, "The International Exhibition of Modern Art" (*Internacionalna razstava moderne umetnosti*), mounted in Ljubljana in the spring of 1986. The substance of the show was fifty paintings and sculptures, each of which was a copy, if not always an exacting one, of a work displayed in the first, far more famous, instantiation of this exhibit—popularly known as the Amory Show and held in New York City in 1913. This first International Exhibition of Modern Art introduced America (much to America's then dismay) to the likes of Marcel Duchamp, Henri Matisse, and Pablo Picasso; the newer version, in contrast, made works by these same artists—all of which were infinitely recognizable by 1986—into vehicles for a distinctly local politics of artistic production. Of the show, one catalog essay extolled:

> The works exhibited are obviously copies; they are not forgeries, because they make no attempt to hide their status as copies: their dates of provenance are all wrong, and their execution is consciously dilettantish. Their anonymous creator has not attempted to reproduce the materiality of the originals in any way, opting to work against it instead. Hence, the copies of

5. A quick glance at the webpages of the *Financial Times* and of *Finance* (Slovenia's financial newspaper, where I worked for a time) can be instructive. You will see that one is a copy of the other and you will guess correctly which copies which.

Joseph Kosuth's *Definitions* are not executed as photo works, but in oil (and dated to 1905), while Duchamp's famous urinal (1971) is a handmade plaster sculpture, and not a ceramic readymade. (Arns 2006, 7–8)

Half a hundred copies of famous art works gathered together in a copy of a famous art show all done in such a way as to avoid the singular effect of that original undertaking. The first Armory show was meant to blow America away; it was sensational, it was shocking, there was huffing and puffing, people walked out, fury pouring from them like cartoon smoke from cartoon ears. The Ljubljana International Exhibition of Modern Art may have been a copy in form and in name, and its contents may equally have been copies, but the intention was to use likenesses to inverse effect. Not to shock and awe via unbridled creativity, but to create something "repetitive, uncreative, and boring": the goal was not "an adventure into the unknown; its voyage rather leads into the known" (Arns 2006, 7). The repetition itself was designed to stand out, over and above any particular works of art.

The likeness here being deliberately pursued was not that of forgery or of deception. Duplication was, rather, undertaken without duplicitous intent. No one was going to buy this Duchampian "Fountain" by accident; there was no mistaking it for the real thing. Rather, both the contents and the fact of the show were principally techniques to open up the space of art for judgments beyond those ordinarily heard at gallery openings or group shows. Gone were questions of aesthetic worth, artistic genius, originality, or skill. In their place arose a different sort of conversation about geopolitical power, about the economies of "high" culture, and most especially about the uses to which history might be put (Bakke 2008). Copies have different effects than originals, but this only works if they are recognizable as *not* being what they pretend at (Arns and Sasse 2006).

"The International Exhibition of Modern Art" of 1986 did not simply frame ideas about geographies and histories, it gave these ideas form. A past New York was transported in an admittedly queer way to then present-day Ljubljana. This was the most obvious folding of time across space, but there was another more noteworthy displacement, one that emerges only in retrospect. "The International Exhibition of Modern Art" was a Yugoslav project, born of an ebullient art scene that tied that nation's capital cities (Ljubljana, Zagreb, Belgrade, Sarajevo) together, as artists and ideas moved across the federation.

In Yugoslavia in the 1980s, after Tito's death but before the wars that would do so much harm to the rest of the country, there were principally Yugoslav artists, of whom Slovenes (marked as much by linguistic distinctiveness as by ethnicity) were a part. It was a decade of common creative flourishing, truncated by war, from which the northernmost piece of Yugoslavia emerged with the capacity to continue a thread of artistic concern, while the other pieces—Croatia, Serbia, Bosnia—wondrous and dynamic, lost this thread. History split. Slovene art, Slovene artists, thus bore these unfinished histories forward in time, not by "completing" them (they could not be completed) but in a combination of mourning, growth, and return. This combination already had a name, "retro-avant-gardism," a phrase invented by Laibach but practiced by a number of Yugoslav artists in the 1980s. What was dynamic and experimental before the Yugoslav wars became a defining characteristic of South Slavic art in their wake.

What is ironic in this slippage of history is that "retro-avant-gardism" as a governing philosophy of artistic practice "imitative of a style or fashion from the recent past" (retro) yet governed by "ideas ahead of their time" (avant-garde) prefigured a truncation of the *Yugoslav* art scene by a war that had not yet come to pass. The work of many of these artists would, in the future, become the object of precisely the same sort of historical-artistic continuations they'd earlier plied on the "historical" avant-garde (Šuvaković 2003, Erjavec 2003). In retrospect it feels like they were prefiguring their own traumatic undoing, as many of the retro-avant-garde's founding figures indeed disappeared into the war or were flung by it into new lives in new countries, their futures as Yugoslav artists lost with the loss of Yugoslavia itself.

Despite the seeming prescience of a movement concerned with disrupted histories, in the 1980s across the east of Europe people understood that communism was changing, ending perhaps, but transforming most certainly (Sher 1977). This was especially true in Yugoslavia, where the interregnum following Tito's death (in Ljubljana in 1980) felt suspiciously like acephalous shatter. There would be no new Tito. The past had already begun to unravel, and the future promised little by way of continuity.

In Slovenia, the starting point of a post-Titoist future was the same as for the other Yugoslav republics. And if Serbia gave rise to the likes of Kazimir Malevich, perhaps the anonymous artist responsible for the "The

International Exhibition of Modern Art," then, in the beginning, Slovenia had Laibach, the seemingly fascist punk band mentioned above.[6]

Laibach emerged in the early 1980s just as punk was fading in Yugoslavia and they were anyway "too different, too crazy" to be properly speaking "punk" (Miha Štamcar, personal conversation, 2002). Unlike other artists working principally with mimicry, including the early Slovene punks whose art was largely a copy of that of their British brethren (Bakke 2007), Laibach didn't copy the avant-garde nor did they copy the disenfranchised youth of a Western European island. Instead they gave voice to fascism, ethnonationalism, and diligent communism. They were in this way provocative, as this untoward mix of ideologies intimates. Laibach, in holding these incompatibles fiercely together seemed to cast light upon the absurdity of each. And though they were a band, playing music upon a stage was the least of their undertakings. Laibach lived the philosophy they championed. They both represented and preached conformity and fanaticism. They spoke with one voice, they eschewed individuality and creativity, they used no proper names, they wore well-designed suspiciously fascist uniforms.[7] All of their songs were covers and yet they could hardly be considered a cover band. They were in many ways terrifying. And though Laibach's earnestness was never in question, there was a fair amount of confusion over just what exactly they were earnest about. Slovene philosopher Mladen Dolar writes: "Laibach . . . shocked the pub-

6. *Laibach*, the German name for Ljubljana, when "dusted off and set in type for rock festival posters within a year of Tito's death functioned as the sheerest provocation in Yugoslavia. . . . It evoked . . . the much longer span of pre-Yugoslav Slovenian history" (Benson 1995). This history of a minority-language community within and under Germanophone governance includes four hundred years as a province in the Austrian (and later Austro-Hungarian) Empire and two years of annexation to the Third Reich (1943–45). This latter period is especially fraught because of claims (and counter-claims) of local collusion with Nazi occupiers, dust and mites under the carpet that the word *Laibach* unsettles into flurries.

7. Says Laibach's Ivan Novak of these outfits: "We wore miner's uniforms (1980–82), Yugoslav army uniforms (82–87), hunting clothes (87–92) and skiing clothes (92–96) . . . But because everyone keep on repeating that Laibach wore 'Nazi uniforms' we finally dressed up in 2003 in Nazi uniforms (clothes used in Yugoslav war films), but also in American military uniforms, repeating the same photo session in both uniforms, sending two different set of photos to media—and they always picked up Laibach dressed in 'Nazi' uniforms, just so they could repeat the claim that Laibach is a Nazi band" (Ivan Novak, personal correspondence, July 2019). What is important here is the desire of others that Laibach conform to their (others') ideas of what might rightly be feared, in this case preferring one horror in particular rather than accepting that it is just one of several available (traumatic) options.

lic because they never once let on that they were making a parody of totalitarian ideology. They exhibited no distance to their own position whatsoever, to their 'totalitarian' form or organization or their ideological proclamations. To all intents and purposes, they resembled a militant group that believed fanatically in their own ideology" (Dolar 2003, 156).

At a moment of hope, a cultural juncture in which democracy or at least a radically reformed communism might be embraced, Laibach belted out nationalist hymns (and vacuous Western pop songs), often in gravelly German. They mixed the words of Hitler, Tito, and Stalin, the images of National Socialist artists, and the pastoral symbolism of right-wing ethnonationalists with a delivery style of neofacist automata. This confusing array of symbols led some to publicly claim the group were ultranationalists, others that they were German imperialists, and still others that they were dangerously utopian communists (Tomc 1994). Each ideology, as it was attributed to them in turn, was hopelessly incongruent with the others. Meanwhile Laibach offered few clues as to where they "really" stood on any of the important issues of communism, fascism, ultranationalism, or even punk rock. They were unflinching and they remain so. For those interested in knowing more, the finest history of Laibach and NSK, the artists' collective they helped to found, is Alexei Monroe's *Interrogation Machine* (2005).

When I saw Laibach in Slovenia in 2002 there were still neo-Nazi fans jammed up against the proscenium, their shaved heads, puffy bomber jackets, and jackboots identifying their subcultural affiliation and their politics. When I saw them in Zagreb in 2001, I was shushed during the concert by aging Croatian aesthetes, with powdered faces and nicely pressed clothes. This was a punk show to be savored; the rules of high art here applied. No talking during the growling grinding out of sound; no interrupting the smashing march of drums. When I saw them in Los Angeles in 2008, they spun the table on their fans who were there for the neofascist hymns, and what they gave them instead was beauty. A single female a cappella ("in the manner of a chapel") number formed the entire first set of the show. A man in lederhosen stamped his feet and booed. When I saw them in Washington DC in 2003, the day that George W. Bush won his second term, the audience was comprised of goth kids there for Goth Night, which would start later in the same space, intermixed with the staff of the Slovene Embassy. The ambassador and his wife had met at a Laibach show decades

Figure 2. Laibach on Mount Triglav, Summer 1988. Mount Triglav, the "three-headed" mountain, is the highest peak in Slovenia's Julian Alps, and is (like the fabled newt) a preeminent symbol of the Slovene nation. It is said every Slovene must hike to its top at least once in their lifetime. Here, Laibach has done it. Photo by Peter Vezjak. Reproduced with permission from Laibach.

earlier, and the group's US tour that year, they told me, had been underwritten by the Slovene government. Laibach had become a sort of Slovene cultural patrimony, whose dissemination on the world stage was supported (in various ways) by the state. In 2015, Laibach were first Western rock band ever invited to play in Pyongyang, North Korea. Now called an "avant-garde industrial band" (by *Rolling Stone*), they performed a set consisting in large part of cover songs from *The Sound of Music* (Grow 2015). "We are not interested," they said, "in making cover versions as another tune of the same song, but in changing history . . . remaking history. We are . . . remaking originals out of copies" (Laibach 1988).

They have, that is to say, through all of this remained remarkably consistent not just in their approach to art as "a noble mission that demands fanaticism" but to a radical copying strategy (Arns 2003, 2) linked to the reanimation of lost futures and to an equally radical overidentification with fearsome ideologies.[8] What history has cut, the retro-avant-garde restores, repositioning an original breaking point as if the dead had not died, as if the East had never split, as if Yugoslavia had remained. "Politics," Laibach says, "is the highest and most all embracing art, and those who create contemporary Slovene art should be considered its politicians."[9] This was not mere lip service: fanaticism and politics were central to their project.

During the 1980s, when Laibach caused such worry, they grew, joining with the painters IRWIN, the theater group Sisters of Scipio Nasica, and the graphic design collective Novi Kolektivizem (New Collectivism) to create

8. On TV in 1983, Laibach were asked what they thought of Edvard Kardelj's idea (Kardelj was the principal architect of Yugoslav self-management and an ethnic Slovene) that neither the state nor the system nor the party can bring happiness to a person, that each person must create his or her own providence. In response Laibach said: "Not the State, not the Party, not God, and not the Devil: happiness lies in the total denial of one's human identity, in people's consciously waiving their personal tastes, belief, judgments, in their free depersonalization, in their ability to make sacrifices, to identify themselves with a higher, superior system, with the masses, the collective, the ideology." Such words from "a group of five men in their early twenties, seated in a row wearing Yugoslav army shirts. Lit from below, as in a horror film, staring straight forward, their faces expressionless under close cropped hair, members of the 'rock' group Laibach had engineered an assembly of generic 'triggers' which, in combination seemed to indicate some unspecified totalitarianism. Each wore an armband with a symmetrical cross—a calculatedly ambiguous symbol. Black leather boots, gleaming buttons, crossed arms and blank eyes completed the effect" (Benson 1995, altered slightly). Thanks to the future having arrived in the interim, you can watch the interview on YouTube. It's amazing. "Laibach—Tv Tednik 1983 (uncut)—Part 1," posted July 9, 2009, video, 6:11, https://www.youtube.com/watch?v=A2WLRAr6nLo; and "Laibach—Tv Tednik 1983 (uncut)—Part 2," posted July 9, 2009, video, 6:50, https://www.youtube.com/watch?v=EmzKcXTGF04.

9. This paraphrase of a 1939 quote by Adolph Hitler was included by Laibach in their response to an interview question by Radio Študent in 1985 about the phrase "*Kunst ist Politisch*," which they appended to one of their productions. Hitler's original statement read: "I am an artist and not a politician. When the Polish question is finally settled I want to end my life as an artist" (Neue Slowenische Kunst 1991, 48).

Neue Slowenische Kunst (NSK). And in 1991, when an impossible future came to pass and Slovenia became an independent country for the first time in its history, NSK reframed their already highly bureaucratic organization into an echo state. Their organization was different from that chosen by Slovenia's politicians, in being more hierarchical and in making no claims to territory. If a state were to operate like a pop-up shop with a strong Internet presence it would look a lot like the NSK state-in-time. They have pop-up embassies and consulates; they have convinced other nations' armies to wear their regalia (if only long enough to take some pictures); they maintain a permanent online passport office which issues passports (you can get one).[10] And for a week or so in 1994, three years into independent statehood, they even ran a post office located in Ljubljana's central post office, such that this building found itself home to two parallel postal endeavors, each offering what appeared to be identical products and services: go to the counter, buy some stamps, and use them to mail some letters. Not all of the stamps, however, had been designed at the behest of nor issued by the then relatively new national postal service. Some had been designed by Novi Kolektivizem (the graphic artists) and priced according to an NSK currency, which did not at that point exist, though it now does.

As with the passports, this false government service was both real and unreal, whether considered in its materials or in its activities (though rumor had it that this ersatz postal service would deliver letters domestically, if the proper NSK-issued postage was affixed). To complicate this entanglement further, several years later the same artists were commissioned by the national postal service to make a "real" postage stamp. This stamp then functioned in an almost identical way to the art-stamps earlier made by the

---

10. These passports, like their stampy brethren, were real-enough-seeming that for many years NSK maintained a mild sort of boastfulness about how people had used their passports to slip out of Yugoslavia during the wars. Thus was this formal document of a state that held no territory mostly an artful means of waging political commentary—until the mid-2000s, when thousands upon thousands of passport applications began rolling in, most from Nigeria. Slovenia (then a member of the EU), the NSK state-in-time, and the possibility of unhindered travel into Europe were collapsed by a single optimistic misunderstanding. It seemed, from afar, that anyone could, for a modest processing fee, purchase a legal European passport on the Internet. The requests trickled into and then flooded the NSK passport service and worried the Slovene government. Many actions hoping to clarify matters were taken and none of then slowed the tide (Arns 2011a, 2011b). If you like, you too can get an NSK passport: https://passport.nsk.si/en/how_to_get_an_NSK_passport.

same collective. One, could in other words, use such a stamp to mail a letter.

Research on Slovenia tends to stop with Neue Slowenische Kunst, the wily weirdness of its art forming a sort of rabbit hole of proclamations and projects that can absorb the whole of a scholar's life. I am indebted to the theorists of NSK who came before me: Inke Arns, Zdenka Badovinac, Michael Benson, Eda Čufer, Mladen Dolar, Marina Gržinić, Alexei Monroe, Slavoj Žižek, and members of NSK themselves among many others. Because of them I can gesture toward the thoroughness and nuance of the group and their work and also move on, for NSK are symptomatic of something else: a cultural proclivity to value a certain kind of obvious copy. Not just any forgery will do—rather, the likenesses that proliferated in Slovenia were those possessing the peculiar capacity to be recognizable *as* copies while also allowing for less nuanced readings. They were, in other words, also "mistakeable" for what they pretended at being.

Think of how American professional wrestling makes it possible to believe it's a sport rather than a sort of theatrical dance of massive men hurling their bodies at one at another (Bakke 2001; Atkinson 2002). Think of how in the early days Stephen Colbert played an (almost) perfect right-wing pundit, or how John Stewart's *The Daily Show* both was and was not a news program (Boyer and Yurchak 2010). Think of those latter-day skinheads at a Laibach concert, waving their flags and *believing* (whilst the singer bent down and with a pointed index finger growled "and we're not here to please you/we have no answers to your questions/yet we can question your demands" (Laibach, "WAT"). Think of a friend of mine, whom you have never met, a Slovene woman with an irrational boss, who said (to deal with him): "I'm just going to do everything he says even more than he wants, so much so that he can't complain any more. I am going to be the best employee he ever had" (Gilen Tengi, personal conversation, 2003). This love affair with likeness, or with overconforming such that conformity is recognizable (or not) as critique—is at its most bombastic and most seductive with NSK, but the swarm of semblances (Tomšič 2018) neither begins nor ends there.

Sometimes the weirdness was more nuanced, less pointed, and harder to recoup into a politics of art or art of politics. Mimesis was, in other words, a broader cultural phenomenon, one which the public-facing NSK drew attention to but did not invent. In 2001, for example, in that perfect piano bar a jaw-droppingly talented young white woman crooned a flawless cover of Nina Simone's civil rights anthem "Young, Gifted, and Black." With eyes shut it was America, 1970, all over again—open them and it all slides sideways; the space, the singer's tiny white self, the impassive audience, the fact that you are drinking strawberry juice, if out of a perfect rocks glass. The situation seems almost designed to clash with itself. Each element placed there to perturb the others, to create a kind of vertigo by means of incongruity. A vertigo that, with time, I would learn to feel as pleasant, homey even.

Artists were not alone in flirting with this andandpersand of unwieldy affiliations. Formal, government-funded institutions were highly complicit and not just the postal service. For example, Tadej Pogačar, a curator and artist, made a museum that worked as a parasite on other museums, occupying them and rearranging the collections to tell different stories.[11] He didn't break in to do this, he was granted access. Including to the tightly ideological Museum of Modern History in Ljubljana, where he crafted an alternate narrative of the Yugoslav past from the museum's collection—musty and moldering artifacts routed out from basement rooms to take the floor. Pogačar approached the project of assembling a new storyline for a new nation not as an historian or a museum might be expected to; rather he was interested in making a muddle, via curatorial intervention, of what might otherwise appear to be the clear, natural, or normal order of things. Even when rearranging the stuff of history as a means of disrupting a given historical narrative he did not so much posit a new whole or an alternate telling but assembled the artifacts he was given access to in such a way that they highlighted the artificiality, arbitrariness, and constructedness of any attempt at a single overarching historical narrative. Tito's death mask was there, unassuming. Before Pogačar was given free reign, it had never been shown. Pogačar took Tito from his shelf and made him into history (Tadej Pogačar, personal conversation, February 2007).

Another group of artists formed themselves into a research institute, acronymed it RIGUSRS (Raziskovalni Institut za Geo-Umetnisko Statistiko

11. Much can be found about the P.A.R.A.S.I.T.E. Museum of Contemporary Art using Google of course, but here is a video presentation (in Slovene) of a retrospective of the project over its decades: "TADEJ POGAČAR & the P.A.R.A.S.I.T.E. Museum of Contemporary Art," posted January 19, 2015, video, 17:41, https://www.youtube.com/watch?v=tdqmctKrKD8. See also Bakke 2008.

Republike Slovenije or Geo-Art Statistics Research Institute of the Republic of Slovenia), and then devoted themselves to producing reports and measures relating to Slovenia's geography and its people.[12] Among these was "the substantiation and promotion of the new international measurement unit, 'Slovenian Mediterranean Metre'" by means of which Slovenia's diminutive coastline could be made to measure a full one hundred kilometers.

Another artist, Apolonija Šuteršič, opened a video club, where you could rent a video; she also made a juice bar, where you could buy a juice; a tiny movie theater where you could buy a popcorn and watch a movie. Yet another artist, Vadim Fiškin, made a hotel, where you could spend the night. Some artists, lots of them, designed the rooms in Ljubljana's then-new youth hostel (formerly the Yugoslav military prison). It has won awards; you can spend the night there; it's affordable and near the train station.[13] Other artists, but mostly Marko Peljhan, now a professor at UC Santa Barbara, built an experimental, portable laboratory totally off the grid, made for doing scientific and atmospheric research. You can apply to be researcher, or an artist-in-residence, there. You can see in figure 3 a picture of me, sitting on the steps of it when it was part of the Venice Biennale, built up on Garbage Island far from the city in the Venice Lagoon. And then Dragan Živadinov, a theater director and also a member of NSK, launched the Slovene space program, later adopted by the state as its own. He got training as a cosmonaut and staged a zero gravity dance performance in low orbit. When the *Challenger* blew up, he was the expert called by the Slovene press to wax intelligent about the event (see also note 24, relating to totemic newts).

It is difficult to explain the slightly eerie sense of always being reminded that a thing both was and wasn't what it was. That a torte, a meter, a democratic system of governance, a hotel, a post office, a cosmonaut, even a yogurt sometimes wasn't (but also sort of was) a torte, a meter, a democratic system of governance, a hotel, a post office, a cosmonaut, or a yogurt. There was, however, no getting away from the fact that Ljubljana's exceptional youthful rappers were white boys (and a girl) raised by Yugoslav socialist parents.

12. These projects and more besides can be seen here: Vuc Cosic, Alenka Pirman, and Irena Wölle, "Slovenian Mediterranean Metre Report," April 5, 1997, http://www.ljudmila.org/~vuk /rigusrs/report.htm; and on Alenka Pirman's page, http://www2.arnes.si/~apirma1/delo.htm.

13. A short history of Celica can be found here: www.hostelcelica.com/en/art-hostel /story-concept-12846.

Figure 3. Makrolab, Marko Peljhan, Venice (on the horizon), 2003. Photo by Daniel V. Roberts.

They were no less remarkable and skilled for this fact, they pulsed their hands in just the right ways as they chanted out Eminem songs with Slovene words, rhymed and timed just right. Watching Shakespeare in Slovenia was amazing; wiping the toilet seat in the Parliament building with the little spritz of disinfectant was amazing. What could be more European really than this tiny ritual of swiping clean that already pristine, intimate porcelain round?

What none of it was was authentic.[14] The play in Slovenia as the nation tipped toward the EU was with resemblances, while care for the true

14. Sean Kingston (1999) points out that authenticity is a "magical effect" created not by transparency but by its opposite: obscurity. "Authenticity is a magical effect similar in many ways to the 'technology of enchantment' Gell (1992) identified as being key to the efficacy of art. Both play on dissonance between the visual experience and the viewer's expectation of what (or how) things generally are. Authenticity only arises when there is some salient aspect of the object which is obscured from the regularities of experience that give rise to unquestioned confidence" (334). Attributions of authenticity, that is to say, are only possible when *something* remains dark; and anxieties over inauthenticity emerge most strongly when that

essences—of *being* rather than pretending at being someone or something—
was purposefully underdetermined. Nor was "looking like" or "acting like"
(smelling like, sounding like, moving like, tasting like) simply unlinked from
what each gesture might be presumed to index—these modes of stumblingly
obvious resemblance were barely standardized at all.[15] As *The Likeness* will
make abundantly clear, there were many ways to approach the problem of
identity, and in Slovenia rarely, if ever, did this mean resorting to a conversation about essences.[16] This was as true of things as of people, of institutions
as of comestibles.

Such claims immediately release a flurrious bevy of entangled concepts
out from Pandora's Box of Well-Tended Ideas. The Authentic, the Sincere,
the Mimetic foremost among these (though once it's opened, the Copy, the
Counterfeit, the Double, the Duplicitous, the Forgery, the Fake, the Ersatz,
the Replicant, the Clone, the Facsimile, the Effigy, the Ditto, the Simulacrum
and its Simulation all also come pouring out and begin to flutter and beat

---

darkness or obscurity of origins is lost. It is this black box of ontological inaccessibility—
located most often in "times and places beyond the immediate horizon ... [or in] mental
phenomena such as intention, belief, or agency" (340)—that lends the notion *and experience*
of authenticity both its real-world charm and its conceptual clout. The move toward revela-
tory transparency characteristic of the early days of a uniting Europe thus, rather than acting
as a salve in a cultural moment when "realness" was experienced as something fading away,
increased the sense of a loss that was both anxiously theorized and oft bemoaned (see especially Baudrillard [all of it] and Debord 1995). In Slovenia, these issues (and attendant anxieties) were far less present because acts rendering exteriors permeable were rarely practiced.
To my delight, when it did occasionally happen that worries about authenticity were voiced
in conversations with Western Europeans, they came off as imitations of "European" concerns, their speakers appearing thus both *as if* Western Europeans (worried about authenticity) and as not Western Europeans (because this worry was worn as a mantel, decorative
rather than "deeply" or authentically felt).

   15. I use "index" throughout this text in the Peircean sense. An index is a sign for which successful signification requires that it "utilize some existential or physical connection between it
and its object," as smoke indexes a fire, a footprint indexes the passing of a barefoot person, or a
larger-than-average molehill indexes a larger than average mole. For a clearish explanation of
Peirce's semiotic theory, see "Peirce's Theory of Signs" in the *Stanford Encyclopedia of
Philosophy*; to get a sense of Peircean semiotics' robust capacities in use, see Kohn 2013.

   16. Michelle Rosaldo writes, of the Ilongots with whom she did research: "What Ilongots
lack from a perspective such as our own, is something like our notion of an inner self continuous through time, a self whose actions can be judged in terms of sincerity, integrity, and
commitment actually involved in his or her by-gone pronouncements. Because Ilongots do
not see their inmost 'hearts' as constant cause, independent of their acts, they have no reason
to commit themselves to future deeds, or feel somehow guilt stricken or in need of an account
when subsequent actions prove their earlier expressions false" (1982, 218).

one about the head). All of these were at play, at one time or another, during my fieldwork. They are all likenesses of a type, though not the same type, and Slovenes were very catholic in the likenesses they'd employ. This book is a testament to this diversity of practice. Far from arguing that there was one true way of being a Slovene or of manufacturing resemblances I hold, with curator and art theorist Igor Zabel, that there was something political—which is to say, pointed and worth taking into account—about sloppy, "'unserious' and 'irresponsible' approach[s]" to "established narratives, activism, art, and professional and scholarly discourses" (n.d.). I expand this claim to include unserious and irresponsible philosophy, hotels, rock bands, politicians, identities, sculptures, and Scotsmen (among others) as these defy narratives of wholeness, intentionality, and truth, enforcing instead an analytic recognition of "the primacy of context over text" (Bakhtin 1981, 428).

Likenesses in Slovenia were, in other words, weighty, emotion-laden things. Equally, likenessness were dull, unremarkable things. Likenesses were humorous; they were comforting; they were eerie; they were omnipresent. This book, which has become about the self, echoes and shimmers with a manifest joy in being and doing what has already been been and been done. As it turned out art, geopolitics and self-expression were critically entangled. How really could it be otherwise?

All of which is to say that I didn't go to Slovenia to study subjectivity, its production, performance, or communication. I was curious rather if there was a relationship between the dogged functionality of Slovenia's approach to geopolitical change and a funny thing or two that seemed to be going on with art. A funniness that is best summed up even now by Laibach's notion (and also guiding principle) that there is no originality in art.[17] They also said, when asked for their definition of an individual, that an individual is: "A multitude of one million divided by one million" (Laibach 1985–90).

17. When members of Laibach were asked in a 2002 interview about the German industrial band Rammstein (which has had greater commercial success than has Laibach) "stealing" from them, they issued the response: "Laibach does not believe in originality . . . . Therefore, Rammstein could not 'steal' much from us. They simply let themselves get inspired by our work, which is absolutely a legitimate process. We are glad that they made it. In a way, they have proven once again that a good 'copy' can make more money on the market than the 'original.' Anyhow, today we share the territory: Rammstein seem to be a kind of Laibach for adolescents and Laibach are Rammstein for 'grown-ups.'" (Litts 2004; Lukes 2013). See also item 7 of "The 10 Items of the Covenant" (Laibach 1983).

There is, to extrapolate, also no originality in individuality. I wondered, did Slovenia's approach to the politics and economics of their relatively speaking peaceful transition out of Yugoslavia and equally efficient if not entirely unerring march into the European Union have something to do with this concerted and politicized lack of differentiation across domains?

Thus, as my first tentative weeks in Slovenia poking about in museums and making myself known at art openings and other *čestitam, čestitam* events (characterized by much congratulatory pattings-on-backs) grew slowly into a year and then two and then three; as I changed (for them) from "American anthropologist" to *tuji element* (foreign element) to a retinal familiar, something beyond art and beyond national upheaval began to gnaw at me. There was, in Slovenia, a decided quietness, almost a discreetness, tied to madness. And in the end, this, an itchy sort of curiosity about the untoward propriety of people I foolishly presumed should demonstrate only crass abandon led to my spinning the entire project on its axis, making this a book about subjectivity, or self-making, in which art and geopolitics also figure as culturally recognizable expressive modes. There was no art, no politics, no cautious acceptance of capitalism, no institution building, nor any alternative to all these things without also and always a carefully crafted carapace of the self.

Thus, though this book is all about concerted plays with "normal" modes of being and behaving, I turn here to sanity's edge, in hopes of bringing into focus for you, the reader, a Slovenia I remained ignorant of all the way until the end of my years there, for it took someone sitting me down and pointing out what every native knew before I could taste the context, the culture that colored this nation and her people.

II. OF SELVES

What I despise in America is the studio actor's logic, as if there is something good in self-expression: do not be oppressed, open yourself, even if you shout and kick the others, everything in order to express and liberate yourself. This stupid idea that behind the mask there is some truth.

Slavoj Žižek with Geert Lovink, "Japan through a Slovenian Looking Glass," 1995

In Slovenia during the period of my fieldwork (2001–3, 2005) one simply didn't see much crazy behavior emitting from crazy people. In point of fact, one didn't see much crazy behavior at all. This, I would later learn, was the more startling anomaly. In public, at least, Slovenes were self-controlled and quietly functional, modest and moderate, so much so that it took me years to even be able to "see" differences in the intensity of belabored adherence to the formal qualities of everyday life. As anywhere, some in Slovenia struggled more than others, but they did so mildly and in silence.

Before having learned to see the careful normalcy of those teetering on sanity's edge, I had operated with a sense of mental illness as a space outside of cultural strictures. It was, as I understood it, a way out; a place of brazenness, of fistfights in libraries and spittle in the face of oppressors, of conversations with private demons in public places. By this rationale, if a society is tight (as Slovenia was) and behavior within it strictly regimented (as it also was in Slovenia) it seemed to me only logical that strangeness, sickness, drunkenness, or craziness would be sites—or social positions—from which one could rebel, rationally or not, against family and friends, bosses and strangers, bus drivers and bank clerks, traffic lights, train schedules, and the requirements of a steady job, of fatherhood, of matching socks. In other words, against pretty much everyone, and all of it. I had understood craziness and other forms of physically invisible abnormality to be a sort of freedom from the tourniquet of normalcy. Yet never, during my years in Slovenia, did I witness a conversation held with no one in particular.

There were loud moments certainly, and startling interactions, but these were always wrapped in combative conviviality. Never a person wigging out alone by him or herself in public. Boisterousness, rather, was performed together with friends. Even aggression felt social. It did happen that drunk men on their own would make a threatening move. These, when directed toward me were, contrary to all my born-and-bred puritan expectations, never sexual in nature. Rather, they were audaciously corrective, like the middle-aged man on a darkened side street late at night who stopped dead in his tracks, mouth silent and agape, to point his finger in felt anger at my pale pink, cherry-stippled kneesocks (lightning rods of ire throughout my time in country). More common were groups of young men, drunk together, lurching jovially through the park late at night, who would move as a mass against random passersby, though rarely in a way that raised hackles of fear, shouting out a "Merry Christmas" in English or, with a note of scorn, *"lepa čelada"* (nice helmet) in Slovene, accompanied by a feigned move to jam something in my bike spokes as I passed.[18]

Drunken interactions such as these were few and far between, always taking place out of doors. They were in equal measure benevolent and malevolent. Even the most shocking of them were aimed more at correcting my aberrant behavior (socks, helmet) than doing any actual harm. In general drunks, especially the chronically drunk, kept their drunkenness well contained, enjoying themselves without making much of a stir. This was noticeable to such a degree that the Lonely Planet's inaugural guidebook to Slovenia refers to the local lushes as "the politest drunks in Europe" (Fallon 1999).

Drunks, however, are not for the most part mentally ill and it was the unfailing silence of the sober I had come to find so puzzling. Was it possible, I wondered, that there weren't any crazy people in Slovenia? Shouldn't somebody start screaming sometime? Lacking anything like an answer to these questions my initial supposition was that everyone with serious neuroses or psychoses was either institutionalized or heavily drugged, that is, not visible because they were not strictly speaking present. Or, in local parlance, they were at "Polje," the large mental institution on Ljubljana's edge where, as rumor had it, certain people—always pointed out with a discrete jab of the index finger in the direction of their receding back—went from time to time.

As my months in Slovenia wore into years, however, I slowly got a feel for aberrant behavior. The too-thin of anorexics became distinguishable from the popular aesthetic, for men and women both, of mild emaciation. I heard stories of "cutters" and then began to notice them, young women especially, with histories of small slices scarring their arms. The suicide statistics—in the early 2000s among the highest in the world for boys and men—and the personal stories behind these took on a new density of importance (STA 2015). And every so often the way that somebody moved down the street felt out of keeping with the norm, a little too slow or with

---

18. After a good fourteen months of diligent bicycle helmet wearing, I finally stopped, as it was definitely more dangerous to ride with it than without.

a distinctive step, something odd about the angle of a head, or the hang of the arms.

In every case, from that of the anorexic to that of a man having difficulty buying bananas at the supermarket, the degree of difference was extremely slight and very mild to the eye; it was often difficult, in fact, to pin down what exactly made "difference" noticeable at all. What I failed to see in this lack of rebellion, in this careful quiet, was a cultural model of mental illness. Against all evidence to the contrary I continued to wait for the explosion of speech and expletive that so characterized the crazy, the drunk, and the ferociously discontented in my own culture.

That is how I came to be sitting in Šent: Slovensko združenje za duševno zdravje, a day care facility for the mentally ill, on my last day in Slovenia. (The Slovene term *duševna zdravnosti* means notably "spiritual health," not "mental health.")[19] I, wedged into the merest of spaces, between the dark edge of a desk and the window, and seated across from me a small woman, Špela Zgonc, who had twenty minutes to spare. Upon hearing my query Ms. Zgonc immediately pointed out that when alone but in public, Slovenes, regardless of their mental health, make no noise: no humming of songs, no uttering of expletives, no half-muttering of sentences, no voicing of shocked memory, no whispering of numbers when counting out money. These everyday silences formed in the interstices of social interactions were the norm, the backdrop, she politely pointed out, against which the silences of the mentally ill should be read.

Starting with this quiet of which I had not even been aware, what Ms. Zgonc offered me in the simplest of ways, was a key. She pulled Slovenia into sharp relief with just a few words while simultaneously making it a place I could hardly imagine—a place so strict in stigma avoidance, so focused on self-control and personal responsibility that it was almost inconceivable to me despite my having lived there, in the midst of it, for nearly three years. Ms. Zgonc made it seem the most sensible thing in the world that crazy people in Slovenia don't talk to themselves; they do not

---

19. *Duša* in Slovene translates into English as "soul" (related to *duha* or "spirit") but the adjectival form *duševno* translates to "mental," a term that gives a more meaty sense of where the soul resides, or alternately, a more airy sense of the nature of the mind.

because sane people do not and to behave otherwise would reflect badly upon them, their families, and friends.[20]

Slovenes, Ms. Zgonc said, looking at me quietly across the cluttered corner of her desk, are self-contained, self-critical, and deeply afraid of stigmatization. They ("we," she said) are judgmental and capable of extreme unkindness toward one another based on the merest infraction of a norm or manifestation of oddity.[21] Then, she explained, when, an individual begins to lose control of him or herself there is an inward turning, a hiding of a madness which manifests in most cases first in phobia or paranoia—mental diseases that keep one indoors and which, by their very nature, limit human contact. Perhaps more important is that these disorders are often understood to be symptomatic of personal failing and individual weakness, both by those afflicted and by their close friends and family (Luhrmann 2004, 2011).

This was Ms. Zgonc's second point: that because of an immense lack of education about mental health, deviations from the norm which in other places might be understood as, for example, symptoms of a chemical imbalance (manic depression) or a social condition (acute anxiety disorder) or as the result of adolescence or genetic diversity are in Slovenia thought to be symptomatic of individual weaknesses of will. If one goes mad—and the importance of this cannot be overestimated, as Ms. Zgonc,

20. The technical term for such conformity to social norms regarding flipping out (or not) is "display rules" and these differ significantly across cultures. Briggs has written a beautiful book about emotional constraint among the Inuit (especially as relates to shown anger) and therein she uses the term "leakiness" (1970, 284). My mother uses the same word to describe stewardesses who get fed up with irritating airline passengers or real estate agents sick of showing houses to certain sorts of people: "They leak," she says. Her meaning is that their emotions spill out through cracks in their slick, hard, but professional façades. Tanya Luhrmann (speaking of Briggs's work) sums this up, saying: "Emotions are powerfully shaped by display rules, but the affect often seeps over the dike" (2006, 352). In Slovenia, the feel was different. Leakage, though evocative, gives a buglike sense of a hard carapace filled with liquid—an inner and outer characterized by distinctly different qualities. Rather, I would say, from my own research that a copy that is poorly accomplished is the one in which one sees the effort of conformity. Here, it is the effort that rings forth, noticeable for own sake (Žižek 1999; Livingston 1990).

21. This conversation is reproduced from field notes rather than from a tape recording. I early gave up the habit of recording conversations because nobody would really say anything with the recorder running. After many long, semi-vacuous taped conversations that only became interesting after the recorder had clicked off, I armed myself, rather, with notebook and pen.

in our short interview, returned to it time and again—it is read both personally and socially as a singular failing of self-control for which the individual is uniquely responsible. Neither social context (with its known ills) nor the chemistry of the body carry the weight of an individual's failings to maintain themselves appropriately.

This was true to such a degree that despite all of my struggles living among Slovenes with my pink socks and much-maligned bike helmet, the simplest explanation for proper, public silence had never occurred to me: everyone struggled, at all costs, to maintain the appearance of normalcy, to not attract attention to themselves, and to not publicly manifest their differences. To be one of the one million divided by one million meant being usual, or in more American terminology, not unusual. From this neither madness as a mode of uncontrolled uniqueness nor sanity provided a space of liberation. There was no stance from which one might have flung a loud and unseemly "Fuck you" outward at the rest of society. For its part, mental illness manifested as an even more extreme version of the self-same management of impression that characterized everyone else. What happens behind apartment doors, Ms. Zgonc said most pointedly, is another matter altogether, but when in public the stigma of difference *regardless of what form that difference takes* was, simply put, anathema. As everywhere, to slip into Judith Butler's (1993) formulation for a moment, everyone is quite busy passing, but only some are explicitly in drag.

What Ms. Zgonc cast in terms of closedness, image management, and self-control, Slavoj Žižek neatly confirms in the quote with which this section opened, though, as is usual for him, through a sort of inversion. Rather than openly lauding a cultural, as much as an individual, need for a self that is *manifestly* under control, Žižek proclaims his distaste for cultures (here glossed as "American") that insist upon self-exposure, self-expression, self-liberation, and more generally, just openness. "[Do] not be oppressed," he says, speaking as if he were an American addressing some imagined army of the introverted, and "open yourself, even if you shout and kick the others . . . everything in order to express and liberate yourself." Changing registers, he ceases playacting and critiques what he has just voiced: "This stupid idea that behind the mask there is some truth."

What is interesting here is that Žižek is clearly expressing a personal opinion, much more so than elsewhere in his scholarly work where he

Figure 4. "Sometimes the only truly subversive thing to do when confronted with a power discourse is to simply to take it at its word" (Žižek 1993a, 237). Melania Trump climbs back into her motorcade after traveling to Texas to visit facilities that house and care for children taken from their parents at the U.S.-Mexico border wearing her I Really Don't Care Do You? jacket. BusinessInsider.com, June 21, 2018. Photo by Chip Somodevilla. Getty Images.

makes similar claims, albeit with far less felt sentiment. In *The Sublime Object of Ideology* (1989), for example, he writes: "The mask is not simply hiding the real state of things; the ideological distortion is written into its very surface" (28). In *The Puppet and the Dwarf* (2003) he again reiterates this idea, saying: "the ultimate idolatry is not the idolizing of the mask, the image, but the belief that there is some hidden positive content beyond the mask" (138). This is not, then, an idle thought, nor is it simply an academic claim. Clearly, Žižek *feels* something strongly about how self-expression works, and more importantly, where it is to be rightly found. One ought not, each of these exemplars enjoins, look for the truth of self on the inside, nor "underneath" some surface thought to mask another more true or more authentic state of being. Rather, and quite to the contrary, the essence of things, people, systems, power relations, ideology is right there and readable on their surfaces. "Sometimes" he says, "the only truly subversive thing to do when confronted with a power discourse is simply to take it at its word" (1993a, 237).[22] The same might be true, one can extrapolate, of individual people. Perhaps rather than searching for the truth-of-self below surface-level expressions the only subversive (read: correct) thing to do is to take these surfaces at their word.

It is not my goal here to provide a lengthy analysis of Žižek and his oeuvre (though I will fall into this trap in chapter 4), but rather to situate him and his work within a distinct cultural context. Žižek is not only an internationally renowned philosopher, he is also a Slovene, whose opinions, aesthetics, and many of his ideas emerged from the family life, street life, and political life of his country during the 1970s and 1980s, as Yugoslav communism began to grow weak in the knees and the Yugoslav retro-avant-garde rose to prominence. Such that, despite the fact that in his theoretical work Žižek speaks about the truths of human behavior (via, in most cases, Lacanian readings of psycho-symbolic processes), he presents this work *as if* it were universally applicable, when, in actuality, it is both grounded in and reflective of a very specific cultural context. This context, while immanent in all of his work, is here in this one quote—from an interview rather than an essay—made palpable.

This unusual degree of emotionality allows for an equally unusual twist of expertise: Špela Zgonc, it turns out, is more of a cultural theorist than is Slavoj Žižek, and he, in turn, is more a native informant whose biases, no matter the terms in which they are cast, serve primarily to prove her point. This reversal of role is one that I want to keep alive throughout this book, limiting Žižek's usefulness, to the degree that it is possible, to the insights he provides without much knowing it and granting the roles of expert and theorist to those Slovenes who were thinking critically about their home culture, regardless of their actual social position.

This is perhaps easier to do in Slovenia than elsewhere because, at least in the years immediately preceding EU accession in 2004, a great many people from all walks of life were thinking about what it was to be Slovene, what constituted Slovene culture, and what if anything granted the nation identi-

---

22. Another example of a similar sentiment is: "it is not ironic imitation, but over identification with it—by bringing to light the obscene superego underside of the system, over-identification suspends its [the system's] efficiency" (Žižek 1993b, 4).

fiable particularity. This quest for national self-knowledge was, and remains, particularly important to Slovenia because of the way it seems to slip too easily from the minds of certain outsiders, usually Western European and North Americans. Even when it is remembered, in a general sort of way, it is often confused in name and occasionally in attribute (like location, language, and historic alliance) with someplace else—Slovakia, Romania, Estonia, Segovia.

At the time, back in the early 2000s, official (i.e., state) and scholarly work on the subject of Slovene particularity tended to focus on elements recognizable to anyone familiar with the history and development of European nationalism and the carving out of discrete European nation-states: a distinctive language, a unique literary tradition, a history of "high" cultural productions, and a clear relationship between the land (as both geography and environment) and the people who inhabit it.[23] A great many artworks, both formal and informal, mimicked these concerns: What will our passport look like? What images will our currency bear? What font best represents us as a people? What shall we call our streets? Can we brand the nation? And if so how? (Or how not?) And, perhaps a space agency might be a nice addition. And so on and &c.

Both Zgonc's and Žižek's commentaries suggest, however, that "Sloveneness" as a practiced category of national particularity might rest in a commonality less likely to be taken up by advocates of national exceptionalism than are a common language, land, cultural patrimony, totemic newts, and historical economies of state.[24] In Slovenia, both Zgonc and

23. There are many classic texts which make this point (see Eley and Suny 1996; Gellner 1983; Brubarker 1992, 1996; Hobsbawn 1992; Luhmann 2002; Tilly 1990; et al.) but my favorite is a nonclassic one: Rajko Muršič, pooh-poohing tropes of authenticity in contemporary rock music, writes, "Nationalism is constructed from . . . the belief in the Nation, the imagined *Volk*, derived from the ancient roots of a people, their control of a land, and shared (authentic) history" (Muršič 2013, 55). Add in a distinct language, which Slovenia has in spades, and this pretty much sums up the standard model for national particularity.

24. Where America had her eagle and Berlin its bear, Slovenia has the *Proteus anguinus*, "a pale stretched cousin of the newt" (divernet.com), which is found almost exclusively in dark pools at the bottom of dark caves in the Slovene karst. It is properly speaking an amphibian, though the only one that does not go through a metamorphosis during its life span. It can both give birth and lay eggs, though neither process has ever been witnessed. And it breathes through three sets of gills (on its sides and on the back of its head) *or* by means of a rudimentary pair of lungs *or* through its skin. It lives for approximately one hundred years, and like humans, reaches sexual maturity in its teens. One specimen was kept in the refrigerator of a Ljubljana lab for twelve years and never fed and did not die—though it

Žižek are claiming (in their own ways), there is a strong relationship between a cultural emphasis on being normal (with all of the lateral as well as hierarchical sanctions this implies) and on the importance, indeed the substantive materiality, of surfaces. Opening oneself is enjoined against, self-expression maligned, while what is given—that is, what is available to the immediacy of the senses—is posited as the correct place to seek to know someone or something for what it, or he, or she really is.[25] Equally, the adoption of unusual elements, like walls or doors, as parts of selves is indexical of a subjectivity that is not merely not individualized (with the *I* and its emotions located principally inside the body; see Lutz 1988) but also not reducible to a social formation (in which the first person plural, *we*, trumps the singular, *I* in constituting an interactional, communitarian sense of self; Kondo 1990; Rosenberger 1994; and for the stinky version, Hankins 2013). Rather, Zgonc describes an entity that makes use of all available contexts, be these material or social, to form the substance of a self (see esp. Kockelman 2013).[26] While Žižek describes a

---

got admittedly thinner—and when, after this time, it was dissected its digestive system was completely, miraculously gone. This "human fish," as the Slovenes call it, because it has a skin color very much like their own, is one of the few things particular to the country and as such it is not uncommon to find it mentioned, pictured, and even occasionally present in situations that are intended to express national particularity. The ten-*stotina* coin had the image of a proteus embossed upon it and several live specimens were brought with the Slovenian national team to the 2002 Summer Olympics in Sydney. The logo for the Slovene Space Agency (SVA) even features a pair of protei, each one in a tiny proteus-sized space helmet. The artist Damijan Kracina used the proteus to form each character of an "autochthonic Slovenian font" designed as a graphical index of Slovene (national) specificity.

25. Far from Slovenia, in the islands of the Pacific, a whole anthropological literature has arisen devoted to the denial of expressive activities related to inner states. Called the "opacity doctrine" (a phrase that always makes me think of the Iron Curtain of the Cold War), it describes those societies "where people are expected to refrain from speculation ... about what others may be thinking" (Robbins and Rumsey 2008, 408). If the opacity of the Iron Curtain gave birth to a culture of spies, slipping behind it in search of truths of culture and power, the "opacity doctrine" has given birth to an intense anthropological interest in Christian confession—when interior states and intentions are expected to be expressed truthfully and aloud. It is here, in this moment of cultural contact related explicitly to religious practice, that opacity as a doctrine becomes most palpable, as local people break (or not) their own rules in order to produce a subjectivity recognizable to others-not-themselves (see esp. Keane 1997, 2002, 2008; Robbins 2001; Schieffelin 2007, 2008).

26. Walls were intensely substantive in Slovenia and doors were like cracks through which things might leak in or out of private spaces; doors were as such sites of great anxiety to be treated with care and touched only by those with keys or codes. I have many alarming

mode of perceiving such a self by taking into account the sort of expressive complexity that would include a shut door, a thin arm, a finger pointed in anger, and cherry-pink socks worn *as if* to draw such ire.

Irregularity in surface-level approximations can, thus, be read off of those surfaces *not* because these necessarily point to "hidden" interior states of presumed distress and disorder, though this is how Americans and Western Europeans would likely read them, using our own thick lens of bias toward hidden yet secretly determinate inner states. Following a more local logic, however, one might say that it is possible to know madness, or other sorts of irregularity, because only the unwell would fail to *appear* normal in precisely these ways. The drama is played out on the surface of persons in those elements (aural, visual, active, olfactory, material, architectural) readily available to the senses.

Likewise, when the drunk threatened violence in response to a bicycle helmet or voice outrage at a particularly garish pair of socks, the very public form such reactions took indexed "drunkenness" (theirs) as a state being made publicly available through discernible actions. Simultaneously, it called attention to, and actively sanctioned, formal inappropriateness (in these cases, my own). But, like the quietness of the mentally ill that so closely mimicked the quietness of the well, the scrawniness of the anorexic that was so nearly undifferentiated from the slimness of the rest, the audacity of the drunk to act upon, and voice, the aspersions cast like arrows from the eyes of the sober points to a concerted attention to type. As the copies which swarm through Slovenia's artistic and social spaces allow one to believe or disbelieve in them, so too with subjectivity. A similar model is in play. Perhaps then what marks Slovene responses to tense situations as culturally particular is a practiced capacity to appear both *as if* other (to oneself) and, simultaneously, as self-identical to whatever one is pretending at. Such that "to be mistaken for" becomes a cultivated element of who

---

and delightful stories about doors, fires, and ropes cordoning things off from other things. Suffice it to say here, however, that the idea that you can just go live in a village and people will invite you in and feed you (this being the staple of anthropological methodology from the earliest days to the present) was not an available mode of entering into community life in Slovenia. Becoming known entailed learning to let them be who they were and one thing they were not was comfortable with strangers passing through doors, from outside to inside most especially.

one is. The complexity and nuance of subjectivity thus abides in the X *and* Y *and* Z of coinciding (but incongruous) identities, present and available for taking and mistaking. Certainly, this has been argued by others, albeit by artists and lay theorists rather than statesmen and scholars. Similarly, Slavoj Žižek doesn't pick on the Americans' insistence on open self-expression because he has a scholarly bone to pick with the whole of that nation, but because he finds the very notion of self-exposure as a route toward truth-of-self misguided.

Subjectivity is, thus, local in that it is both learned and instilled (Herder 2007 [1792]), and it is entropic, which is to say, it takes energy to maintain. Cultural contact, geopolitical transition, and socioeconomic conversions are all challenges to the hard social work of maintaining recognizable versions of selves and worlds over time and, as such, these tend to be central aspects of anthropological studies of subjectivity. They are also part, but not the whole, of the story *The Likeness* sets out to tell.[27] For, once you begin to get a feel for the Slovene insistence on the substantive materiality of surfaces as the right way for knowing someone such as they are, a set of more philosophical—and artful—practices emerges.

Half, then, of what I am attempting in this book is to communicate the flavor of this tremendous bloom, this understanding, from nose-to-toes, of subjectivity done otherwise.[28] My hope is that by the end you too might find yourself asking yourself if it really does matter if Melania Trump, wife

27. Luhrmann writes that "subjectivity is a term loosely used by anthropologists to refer to the shared inner life of the subject, the way subjects feel, respond, experience . . . [their] 'thoughts, sentiments, and embodied sensibilities, and especially their sense of self and self-world relations'" (Holland and Leander 2004, 127, quoted in Luhrmann 2006, 345). This is the basis, the starting point that grows immediately more nuanced with the claim that "subjectivity implies the *emotional* experience of a *political* subject, the subject caught up in a world of violence, state authority, and pain, the subject's distress under the authority of another" (326, emphasis in the original). I agree that subjectivity emerges into view in moments of "political domination and social suffering" (Biehl, Good, and Kleinman 2007, 1) but not only then, as Rosaldo's eloquent argument about another people (Ilongot headhunters) without an operative relationship to the inner self points out (1980, 1982).

28. There are as many texts explicating the history and form of the "Western self" as there are leaves on the trees, but one common feature is nicely summed up by Andrea Henderson, who, in her reading of William Wordsworth's *The Borderers*, argues that "*looking into* the depths of the human souls amounts to *forging* a depth" (1996, 165). In other words, feeling that one has an essential inner self is for Wordsworth the explicit product of looking for it. The more one tries to know oneself, the more substantive the self-to-be-known feels; acts of knowing come to be indistinguishable from acts of making.

to the American president (and not incidentally, Slovene), uses a body double. It certainly matters to Americans, aghast that the First Lady might occasionally be played by an actress, but again that just tells us something about Americans, about whom we already know so much. Turn the attribution around and you can glimpse a parallel world in which this mannikin played by another is exactly right, with the added benefit of being pretty funny. Have you seen the pictures? She, the wife/not-wife, gives every appearance of wearing a pair of Groucho Marx glasses, false nose and all.[29] What, in other words, if integrity is not linked to a normative sense of accord between what is earnestly presented and what is essentially felt or known? What if, and this is pure supposition mind you, the swap was supposed to have been noticed? What if the joke is on the American press and public? Their outrage planned and planted? *That* would feel like a masterful Slovene occupation of a role understood as such.

If Melania reminds us of anything, day in and day out, it's that "wife to the American president" is a part to be played and as such she can choose to play it poorly. The nuance of her persona is not in the way that her distaste for her job and her husband is made evident through her behavior (the secreted-essence-faithfully-represented model), it's in the fact that she never lets us forget that she is acting (the surface-level-complexity model). She is acting and doing so in precisely such a way that we know that it is an act. The arrival of an inauthentic double as one aspect of this performance makes her more complex, so long as we are sticking with the faceting of surfaces as the site for the big reveal of personal nuance.

In the early 2000s, Christine Cornea made a similar argument about Arnold Schwarzenegger's *Terminator*. His flatness in this role wasn't, she said, the result of his being a bad actor, but of a concerted and largely successful attempt to depict the attenuated inner life of a robot (2003). Not a Slovene but an Austrian, Schwarzenegger was born and raised in what are considered traditionally Slovene lands, in a village about thirty-five miles

29. Wonderfully conspiratorial images can be found here: Alex Abad-Santos, "The 'Fake Melania' Conspiracy Theory, Explained," *Vox*, October 20, 2017, https://www.vox.com /culture/2017/10/20/16503870/fake-melania-conspiracy-theory-explained. Commenter Ricky Davila weighs in and sums up: "After seeing this clip over 20 times, I have to say, I wouldn't be surprised if they used a Melania double. Fake Trash do things like that."

north of the present-day border between these two nation-states so long conjoined in a Central European empire of repute.

My argument here is not that Schwarzenegger is secretly Slovene, or that those thirty-five miles and a century of history do or do not matter in some substantive way, but rather that the idea of approaching the performance of a role, *any* role, in a way that articulates a poverty of interiority is a culturally available mode of being. It can be a way of protesting expectations (or of living up to them). It was certainly available to Mrs. Trump and likely also to Mr. Schwarzenegger; it was certainly available to Mr. Žižek and to an almost infinite list of other persons I encountered during my fieldwork.[30] It is also available to us. For it's not as if modes of subjectivity stick to geography the way mountains stick to fault lines (Erjavec 1994). It is easy enough to see, not only from Melania's improper way of being a First Lady but also from her husband's infinite humbug—which also betrays a "wrong" approach to subjectivity—that self-conception and self-practice is both normatively enforced and given to immense variety. You too can practice being a robot on the inside, feel the flatness, bask in it, share it with friends over beer.

What is curious, thus, in all of this is that being one's own self appears to be as subject to play as would a more formal social role (like First Lady) or even a theatrical one (like the Terminator) or a material one (like a piano bar) or an institutional one (like a post office or a European welfare state). Identity is wrought, it's in play. Identity is, in other words, something one does or deploys every bit as much as something that one is (Goffman 1990 [1959]).

There are, however, stakes to ways of being a self that are linked less to modes of performance and more to matrixes of recognition. If Slovenes look shamefaced, to outsiders, in their refusal to self-represent or if the First Lady seems truculent in her less-than-passionate embrace of her role, or if the governor is popularly understood as a bad actor, it no longer

---

30. It was also available to a certain Weird Al Yankovic, born in Ohio to a family of Yugoslav, though not Slovene, origin. Despite this, many Slovenes claimed during my time in country that he was the son of the famous Slovene polka musician Frankie Yankovic (who, though likely the all-time most famous Slovene polka player, is from West Virginia). The two are not related, though Frankie Yankovic has played the accordion on some of Weird Al Yankovic's tracks. For a detailed hagiography (and history) of Weird Al, see Demento 1994.

matters that he might be a particularly nuanced one, or that she might grow more resplendent by being doubled, or that a silent refusal to live up to expectations might be a political act.[31] All of this is all lost in interpretation without those doing the interpreting ever being the wiser. Misreadings of local subtleties mean that these lives, dynamic and peculiar, are understood simply as failures when judged according to other people's narratives. As for these other people, it really did seem, in Slovenia, that these judgers and misjudgers harked from certain foreign lands, those places of easy capitalism, those places that postsocialist states like Slovenia were supposed to be orienting themselves towards, worse, those places they had set themselves to becoming if not identical to, than at least kin with. Joining the EU and being recognizable as belonging to it was the explicit goal of the Slovene state during the period of my fieldwork, and that project—largely bureaucratic—hinged upon being recognizable to Europeans as European-enough to not disrupt the values and laws of that union, and to be ethically (and ethnically) identifiable in ways supportive of an easy merge.

This then is the second half of what I am after in this brief volume. I will attempt to convince you that particularity, whether national or individual, might just as well stem from modes of appropriation as from the pointed expression of a minutiae of differences. And that such appropriations allow for a mode of subjectivity that works perfectly well without recourse to a doubled, if divided, outer (accessible) and inner (hidden) self, but rather congeals the complexities of being into that which is readily available to the senses. Slovenes then are apt to play with form when playing with selves; and, when asked to perform themselves in ways indexical of an interiority hidden from view, often become angry and, in various subtle ways, protest the division.

I do not make this argument for radically different modes of subject formation right under certain noses as an anthropological exercise, the aims of which might be to prove, yet again, to a crowd of dubious doubters that cultural diversity does in fact exist, even among middle-class, white

---

31. The fact that Mr. Schwarzenegger's most enduring and endearing appellation is a mix of a political role and a theatrical one acknowledges at least that his "self" is always already performance—in life as in fiction.

Europeans who all look and act pretty much alike (which in the Slovene case was pretty much the point). Instead my aim is to illustrate with some force that changes of economic system and of geopolitical alliance necessitate changes in both self-conception and self-expression. And that resistance to these can come in a number of forms and at a number of scales. Refusing to be a certain kind of someone is one of them (Dunn 2003, 2004, 2005; Keane 1997, 2002).

Thus, rather than seeking the truth of a being beneath its surface or inside its body in psyche, soul, or essence, in Slovenia I found something thicker and more nuanced happening with the substances of enclosure: skin, behavior, dress, sweat, coiffure, gait, and all the subtle interactions one has with the built environment. What one uses to accomplish self-expression—which, in Slovenia, was most often a simultaneous broadcast of hypertrophic conventionality—became, when considered thusly, the apperceivable substance of self. Not one model to rule them all, but a diversity of practices that relied upon an active turning away from the notion that anything besides a massive spill of blood (see chapter 5) will result from opening oneself to (self-) examination.

A Break in the Pattern

Because Slovenes play so gracefully with form and because I have learned from them that what truly matters to a thing happens in its formal quali- ties, I've taken some liberties in this book. There are hints of silliness throughout. I won't give them away here, but if your eye catches at play with language, lexicon, punctuation, and citation that is because these things that give shape to an argument are mine to bully and sprout. I have felt lucky that the writing of it (a project that has been ongoing for the past decade) has happened in parallel to a heartening move in anthropology toward experimentation in writing, not just crazy fonts or spitting and swearing (lots of this though, in chapter 4), but also attempts to knit the formal qualities of a written work to its argument and its point. This is an intellectual moment that goes beyond *Writing Culture* (Clifford and Marcus 1986), in that reflexivity is (if assumed) not central. What is wrought in the writing has rather more to do with form and genre as quiet, minor moments that don't quite add up, but that nevertheless work in some way, warm in some way the intellectual cockles of our hearts. I have been party to some of these trial balloons and peripheral to others, but I am appreciative in practice and in mind to all those with whom I play in parallel with what ethnography is and what great scholarly writing can be:

Marina Peterson, Katie Stewart, Lisa Stevenson, Stuart McLean, Craig Campbell, Anand Pandian, Shane Greene, Karen Pinkus, and Hugh Raffles among many others.[1]

I've also taken two biases to heart in penning the thing. First is that it's harder to write a short book than a long one. At every turn I have asked myself, What is the minimal amount of information, discourse, and data necessary to make a point, elegantly, fully, and convincingly? I have cut words, paragraphs, and pages upon pages in single-minded fidelity to an attempt to make less be more. In my mind this often took the form of "Nobody really wants to read a whole book about Slovenia." It's such a small, copacetic place. I give it then, to the best of my capacity, a small, copacetic book of its own.

Second, as much as I adore anthropology there is one tendency in particular that I felt it necessary to counter here. All too often the people with whom anthropologists do research become a source of data—in all its myriad and wondrously messy forms—while the people who structure academic debates, most of whom were educated within the European and North American academies, become a source for the analytic mangle through which this data is wrung. To my mind this wringing can only produce certain sorts of insights, communicable because palatable and familiar to readers who also live and think within this circumscribed academic world.

1. A debt of gratitude is owed to all those who helped make this book, in Slovenia and also in the years of writing that followed. Thank yous, then, to Lila Abu Lughod, Inke Arns, Marcus Aurin, Michael Benson, Vicki Brennan, Rachel Burger, Jenny Burman, Eda Čufer, Benjamin Eastman, Tana French (for the title), Victor Friedman, Andrew Gilbert, Jessica Greenberg, IRWIN, Eva-Lynn Jagoe, Janez Janša (and everyone at *Maska*), Anne-Elise Keen, John Kelly, Jurij Krpan (and Galerija Kapelica), Špela Kučan (and everyone at Ljudmila.org), Sheetal Lodhia, Katherine Lemons, Laibach (and most especially Ivo Saliger), Eric Lewis, Tanya Lurhmann, Sebastijan Maček, Peter Mlakar, Alexie Monroe, Andrea Muehlebach, Rajko Muršič, Tadej Pogačar, Timothey Pogacar (and with him, the Society for Slovene Studies), Elizabeth Povinelli, Tom Preistly, Maple Raza, Alenka Razboršek, Daniel Roberts, Danilyn Rutherford, Michael Silverstein, Marko Snoj, Igor Španjol (and Moderna Galerija), Jonathan Stern, Teresa Ventura, Margot Weiss, Matthew Wyman-McCarthy, Dragan Živadinov, Marko Živković; all members of the Center for the Humanities at Wesleyan University 2008–2009, where this book in its current form was begun; and to the staff and editors at University of California Press, including the reviewers whose comments helped push this manuscript into final form. Lastly, to Julien Weiss, who didn't think it was possible that any book could take longer than my last book: here is to small victories in good company.

Though it is imperfectly accomplished, my aim here was to gather data from my time in Slovenia and also to use Slovene thinkers as the principal means of providing analysis of this data. I have done this largely because a local point of view, or stance, emerges much more forcefully by these means. In Slovenia this was easy, since one of their primary exports is world-class philosophers (with even more of them tumbling about locally than one can realistically imagine). This wealth of critical thought and critical thinkers allowed me to keep the interpretive circle tight. In chapter 5, where I talk at length about colonialism and the "capitalist conversions" this has wrought, I have had to step away from this commitment to local theorists, further away than I would have liked. But the impulse was always there to stick as tight to Slovene lands and minds as I could.

Structurally the book is written like a mountain path: it is meant to get harder as it goes on. It starts out easy, gaining in complexity and tension until a peak somewhere in the middle (right around the subsection entitled "This Is Going to Hurt a Little"). It then tumbles back down to flatland in a sort of release that is still muscular, through to the end. Though the path downward from the midpoint is more easygoing, the subject matter continues to become more emotionally and viscerally extreme. In this way the book mimics not just the project of climbing up and then down a mountain, but somehow also the process of fieldwork (my own): it starts with the easily accessible stuff, friendly and on the surface, and then proceeds to what is also there, but less often shared, and from there it gets gory, lustful, and homey. If it feels simplistic at the start then just keep reading. If it makes sense, then dive on in, it will chew you up. I hope. Slovenia chewed me up and part of a good ethnography is to give this gift from researcher to reader. I write with humor for this reason as well, because a lot of what was going on in Slovenia during my time there was funny on purpose, but also because levity is a very local way of steering clear of irony. And irony was the stance most notably missing in all of this (Boyer and Yurchak 2010). I have tried to capture some of the doubled edge of earnestness and playfulness in my own writing as well.

Very briefly, for those who are interested in skipping any part of the climb or descent, here is an overview of the book as a whole. Chapter 1 introduces the notion that subjectivity can be complex and nuanced without reference to an inner self. It does so mostly through an extended analysis of a lecture Walter Benjamin gave on the late works of Piet Mondrian in Ljubljana in 1986. Chapter 2 uses Mladen Dolar's work on the voice to examine the shirking, hiding, and slouching of Slovene artists when asked to self-represent publicly by non-Slovenes visiting from the West. The argument here, inside the case study is that though the voice may come from inside the body, it is not proof *in the least* of a quintessential innerness linkable to special-flower subjectivity. Chapter 3 turns again to art, in this case the project *Name Readymade* by Janez Janša, Janez Janša, and Janez Janša (in part I), and to the particularities of Slovene grammar (in part II) to investigate doubleness as a comfortable category of operation. In Chapter 4, I come at last to Slavoj Žižek in earnest and to shit, also in earnest, asking what draws these two together. Here I make the claim that Žižek forces an attentiveness to context upon everyone, regardless of whether they want the job or not. In part II of this chapter I trace out the history of what some might call the Western self. That might (or might not) be the right way to say it, but certainly, the self that came at the end of the era of kings and in the early days of factory capitalism. If you are interested in that, skip ahead, but you'll still have to deal with rather a lot of bullshit on your way there. In Chapter 5, I turn again to art, in this case a series of surgical performances by Ive Tabar entitled *Evropa (I–V)*. The politics of European integration are at last brought to bear on the ferocity of Slovene refusals to be *that* kind of person. The afterword is mostly just for fun. Here I take to task American analyses of Melania Trump, hoping to have shown via the rest of the book that if you change your angle of attack, and add some robust local analysis, you get a Melania who is doing herself and everything else exactly right.

Chapter 1

June 1986; Tito is six years dead and Yugoslavia is in economic collapse, though it has not yet turned terminal, turned against and eviscerated itself. Indeed, there was little reason to believe, in 1986, that the nation might not still be salvaged: reformers were everywhere, warriors were few, and communism had yet to implode across the rest of Eastern Europe. That collapse was still three years in the future and utterly unimaginable in its scope. In June of 1986 in Ljubljana, Slovenia's capital city, Walter Benjamin stood before a crowd of a modest size and spoke about the so-called "later works" of Piet Mondrian, the dead Dutch painter of some renown. Of course, Benjamin too was dead by 1986—forty-six years dead. Four years after Benjamin's death in the autumn of 1940 (perhaps by his own hand, perhaps by Stalinist thugs), Mondrian collapsed from pneumonia in New York City and he too died.

The paintings under discussion that spring day in Ljubljana were, however, dated between 1963 and 1997. The earliest, thus, had seen brush to canvas some twenty-one years *after* Mondrian's death, while the last was completed eleven years *after* the date of the lecture in question. Rather

Figure 5. Walter Benjamin, public lecture, Ljubljana, 1986. Photo by Moholy-Nagy.

than delivering a treatise focused solely on the artistic merit of these "later works" and rather than formulating a plausible set of Benjaminesque musings that could be mistaken for those of the original name-bearer, this Benjamin took a different route: he led his audience into a ridiculous, metaphysical, earthquake-riddled scenario, at a museum of all places, in order to make a point not about Mondrian but about the nature of the copy, of which he was, of course, also one.

"One sunny day," Benjamin said (and I begin quoting here from some-where in the middle of the lecture), "we set off for the national museum. And," he continued,

> . . . suddenly we have the feeling that we have seen something familiar. We are sure it is a mistake or an error, and at first we reject the idea that we have already seen the painting we are observing. . . . We rub our eyes and look again. Quite definitely Mondrian. And it is the same Mondrian we saw a few decades earlier. . . . Suddenly, we feel the earth has begun to shake. We quickly look at the wall. It too is shaking. We are struck by a thought: earthquake! . . . But what is happening to our painting? With that other Mondrian painting? It is completely still—it is actually floating in

its nonexistent space, as though what is happening around it does not concern it.

(. . .)

Still shaken by the previous dramatic events we make ourselves a cup of coffee, sit on the floor, light a cigarette; and when we think about everything that has happened, our eyes accidentally, almost absentmindedly, flow off to the wall where we have placed the painting. In an almost empty and half-lit room, on a wall which once was white, two Mondrians are hung; an original and a copy. We would not be even slightly surprised by their similarity. Formally they are actually two, the same paintings. But we know that only one is the original, painted as a result of Mondrian's interest in the problems of space, plans, verticals, horizontals, primary colors, gray, black, yellow and red. And all this can be seen in the painting. We look at the copy: everything about it is just as it was in the original. . . . But we can say for sure that the unknown painter of the copy was not concerned with horizontals, verticals, colors, and background when making the painting. . . . We say that the sole sensible reason for this copy being made was the fact that copying Mondrian is nonsensical. The subject of the artist's interest was in the copy itself and its relation to the original. What we have before us, therefore, are two paintings, which are the same, but with two completely different ideas hidden behind them. We can see in the original what its idea is, but we cannot say the same of the copy. This means that the copy contains an idea of its ideal, as well as its own idea: the idea of a copy. Hence it follows, paradoxically, although seemingly truly, that the copy can be multilayered in its meanings and more complex than its original. (Gržinić 2000, 81–82)

Of the many curious things going on in these passages, two are consequent to the current argument. First, something decidedly odd has happened to the individual as it is performed by Benjamin—already a copy who speaks of copies. Despite being singular in form he is plural in person, indeed doubly so. His appellation marks him as other than himself—technically this form of personage is called a "multiple single" and it is commonly used by Slovene artists. Second, his use of language spreads him out into the crowd until, not unlike the king, he narrates with one voice the purported experiences of a plurality. That is, he consistently speaks in the plural and by this means includes us (us here now) as much as the Ljubljanites (there then) in his account. It is not Walter Benjamin—doubly not, as Walter Benjamin is dead—who sets off to the museum but, we are told, we do it, as if we had been there with him. *We* see the same

Mondrian we saw a few decades earlier; *we* feel the earth begin to quake and the walls begin to shake, and *we* see the painting floating in its nonexistent space, except that (as we all know well enough) we were not there. What's more, our "not-thereness" is indexed by the form of the lecture itself. Despite Benjamin's first-person-plural narration, had we been there we might well find ourselves attending a therapy circle or church event together to discuss the quaky-uncanniness of it but it would be unlikely that we would need to be preached to about it in such a faux art-historical way. No, we would remember all of it well enough ourselves.

Nor is the swapping out of the singular for the plural the only odd thing that Benjamin has done with his person and with that of his audience in this lecture. He also makes it clear that, though he has but one body, this body is shared. It is "his" body, in fact, that affords the rest a common experiential nexus. And though it may be singular, we are not. Thus, phrases like "we make ourselves a cup of coffee" prompt the literalist among us to wonder if a single cup will be enough. Likewise with the cigarette. It was after all a traumatic event, our mouth might not be content with a single cigarette. And when our eyes wander and alight absentmindedly upon the one painting turned to two, our eyes like our absentmindedness have been claimed for the collective.[1] Even if unintentional, the lexical awkwardness of Benjamin's attempt to adequately meld both himself and us into a sensible entity lends a certain structural support to his final point on the multilayeredness of meanings and the inherent complexity of copies. He, a copy himself, is more than the original Benjamin was, and we, made to be part of him, add to the complexity of his person. In acting, in falsifying, in pluralizing, and in multiplying he facets himself, becoming a more difficult entity without becoming a deeper one.

While all of this is quite interesting, it was also, in Slovenia in the years leading up to EU accession, quite common. One was constantly being told how one felt about what one was experiencing, most especially when culture was in question. A more contemporary example comes from *Vulgata, The Third Triennial of Slovene Contemporary Art*. This exhibition occupied the

---

1. In chapter 7 of her book *Bodies in Formation: An Ethnography of Anatomy and Surgery Education* (2012), Rachel Prentice describes exactly this sort of a subjective smudging that emerges (in her case and mine) when speakers develop an intense intimacy with digital or other fantasy (fantastical) worlds.

creaking halls of Moderna Galerija, Slovenia's national museum of modern art, during the long and dreary winter months of 2001. In the exhibition's catalogue one finds a short, four-hundred word, exegesis on the contemporary video work of Maja Licul. Licul, though represented at *Vulgata* by a video installation, is best known for having helped design a national currency for Slovenia after its exit from Yugoslavia. Later, she would do the same work for the "Slovenia" side of the one-euro coin. She is now a jeweler.

The catalog, however, tells its own story, which follows a narrative path eerily similar to that paved by the Slovene Benjamin. It begins: "Maja Licul's video work *Untitled* (1999) shows the artist on a small monitor facing the camera, talking and gesticulating. A pair of headphones transmits Licul's voice: one ear pad conveys the speech whereas the other gives the listener the impression of Licul talking with the other voice . . . The other voice makes fun of Licul's statements, smiles at the pompous tone of her voice . . ." And then, from the middle: "The deconstruction and alteration of the time structure of the narration, based on an antithesis of the narration and a synchronicity, distances the viewer from his voyeuristic look. . ." And at the end: "Here the subjective returns to itself, which lends an oppressive openness to the work. We are forced to realize that *anything goes* does not necessarily mean that anything is possible: we are trapped in the conditionalities of different worlds" (47–48; italics in original).[2]

All the elements are in place. Fifteen years after the Ljubljana Benjamin, five years after Žižek's published complaints to Geert Lovink on the pushing and kicking of self-expression, and five years before my conversation with Špela Zgonc about closed doors, Gregor Podnar, *Vulgata*'s head curator, describes a video work in terms of its oppressive openness. A queer phrasing, perhaps, but the sentiment should already be becoming a familiar one.

---

2. The Slovene of the final section reads: *"Subjectivno se pri Maji Licul vrača k samemu sebi, in to daje delu mučno odprtost, saj moremo spoznati, da anything goes Še dolgo ne pomeni, da vse mogoče, ker smo ujeti v pogojenosti različnih svetov."* This should not, however, be taken as a truer version than the English provided above. Both were translated, or at least, translators are credited for both the English and the Slovene texts. Podnar, the author, while Slovene, was raised and educated in Germany; it is likely then, that the original— invisible to the reader—is in German.

Figure 6. Maja Licul, "Untitled" (1999), from *Vulgata, The Third Triennial of Slovene Contemporary Art* (2000).

More relevant to the immediate point, however, is the increasingly dictatorial way in which one's experience of the artwork is narrated. In the first paragraph, an ear pad *"gives the listener an impression"*—a notion which is feasible, though, of course, simultaneously arguable. Were the work there in that room where you now sit, for you to listen to, some among you might listen and be given the impression implied and others might be given a different impression all together. Indeed, some might just find it dull, while others for more personal and unfathomable reasons might decide to take off the ear pad and wander away. This, it should be noted, was the most frequent reaction of visitors to the exhibit.

Several sentences later, however, the audience's situation has become more dire, for it turns out that the time structure of the narration *"distances the viewer from his voyeuristic look."* How exactly, one might ask, does "an antithesis of the narration and a synchronicity" work to split the viewer off from his voyeuristic look? How, more fundamentally, did it come to pass that the viewer is male, photographic evidence to the contrary? And, at what point in "his" stroll through the gallery participating in the art in a proper sort of way—stopping to look, realizing he should put on the head phones, actually putting them on, and listening for a bit to the contradictory speech within—did his "look" transform from an appropriate mode of interacting with art to a perverse one? What is gained by accusing the viewer of voyeurism, even if it is a voyeurism subverted and diverted by the viewer's interactions with the artwork?

All of these, of course, are the wrong questions to be asking. But it is through asking them that a misunderstanding about the nature of this "catalog essay" as a catalog essay emerges into visibility. It is neither objective nor is it descriptive. It provides very little useful information about the work of art, revealing neither its history nor its inspirations. It says nothing of the artist's intentions or the aesthetics of the piece, nor does it elucidate the reasoning of the curator (who is, in this case, also the author) for including it in the exhibit. Formally, then, it is a catalog essay—it's published in a catalog, it's laid out in an artful manner, the fonts are considered, the words arranged in groups that resemble sentences, footnotes cite famous Frenchmen, an illustrative image accompanies the text, a translator is mentioned. In much the same way that Benjamin's "art historical" lecture on the later works of Mondrian resembles an art historical lecture without actually being one, the content of this catalog essay fails to conform to its form.

Even the Slovene Benjamin plays this line between expectation and actuation of an ideal type. For, despite his choice of appellation, this Benjamin has taken no care to resemble the historical Benjamin. He looks, rather, like a midlevel functionary in a large, nondescript government agency, an average man in a suit—here there is no mustache, no glasses, no unruly hair, none of the first Benjamin's characteristic heft— this Benjamin is in fact so average as if to suggest that he has taken "averageness" as his model more than the historical personage of his namesake, who was not, by all accounts, average-looking at all. This Benjamin, the false one, does not trouble the eye.

It should now be clear that fidelity to those essential qualities of a form that would serve to make it a *believable* exemplar of an ideal type is not what Benjamin, Licul, and Podnar (the list will grow) are after in fashioning objects, persons, texts, performances, and perhaps even themselves.

This conclusion is reached without the need to read "into" the works and personages given—just reading them is sufficient; their infidelity is both abundant and amply evident right on the surface. And though foreigners in Slovenia had the tendency to scrape obsessively at unconvincing surfaces in search of the *true, authentic, real* roots of a given form, what is both more curious and more relevant to the current discussion is to ask what the positive content of these works and persons reveals.[3]

To do this we turn for a moment to another sort of document entirely. Like the "art historical lecture," the philosophical treatise is form of public address quite popular in Slovenia and it too follows a distinctly local formula: one part continental philosophy, with a strong preference for the Germans (Kant, Hegel, Neitzsche), to which is added one part Lacanian psychoanalysis.[4] This is shaken well and poured through a fine filter of popular culture; the visual (film, photographs) and the base (jokes, anecdotes) are preferred. The product that results can be spoken (in a lecture) or written (in an article or book) or even, on occasion, may seep out as quips in everyday conversation. But its form, its container, if you will, is words.

Slavoj Žižek is the most renown practitioner of this formula, but he is far from the only one to have made his career from its earnest practice. His ex-wife Renata Salecl is equally adept if not so well known abroad and Mladen Dolar (a colleague and a peer) is perhaps more respected locally for the quality of his thought and work in this genre than is Žižek himself; the same could be said of Žižek's bearded near-doppelganger Rastko Močnik. Add (from a slightly younger generation) Alenka Župančič and Miran Božovič, art theorist Marina Gržinić, and those who give public lectures on Lacan (e.g., Aljoša Kolenec)—a surprisingly common occurrence in Ljubljana—and you have the makings not just of a cohort, but of a recognizable, reproducible social form for fashioning and thinking the world. It even has a name: the Ljubljana school of psychoanalysis. And

3. Župančič (2003) notes that "Nietzsche defines nihilism as the psychological state that makes us search for meaning or sense in everything that happens. In other words, it is not simply statements about the meaninglessness of everything that are nihilistic—the very need that we experience for all things to have a meaning is the height of nihilism" (153).

4. When speaking of Žižek one would also need to include Marx on this list, but in this he is idiosyncratic.

while many of these thinkers will be treated in some detail later in this book, it is only right to add here a story, almost a parable, told by Župančič in the addendum to her 2003 monograph *Shortest Shadow: Nietzsche's Philosophy of the Two*. This is the story of the false Hitler:

> At the beginning of the film [*To Be or Not To Be* (dir. Ernst Lubitsch, 1942)] there is a brilliant scene in which a group of actors are rehearsing a play featuring Hitler. The director is complaining about the appearance of the actor who plays Hitler, insisting that his makeup is bad, and that he doesn't look like Hitler at all . . . what he sees in front of him is an ordinary man. . . . not satisfied [the director] . . . is trying desperately to name the "something more" that distinguishes the appearance of Hitler from the appearance of the actor in front of him. He searches and searches; finally he notices a picture (a photograph) of Hitler on the wall, and cries out triumphantly: "That's it! That is what Hitler looks like!" "But sir" replies the actor, "that is a picture of me!" (Župančič 2003, 169–70)

Benjamin, neither the false nor the real, is not Hitler. But the story of Hitler's double as Župančič tells it is very similar to that played by the false Benjamin. Here is an ordinary man whose role is to double an extraordinary one, who does so in such a way that he does not become less ordinary, and yet, despite this, whose self-as-copy effectively stands in for the original. He both resembles and does not resemble what he pretends at. He can be both mistaken for and not taken as that which he mimics. In both cases there is something comic in this procedure as each plays with pretense, (non)resemblance, staging, delivery, the lodging of various tongues in various cheeks. When I tell the story of the false Benjamin people invariably laugh. It's funny, actually. And of Lubitsch's Hitler, Župančič also says: "This . . . is quite funny, especially since we ourselves, as spectators, were taken in by the enthusiasm of the director who saw something in the picture quite different from this poor actor (whose status in the company is not that of a true actor or a star, but of a simple walk-on). Here we can grasp very well the meaning of 'minimal difference,' a difference that is 'a mere nothing,' yet a nothing that is very real" (170).

Rather than considering difference as something remarkable—that is, something to be remarked upon—or as something (following Bateson's famous formulation) that makes a difference, instances of which might be gathered and assembled into that most weighty component of modern life (i.e., information), Županič turns her analysis in the opposite direction.[5] Far from being some *thing*, for Županič difference, especially minimal difference, is "a mere nothing." This nothing is nevertheless a sort of substance—"a nothing that is very real." And it is this "mere nothing" that differentiates a catalog essay, an art historical lecture, a Mondrian, a Benjamin, and a Hitler from a catalog essay, an art historical lecture, Mondrian, Benjamin, and Hitler. Each is almost, but not quite, nearly, but not exactly. Each stops short or veers ever so subtly in another direction. The point here is that, as conceptualized by Županič, resemblance is not about perfection or exactitude, nor is it about the failure to achieve these things. Rather, it is about creating just enough space between an assumed-to-be-known form (Hitler) and its double (ordinary man) that discord can be remade as a *funny* sort of ontological play. Or, in Županič's own Lacanian-inflected words: "instead of playing on the difference or discordance between the appearance of the Thing and its real residue or its Void, comedies usually do something else: they reduplicate/redouble the Thing, and play on (or with) the difference between its two doubles. In other words, the difference that constitutes the motor of the comic movement is

5. In Bateson's estimation even the smallest difference can be understood as a sort of particulate that can be gathered or patterned; it can accrue or be made meaningful. Far from being nothing a difference is the smallest individual unit of something: "'What is it in the territory that gets onto the map?' We know the territory does not get onto the map. That is the central point about which we here are all agreed. . . . What gets onto the map, in fact, is difference, be it a difference in altitude, a difference in vegetation, a difference in population structure, difference in surface, or whatever. . . . There are many differences between them—of colour, texture, shape, etc. . . . Of this infinitude, we select a very limited number which become information. In fact, what we mean by information—the elementary unit of information—is a difference which makes a difference" (Bateson 2000 [1972], 455–59). Županič, in contrast, takes a similar situation and looks at the minimal (of minimal difference) as just that: "minimal," a "mere nothing." It cannot be gathered or accrued; it is not additive, it cannot be made into something big, extractable, malleable, or meaningful because its realness is pointedly not a sort of thingness but rather a sort of nothingness. I bring up this difference between Bateson's (American) cybernetic reading of difference and Županič's (Slovenian) Lacanian take on the same because of the ways in which these two reveal cultural differences in interpretive strategy. Even when the base material is decidedly similar—both are concerned with minimal difference—opposite conclusions about something so fundamental as the substance (or lack thereof) of a thing can be (and have been) reached.

not the difference between the Thing in itself and its appearance, but rather the difference between two appearances" (167). This is "truth as a montage of two semblances/appearances" (165) and pointedly not "truth" to be found below the surface of things.

Again and again, then, the same pattern redoubles and repeats itself. In performance art, in philosophy and the readings of the world it proposes, in paintings, in texts, and—as we shall see—in public lectures, audiences are enjoined to consider selves that are faceted by others; subjectivities that stretch outward, collapsing what they touch back into an apperceivable form (the collective, for example, can enjoy a cigarette); beings that are condyles not only of each other but of the things with which they come into relationship. It is not only the false Benjamin who shows us this, almost *as if* in jest. We also see it as Maja Licul's commentator first transfers agency from the art object to the human (*it* gives an impression that lexically, at least, is not to be refused) and later collapses the generic ("listener," "viewer") into the male, and later still the singular into the plural (by the end it is not "he" but "*we*" who are forced . . . and *we* who are trapped), and finally, the animate into the inanimate, as the subject returns to *it*self. The form and the various substances that constitute a person, while mutable, are not made so by means of references to essences and insides, but always by the complexity, and the imperative, of bindings beyond the singular.

II. WALTER BENJAMIN (ET AL.) SPEAKS HIS MIND, LJUBLJANA, 1986 (2001, 2003)

> The way in which I create myself is by means of a quest. I go out into the world in order to come back with a self. I "live into" another consciousness; I see the world through that other's eyes, but I must never completely meld with that version of things . . .
>
> Katarina Clark and Michael Holquist, *Mikhail Bakhtin*, 1984

There are proofs that have not yet been offered. In fact, some of the most interesting moments of the evidence supplied have, thus far, been ignored.

I have said only that persons are complex but not deep, that they shimmer in unusual ways on the surface and that they recruit unusual elements, philosophical and physical, to complicate these surfaces. I have spoken of averageness but not of sweat, of Maja Licul without pointing out that she despite being naught but a head pictured on a TV screen is also doubled. I have barely mentioned copies, though they are of the essence, and Lacan with his notion of the "subject as void" is almost entirely absent. I have not mentioned twoness, doubleness, as one of the quintessential concepts of Slovene life and grammar. Nor have I have raised the problem, an immense problem, of how, and under what circumstance, one speaks for oneself. Before this book comes to it close I will address these omissions. Here, however, I enjoin you to consider the last of them, though in order to do so we must return again to Benjamin—though not so long-windedly as before—and to the double problem of knowing others and of speaking for oneself.

We know Mondrian, the Slovene Benjamin tells us, just by looking at the paintings. We see him in them. It is not his skin that we see in their skin; this is not a moment of formal self-portraiture. We see, rather, something more essential and more difficult to grasp than a visage. We see painted there, on the surfaces of his paintings, his interest. His interest in the problems of space, of plans, of verticals and horizontals. We see his interest in primary colors, in gray, black, yellow, and red. And all this, we are told, can be found in the painting itself. We do not need the artist to explain himself. We do not need the artist at all. He is after all, and despite Benjamin's temporal claims to the contrary, dead. Yet because he is present in the thing, we can know him in ways that are both fundamental and nuanced.

This sentiment should be familiar to students of the history of art. There is (or was) a sort of magic attributed to the artist's hand, such that when he touched brush to paint and paint to canvas something essential of himself was transferred onto the object and, in daubs and smears, made manifest upon it. There was another Benjamin, as some might recall, who once, long ago, spoke about this phenomenon at length (1968, 217–52). And though there is a different evidentiary logic at work in the two arguments, the resulting claims are much the same. The object, as it is read by Benjamin, is not other than Mondrian.

Likewise, when "we" look at the copy, we know "for sure . . . that the unknown painter of the copy was not concerned with horizontals, verticals, colors, and background when making the painting." "We say," just by looking at the copy, "that the sole sensible reason for this copy being made was the fact that copying Mondrian is nonsensical" (82). How do we know this? Not by speaking to the artist; not by demanding that he express in words what his motivations, his interests, and his curiosities were. Indeed, we do not know who this artist is. We do not even know if he is singular or, for that matter, male. Yet, despite the fact that there are many reasons one might copy a Mondrian, we know unequivocally from Benjamin that the artist's interest was in "the copy itself and its relation to the original." And we know this too from the surface of the painting: the artist's interest is just as self-evident as Mondrian's and his being is every bit as coterminous with his product. The two paintings may be all but indistinguishable, but this does not prevent the two artists present in them from appearing as discrete entities, knowable as such (an argument with an august history, see esp. Boas 1940).

The certainty that I attach to this point proceeds from Benjamin's own, for it is here at the very end of his lecturing that he exits the frame of fantasy and speaks firmly, with the universalizing voice of authority. His assertion that "the subject of the artist's interest was in the copy itself and its relation to the original" is one of only three in the whole of his performance (which is much longer than the excerpts I have provided here) in which he makes a firm statement. Gone, for the space of a single breath, is the equivocation, the plural self, the rhetorical questioning, and the theatrical extravagancies that characterize the rest of the event. Benjamin says: "This means that the copy contains an idea of its ideal, as well as its own idea: the idea of a copy. Hence it follows, paradoxically, although seemingly truly, that the copy can be multilayered in its meanings and more complex than its original."[6]

6. There is only one other point in the performance when Benjamin speaks with such firm-footed surety: toward the very beginning he says, "The paintings are dated with the numbers 63, 79, 83, 92, 96. This means the earliest was painted in 1963" (Gržinić 2000, 79).

His point having been made—this is after all the dénouement of the performance—he slips back into character and subjective complexity again and continues: "Can we now imagine what good old Mondrian would have to say about all of this?" (note that equivocation, the plural self, rhetorical questioning, and theater are all brought back here, in one fell swoop, recentering us and him firmly within the framework of a performance).

He speaks, in these few instances, *not* as a performer who utters the words of others faithfully such that the show might go on, nor as the man we might presume him to be when not "on stage." Rather, he speaks with surety—of and for himself—as the ersatz Benjamin. A clarification, though hopefully not a necessary one: He is not here, in this instant, pretending to be Benjamin—all the trappings of theater have been thrown momentarily away—he is actually *being* an impersonation of Benjamin. And it is at this point when he is most thoroughly aligned with the copy, indeed almost indistinguishable from it, that he speaks his mind—his mind, which is the mind of a copy. Here, he voices his own opinions, which are likewise the opinions of a copy, albeit a lively and quite self-conscious one. In claiming for the copy a multilayered complexity of meaning absent from the original, he is claiming the same for himself. If nothing else is indubitable, this one thing is: Benjamin grants the copy (himself included) a complexity that supersedes that of the original.[7] The false betters the true.

7. Nor was he alone in this. In an open letter to *Art in America* (also in 1986) on the occasion of his *Last Futurist Exhibition 0.10*, Kazimir Malevich wrote: "I kept on thinking for years to do the same exhibition again. Since, for obvious reasons, it was not possible to do it in Petrograd, I decided to make 'The last Futurist Exhibition' again exactly 70 years later (Dec. 17, 1985—Jan. 19, 1986) in a small apartment in the beautiful town of Belgrade. One part of the exhibition was the exact replica of the Petrograd installation. But this time, no papers with the titles on the walls, no numbers, no chair. Another part of this exhibition presented some of my recent, neo-Suprematist works: Suprematist icons on ancient reliefs and sculptures. Suprematist icons in needlepoint. I think you can get a better impression from the picture. I know that for most of you this letter will come as a great surprise, since it is generally believed that I died in 1935! I know . . . Suetin's coffin . . . the great burial procession along the streets of Leningrad . . . the Black Square on the grave . . . Yes, there are many people thinking that I died. But, did I?" (quoted in Arns 2006, 9). Inke Arns notes that "the total identification with the copied works and with the artist whose work was being copied" makes Malevich (and Walter Benjamin) different from appropriation artists in America, like Sherrie Levine and David Diao, who put their own names on borrowed images. With

Were this the only moment at which what might be termed "earnest self-representation" was performed in an unexpected way it would not necessitate such ado. It was, however, in the few examples provided thus far, a common technique. As was noted above, in the text on Maja Licul's work, both the Slovene version and the English one have translators listed. There is information, opinion, and even the lexical construction of a generic social body, but no original. In both cases—the Slovene and the English—it is the copy that speaks for and as itself. Likewise, when Maja Licul speaks, it is with two voices. Both are her own, but neither is fully intelligible because one is constantly interrupting and commenting upon the other. Even if one were to insist upon untangling these texts in order to "get at" the truth of them, the twinning of subjectivity is complex enough that a consideration of each element independently of the other would render invisible the essence of the work, which abides in the confusion of sounds emanating from what appears to be a singular subject. Of course, even this is illusion, for it is not actually Maja Licul who is speaking; it is her head, alone, that speaks. Even this head alone is at a degree of technological remove from her person. It is her head on a TV. It is a copy of her that speaks in her voice, twice over.

Strange subjectivities abound. A veritable tome of exemplars could be provided, some much weirder than these—some horrifying—and others much simpler, pleasant, even giggle inducing. There are people whom I presumed existed, like the occasionally quoted student of Slovenian art Luther Blisset, who turned out to be (almost) entirely fictive.[8] Others whom I presumed did not exist, did, like the mythic Irine Wölle, who despite any positive proof to the contrary I have been consistently assured is real and lives and breathes, if somewhere beyond the bounds of my

Malevich and others of his ilk we see the "complete disappearance or dissolution of the artist or author in the identity appropriated." This move is more than common literary mystification, in which "the anonymous author appears in a two-fold sense: he does not only invent 'a text, but also its creator.' (Frank et al 2001, 8)." Here, "not only the object (i.e. the text) undergoes mystification, but so does the subject (i.e. the text's fake author)" (9).

8. Blisset authored a remarkably prescient little essay entitled "L'artista sloveno," (1995/96). And though there is no evidence that this source exists, the English translation can be found on the web page of the Geo-Art Statistics Research Institute of the Republic of Slovenia, which is an institute, though a false one, devoted to the production of

perceptual experience. What these plays with subjectivity hold in common are procedures, much like those detailed above, that distance the individual from him or herself by multiplying surface-level complexity while simultaneously voiding the center of any positive content. Were Slovenes just speaking among themselves and to other locals, usually culturally and linguistically integrated Croats, none of this would matter very much. My role would be little more than that of a documentarian entering an academic debate about how people in different cultures self-constitute and self-represent differently.[9]

The stakes however were much higher. As Slovenia moved into Europe, a process for which there was significant popular support, it became common for outsiders (like myself) to visit and blithely demand that individuals speak for themselves, not for collectives, not *as if* others, not in their roles, not hidden behind bits of available architecture, not on videotape, in books, or on the web, but for *and as* themselves. Slovenes were to have been self-representing individuals. This was especially true when interactions were with artists and other cognoscenti of the cultural world. What such demands produced in the early years of the new millennium were a series of mysteriously absurd (often, even, absurdist) interactions as locals attempted to conform "formally" to foreign expectations while outsiders naïvely expected to find familiar (to them) habits of

---

reports and measures relating to Slovenia's geography and its artists. Note this Blisset and the more well-known Blissett, author and footballer, have much but not everything in common.

9. Catherine Lutz sums these up nicely: "A number of ethnographic studies have in fact demonstrated the interpenetration of concepts of the person with virtually every aspect of cultural knowledge, from that concerning divisions of labor to notions of time and history, to ideas organizing politics (e.g. Geertz 1973, Heelas and Lock 1981; Marcella, DeVos, and Hsu 1985; Kirkpatrick 1983; Myers 1979; Rosaldo 1980; Shore 1982; White and Kirkpatrick 1985)" (Lutz 1998, 83). An august list to which I must add: Mauss 1985 [1938]; Willis 1977; Riesman 1992; Pesmen 2000; Ortner 2005; Biel, Good, and Kleinman 2007; Pinney 2008; Wilf 2011; Stevenson 2014; Kockelman and Enfield 2017. There are also many exceptional nonethnographic works on the cultural development of the inner self; those which proved most insightful to me during the course of this study though they are not otherwise cited herein were Greenblatt 1980; Krauss 1986; Deleuze 1994; Pfister 1995; Haugeland 1998; Link 1999, 2004; Metzinger 2003; and Maus 2004.

self-promotion, self-representation, and open self-expression. These moments are collected here, to show the grinding of gears as Slovenes were greeted with a particular sort of failure as they approached, mano a mano, European cultural integration as if it were primarily a mimetic process.[10]

10. Mimesis for most people simply means imitation. A leaf is green; a lizard is the same green. A parent eats noodles by spinning a fork around in a bowl full of them; a child eats noodles by spinning a fork around in a bowl that is similarly full. Life is attentive to its surroundings in various ways, sometime with cognition, sometimes without, and fitting to those surroundings often takes the form of likeness. Whether in color, in motion, in form, in smell, in size, in song, life is mimetic and imitation is a mode of fitting to context; this is true of culture and nature, societies and ecosystems. Of course, when humans get involved meaning begins to wend its way through these processes, knitting worlds as it goes. What is knit is sameness *with* difference, an elegant toggle, "pulling you this way and that; mimesis plays the trick of dancing between the very same and the very different. An impossible but necessary, indeed everyday affair, mimesis registers both sameness and difference, of being like and of being other." Creating stability from instability is no small task, "yet all identity formation is engaged in this habitually bracing activity in which the issue is not so much staying the same, but maintaining sameness through alterity" (Taussig 1993, 129). In other words, we are not like you, but because of you, we are like us.

Chapter 2

I. TECHNOLOGIES OF SELF-PROTECTION

> This is then not exactly the psychic armored ego but, instead,
> the social ego formed from the outside in, its social substitute
> skin forming its insectlike exoskeleton.

Mark Seltzer, "Serial Killers (II)," 1995

Jurij Krpan, Kapelica Galerija's head curator and the curator of the
Slovene pavilion at the 2003 Venice Biennale, often bemoaned how hard
it was to get Slovene artists to stand up in front of an audience and talk
about their work. They were content to offer lectures as themselves but on
the work of others or, while impersonating others, they would talk about
almost anything. But getting them to represent themselves *as themselves*
publicly was, Krpan claimed, nearly impossible.

Indeed, in Ljubljana in the early 2000s, where public lectures with cultural overtones were common—with one to three a week (except in August
when everyone is on vacation)—I only once witnessed a Slovene artist talk
before a room full of people about his work, albeit in an unusual way.
Marko Peljhan, the artist in question, sat as he spoke behind a veritable

Figure 7. Laibach *as if* shopping at the mall (EINKAUF action), Ljubljana, 2003. Reproduced with permission from Laibach.

wall of technology. Though he had brought along these many machines (speakers and cameras and projectors and screens) to augment the presentation, they had a secondary purpose. They also blocked him almost entirely from view. In this, Peljhan was not alone.

In their art, as in their public lives, Slovene artists almost universally shied away from acts of self-representation, frequently by placing some substance between themselves and their audiences and, as often as not, also adopting a false role or invented persona. Marko Kovačič, for example, put on a white lab coat and the guise of Dr. Jevgenij Skavčenko when presenting his *Plastos Civilization* (Bakke 2007). The four (and sometimes five) individual members of Laibach not only use the collective eponym "Laibach" but also have over the course of almost thirty years worn quasi-military uniforms when in public. This "space" of performance in these cases extended well beyond the typical venues of concerts, photo shoots, and public interviews to encompass the after party and just roaming around town.

Someone from the Geo-Art Statistics Research Institute of the Republic of Slovenia (RISGURS) wrote with the authoritative voice of an expert on "Slovenian-Mediterranean Artists" as if he or she were Luther Blisset. This adopted identity was then embedded deep into the faux-institutional form of the arts collective itself. Painter Žiga Kariž took to spending his nights and taking his meals in the gallery where his art was hung. Yet despite the fact that he could hear everything happening in the gallery below, he was himself invisible, protected from public view by the walls surrounding his enclave.[1] Theater director Dragan Živadinov, well-enough known in Ljubljana to be considered a public figure, often wore something akin to a uniform. This uniform bore great resemblance to the costumes he clothed his actors in on stage. Thus, though each of these artists and a great many others both like and unlike them integrated themselves into their artworks in personal and often also bodily ways, each also pulled away from overt acts of public self-representation.

Within these patterns of (hedged) self-presentation there were certain constants, most notably: a false identity, a uniform, hiding in darkness, and at the most extreme, hiding behind walls. There were also other slightly more complex clusterings of tools used by Slovene artists to shield themselves, like cell phones, Internet connections, and webcams; indeed, certain of these seem to have been designed for maintaining a delicate balance between self-exposure and self-protection. All pointedly allow for, indeed facilitate, communication while staving off direct physical contact. Wireless and satellite technologies were not originally intended for use between bunkmates lounging a half-meter from one another, as they were employed in Peljhan's masterful artwork-as-research laboratory, *Makrolab*. They can however, without much stretch of the imagination, be used in exactly this way as well as in other situations of close physical proximity (text messaging a neighbor at school; Skyping with someone in the next room, &c.).[2] A more curious treatment of mediating technolo-

1. The Slovene contemporary art gossip-mill was abuzz with the fact that at some point late in the 2003 Venice Bienalle, Kariž had taken to sleeping, eating, living in the upstairs of A+A, much to the (Venetian) gallery owner's horror. It took, they say, three weeks to move him out.

2. "One day I arrived at *Makrolab* after a 24-hour interval dripping wet from the hill, entering the hydraulic hatch to find the lab's inhabitants all staring at screens, on beds, at the workstations, a silence punctuated by the odd muffled giggle. Hi everyone, how's it going?

gies than proximate communication via devices designed for bridging distance was the means by which these devices were often reduced by Slovene artists to their materiality—their "objectness"—and then placed "in the way."

As most anyone living in places dense with personal electronics knows, "togetherness" in the here-and-now has sprung something of a spatiotemporal leak, as mediating objects—phones, cameras, tablets, MP3 players, electronic books, and other portable devices which maintain constant access to the Internet—have become as common as clothes and keys. Unlike clothes and keys, such devices force the present open; they accomplish this as much by inserting elsewheres into it as by shutting out, even if only momentarily, more immediate persons, objects, and relations. That is to say, most of the interruptive potential of mobile technologies, while common in Slovene culture, was far from specific to it.

What was unique, however, was the way in which mediating devices (cell phones, cameras, computers, and projectors of various sorts) were placed physically between people and thus used to fracture *visual* contact. In other words, high-tech devices can be used not only to incorporate an elsewhere (and an elsewhen) into proximate interactions, they can also—via their placement alone—prevent people from seeing one another. This use of technology as clutter was especially common in Slovenia in situations when public self-representation was expected and when the other easy means of cordoning oneself off from others (like a false identity, a uniform, darkness, &c.) were not immediately available or situationally viable.

For example, in the public lecture given by Peljhan mentioned above so many things had been gathered together and placed between him and his audience, including a slide projector, a video projector, an overhead projector, a television set, a video camera on a tripod, a laptop computer, and a microphone, that they formed an asteroid belt of electronics between us

---

No answer. After 5 minutes of being ignored I check the nearest screen. Lines of text—'Rob just came in, he's dripping wet'. Next line. 'I wonder if he'll make coffee'. There was an animated electronic conversation raging between people a metre away from each other. The lab had become a hive. Then I realized the hive extends all the way to Antarctica, all wondering if I am going to make coffee. I am tending a node of a global organism. I unloaded the food and made coffee." Rob La Frenais, curator of *Makrolab* in Scotland, quoted in Peljhan and Projekt Atol Institute (2003, 55).

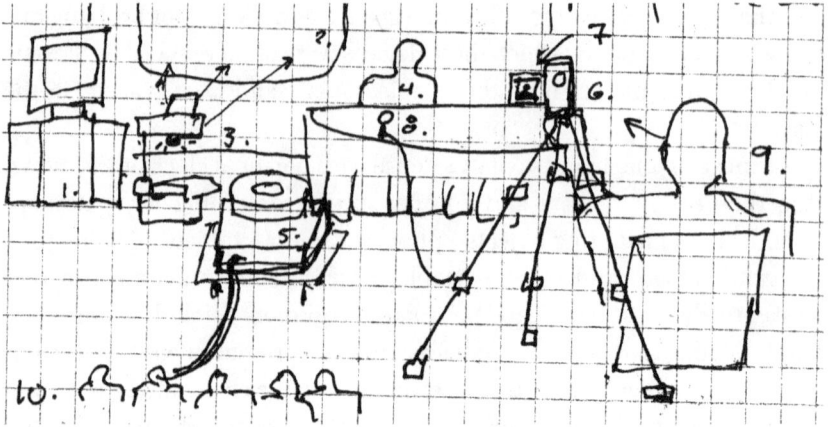

Figure 8. Marko Peljhan lecture, Ljubljana, 2003. (1) TV set and stand, (2) white screen, (3) overhead projector, (4) Peljhan, (5) slide projector, (6) video camera, (7) camera image of Peljhan, (8) microphone, (9) man operating video camera, (10) audience. Drawing by the author.

and him. Everyone in the room could easily see the white screen behind Peljhan's head upon which videos, slides, and text were projected, and everyone in the room could hear him clearly when he spoke. This was in part thanks to the high-quality, permanently installed sound system in the room, the speakers of which made up part of the clutter. It was only the speaking body of Peljhan that could not be seen. This lack of visual reference did not in the least detract from the lecture. His points were still well and interestingly made and his visual aids contributed to both the depth and the entertainment value of his presentation.

Certain of the devices used by Peljhan in this talk—such as a large white projection screen and a decent sound system—were omnipresent at performances and public lectures in Slovenia, as they are elsewhere. Other high-tech objects, especially those placed between audiences and performers, increased and decreased in number and differed in their placement depending upon the event. It was not therefore a personal proclivity of Peljhan's to maximize the interruptive potential of these sorts of things. Rather, his being the only public lecture given by a Slovene artist on his own work during my time in country (save one by Apolonija Šušteršič, which was held entirely in darkness) make this a rare example of a local mode of public self-representation.

There was, however, one other occasion when local professionals with some power and strongly held opinions (about each other if not always about the questions at hand) were expected to represent themselves publicly. This was at the two-day mini-conference entitled What Does Contemporary Art Demand of Its Institution? (*Kaj sodobna umetnost zahteva od svojih institucij?*) in 2003.

This conference, held in Moderna Galerija's basement "information center," was structured such that Slovenia's most prominent curators, directors of art institutions, and representatives of the Ministry of Culture might address each other formally and publicly, as well as intermingle with invited counterparts from abroad. The speakers at this conference (which included most everyone in the room at one point or another) had been organized onto panels. And each set of panelists spent several hours at a long table set up at the far end of the room. While there, ostensibly in plain view, these presenters were rendered almost completely invisible to the audience by an immense array of techno-clutter. So many recording and projecting devices had been erected in the three feet or so between speakers and audience members that in certain cases only an ear, or the top of someone's head, could be seen by those who had come to hear what the speakers had to say about contemporary problems of contemporary (art) museums.

An argument could be made that these machines were necessary to the success of the event. Some devices were there to record the goings-on for later dispersal (still cameras, video cameras, and audio recorders). Others brought past events and faraway places to bear upon the arguments being made (video projectors, slide projects, and computers with PowerPoint presentations, web pages, audio clips, &c.). Still others assured the success of the event in the instant (microphones, mounted speakers, and the equipment necessary for simultaneous translation). Certain of these objects were primarily symbolic, though no less important for this. The microphones for example, were slim, shiny, tubular things which could be twisted and turned in various directions by whomever was speaking. These served to index up-to-dateness in their form, material, design, and flexibility. However, their long, skinny, twisty shape also more effectively interrupted the face of the speaker than a standard mike on a stand would have. Indeed, from the audience's point of view these modern mics bifurcated the speaker's head pretty much in two. Nor did the size of the room (modest) or the size of the audience (twenty to thirty people, depending on the time of day) really necessitate the use of microphones. Were it not for all of the other technological devices impeding a clear line of vision, few if any of those present would have had difficulty following the presentations without benefit of a speaker system. Likewise, the video recordings of the proceedings—two were made, one by RTV Slovenia and one by Moderna Galerija, each with their own camera—could have been made with the cameras placed at the back of the room rather than between the viewing audience and those presenting their work, had it not been for all the other sundry machinery standing in the way.

More curious even than their positioning was that, at both Moderna Galerija and its doppelgänger Galerija Kapelica, the videotapes these cameras produced could not really be watched after the fact. The tapes were there but neither gallery had the machinery necessary to replay them, except via the cumbersome means of hooking the camera itself up to a TV. Thus, although the videotaped events were, in theory, being preserved for future viewers at the expense of those co-present, this process produced little more than numerous small rectangles of plastic. These were kept (in Kapelica's case) in cardboard boxes in the gallery's office or (in Moderna's) on the shelves of the video library (see figure 9). Many of these tapes, at least among those in Moderna Galerija's collection, had never been watched and were neither labeled nor categorized. Thus, the spatial privileging of the technological over the human was neither straightforwardly nor logically explainable by necessity alone.

The explanation Slovenia's most famous son, Slavoj Žižek, would likely give for this type of behavior is that of "interpassivity." According to this formulation the object, and most especially the device, has experiences in the subject's stead. For example, here it might be said that the camera was there to "watch" the presentations on behalf of the audience, such that the audience was freed up from having to do this themselves, as an answering machine might "listen" and indeed even "speak" for its owner. More than acting *as if* eyes, *as if* ears, *as if* (in the case of the laugh track) the subject's

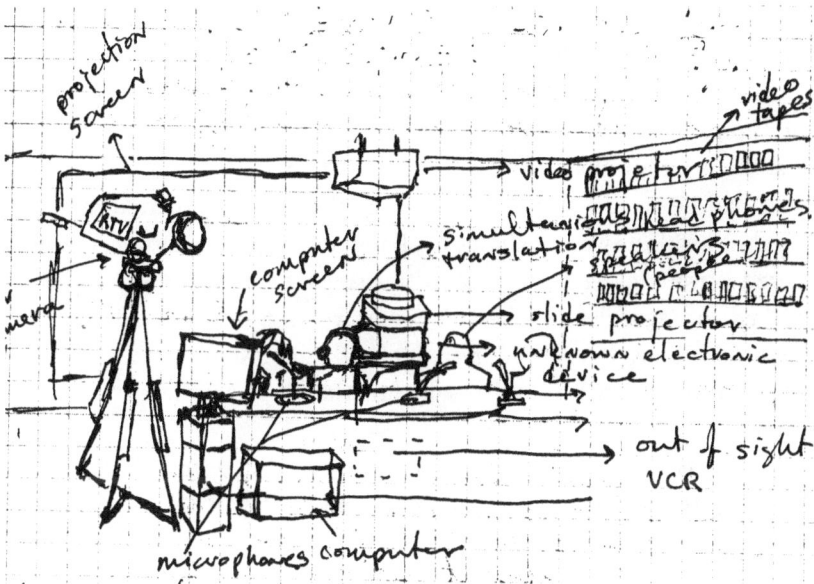

Figure 9. "What Does Contemporary Art Demand of Its Institution?," Ljubljana, 2003. Drawing by the author.

own laughter, Žižek claims that these things actually fulfill an emotional duty, an "ought" of attentiveness with which the modern world is overfull. Our machines enjoy for us, leaving us free not to enjoy, not to laugh, not to chat with people we care for and about, and not to watch what might otherwise give us pleasure. It "is the object itself," he says, "which 'enjoys the show' instead of me, relieving me of the superego duty to enjoy [it] myself. . . ."[3]

3. He continues: "Every VCR aficionado who compulsively records hundreds of movies (myself among them) is well aware that the immediate effect of owning a VCR is that one effectively watches less [*sic*] films than in the good old days of a simple TV set without a VCR; one never has time for TV, so, instead of losing a precious evening, one simply tapes the film and stores it for a future viewing (for which, of course, there is almost never time . . .). So, although I do not actually watch films, the very awareness that the films I love are stored in my video library gives me a profound satisfaction and, occasionally, enables me to simply relax and indulge in the exquisite art of *far'niente*—as if the VCR is in a way watching them for me, in my place" (Žižek 1998). See also Johnson 1988.

Extrapolated to the case at hand, one could say that the cameras watch for the audience and the microphones listen for them. Even better, another person had, in this case, been tasked with listening. In the back of the room, in a plywood "soundproof" (but actually quite sound-leaky) box, there sat a translator who listened and an instant later reproduced what had been said, in Slovene or in English as the situation dictated. Wireless headsets were available to all members of the audience, however these too went largely unused as, with a single exception, everyone spoke in English, regardless of their national origin. Since the audience was composed almost entirely of presenters and others active in the European art world they were also universally functional—if not elegant—English users.[4]

What is curious about all this, if one is thinking in terms of interpassivity, is that the equipment for "watching" and "enjoying" the conference in the attendees' stead made it very difficult for them to watch and enjoy it for themselves. The equivalent in Žižek's schema would be placing the VCR in front of the TV such that it blocked the screen and prevented—in the moment of recording—the viewer from seeing it. Interpassivity, that is to say, is an analytic of audiences. One doesn't think of how the TV show manages itself not to be watched, or how the laugh track might react to not being laughed along with. Agency (in the act of delegating enjoyment to another), particularity (in the ways one can and does choose to do so), and petulance (in not wanting that enjoyment to adhere to oneself in the first place) are all properties of the would-be viewer, or listener, or laugher. "Interpassivity" speaks to deligation. It transfers the obligation of an audience to enjoy, or at the very least be attentive, over to a device. While this may serve as a super-adequate explanation for all of those unlabeled, unwatched, and unwatchable video tapes on Moderna Galerija's shelves and in cardboard boxes on top of filing cabinets at Galerija Kapelica, it

4. Dragan Živadinov did wear a headset for most of the time he was in attendance, though he speaks English as well as many who were present (and slightly better than some). One can take this as a desire to be comfortable in understanding what he would quite likely have understood anyway, but with more effort, without the device. Or one can take it as a moment of language ideology (Irvine and Gal 2000) in profligate action. Likely, it was a bit of both.

offers little of analytic usefulness when it is the speaking subject who man-
ufactures, and profits from, the blind. Or, to say the same thing with fewer
words. If the audience didn't want to be there they would watch the videotapes—or at very least rely upon the idea of these tapes as there to be
watched. Yet the audience *is* there, co-present in the moment. They were
"enjoying" (if only aurally) the exchange of ideas. The wall of technology
did not serve to enjoy in their stead. At best, it enjoyed in their company,
but for the most part it was just in the way.

What's more, it was not universally true that objects were made to clutter the near orbit of speakers. Situations in which persons were *not* being
asked to represent themselves as themselves nor to voice their own opinions were characterized by much less, and much less intrusively placed,
machinery. For example, at a series of public lectures on Lacanian psycho-
analytics, held in 2002 at Galerija Kapelica, the young professor Aljoša
Kolenec used no technological accoutrements nor any other tropes common to public art events, like body paint, darkness, or a covered head.
Neither, however, did Kolenec make claims construable as his own.
Rather, in a manner that might best be described as "Žižekian," he devoted
himself to explanations of Lacan's positions, analytics, and approaches to
human beings as if these were both universal and absolute. Not his, but
everyone's. He quoted, he used references to popular films, he interpreted;
he was more of a translator than an author. His opinions were neither
individual nor idiosyncratic.

Likewise, on that day in 1986 when the false Benjamin spoke on the
late paintings of Piet Mondrian, he was, in stark contrast to those presentations mentioned above, photographed from the back of the room. The
camera was positioned behind the audience, leaving "Benjamin" and the
paintings in question entirely open to the audience's view (see figure 5).
When the Italian/British performance artist Franko B. performed his
nude promenade and bleeding performance *I Miss You* live in Ljubljana
in 2002, he was covered from head to foot in white greasepaint. The press
waited at the end of the catwalk, while the audience was seated along its
long edges, their views entirely unobscured. When Apolonija Šušteršič
presented a retrospective of her work she used only a computer, a
projector—mounted in this case on the ceiling (not in the way)—and the

ubiquitous white screen. This setup would have left her in clear view had the lights not been turned off for her entire lecture. Since Šušteršič spoke her presentation from memory rather than read it aloud she was not even identifiable in the pinprick of light otherwise offered by a reading lamp; her voice rather provided a disembodied, though easily heard, accompaniment to her visual aids.

In radical contrast, those invited to speak at What Does Contemporary Art Demand of Its Institution? had no recourse to roles other than their own nor permission to address topics beyond their own area of expertise. Nor could they simply shut off the lights for the duration of their presentations. To make the situation even more delicate, they had been asked to perform the task of "self-representation" before an audience of foreigners and other locals, many of whom were held in high regard. (Among others Nicolas Bourriaud, in from France, thin as a rail and smoking like a chimney; most of the artist's collective IRWIN; Dragan Živadinov, given to uttering loud exasperated sighs whenever anyone went on at too great length about things he [presumably] disagreed with; the occasionally present then-minister of culture and her omnipresent spokesman, Simon Kardum; Joseph Ortner, the cofounder of the *Museum in Progress* in Vienna; and Lars Grambye, the director of the Danish Contemporary Art Foundation.)[5] In other words, in this particular case, it was precisely self-representation that was demanded from all parties at all times while very little was made available to hide behind, or within, save the copious machine clutter.[6]

5. The English webpage of the *Museum in Progress* can be found at www.mip.at/en/index.html, accessed July 2019).

6. Even the formulation of the conference title: "What does contemporary art demand of its institution?" (*Kaj sodobna umetnost zahteva od svojih institucij?*) obscures persons. It is the contemporary art that demands, not the contemporary artist, though he or she shapes this art in ways that do or do not fit into traditional spaces and formats of display. Likewise, the art is not making demands upon curators and others whose efforts support and allow institutions of art to function. Rather the art makes its demands upon the institution itself. The inanimates are here in relationships of demand, frustration, belonging. The people are secondary—to the degree that one might (or perhaps must) imagine them existing at all.

II. "BY THE VERY CUNNING OF THE SCENE"

More than just a body seen or an opinion voiced, the sticking point in many of the interactions and performances described above lay precisely in their combination: the voice, when separated from the body, tended to flow easily; and the body, when separated from its (voiced) opinions, was often and pointedly presented for public view. It was only when these two were combined into one thoroughgoing act of "body plus voiced opinion" that lines of slight began to be shut down or obscured in various ways (Salecl and Žižek 1996). Though one could easily speak here of self-reflexivity or of "the mirror stage" (Lacan 2006), the act of individuation that concerns me was not that of coming to know oneself as something—or rather some*one*—specific and unique. Rather, it was that of presenting and representing that someone to others in a public forum. Responsibility for self here appears to be as much at issue as individuality or particularity per se. The two sorts of selves (voice and body) existed well on their own, as Walter Benjamin the Second, Maja Licul, Marko Peljhan, Apolonija Šušteršič, et al. made clear above. Only when brought together into one "subject" that both speaks for (with its own voice) and represents (with its own body, role, profession, expertise) itself did balking and hedging commence.

That a visible anxiety might arise where opinion and persona coincide should not come as a total surprise given the immense importance in Slovenia of modally inflected gossip, the distress that marked imperatives for open self-expression, and the gravity attendant on individual variations from the norm. What is curious is not that individuals, each unique in many ways, might shy away from appearing as such among their peers. Rather, given the value placed upon individualism, personal accomplishment, and distinction within the European art world, it felt remarkable that Slovene artists, curators, and administrators might shun appearing as distinct and accomplished individuals. This was most obvious when they were asked to do so live and in person.

At first glance the self-representative split here would not seem to be between an inner and outer self, but between a body and a voice—between being seen *and* being heard; speaking for *and* as oneself was anathema. One might easily, and perhaps even correctly, claim that there is a fragility or vulnerability inherent to seeing a voice emerge from inside a body. How can one disown something so incontrovertibly intimate as one's own voice, spoken from between the breathing lips of one's own mouth, past the brief hard hint of one's own teeth, pushed outward from the body with the stink of one's own warm breath? There is a physiological intimacy, akin to that of excretion, to speech. Something from inside exits the body, but rather than disappearing like shit into a hole, flushed neatly away into a city's sewers, the voice carries forth. It touches, figuratively and in wave form, all proximate ears, all proximate bodies, all proximate persons. Before issuing a critique of Slovene shyness in this regard one might ask why more people don't care about the intimacies of speaking. Drunks, the mad, Americans— they all talk with indiscriminate ease. Open self-expression, that is to say, might be linked, in an admittedly facile conjunction, to opening the mouth and letting sound pour forth.

Mladen Dolar, the philosopher we met in the preface, addresses these questions explicitly. In *A Voice and Nothing More* (2006), Dolar does not speak of Slovenes hunkered behind laptops or shutting off all the lights before opening their mouths. The issues he raises are, however, linked to the intense bodily discomfort displayed by Slovene artists when asked to speak for, and as, themselves.

Nor is Dolar, when teaching or presenting his work in public, so different. He reads rather than speaks extemporaneously. His head bowed, his notes tightly written in a tiny script, he aims his mouth at his paper and chews his way through his prepared text. He too wears a microphone, even in a classroom situation, clipped neatly to his collar so that the voice that spreads his words does not come to audiences from his breath or his body but from speakers mounted in the far corners of the room. When he speaks, his mouth remains almost always invisible to the observer, his words directed not outward but down toward the dot of the microphone, his papers, and then pretty much directly to his shoes as if these were the intended audience for many a well-thought out treatise on psychoanalytic and philosophical thought.

For Dolar this is not just a way of being, it is analytic fodder, and in his slight and careful book on the voice he is intensely concerned with a misapprehension hinted at above. The voice, because it emerges from inside the body, is easily mistaken as representative of an otherwise inaccessible psychic, rather than a more commonsensical physiological, innerness. This is, for Dolar, who sees the voice as immanently biological yet replete with ascribed meanings, a mistake. The body is "a mechanism emitting voice" (10), he says. Yet this voice is often mistaken for the sound (here quoting Aristotle) "of what has a soul in it" (24).[7] Simply put, the voice—a product of the flesh—becomes homologous to an insubstantial but presumed form of being. Neither voice nor soul are flesh, but both find their home in flesh. Neither are knowable in their essence, yet both find expression in the mass of the body's emotive material. Which is to say that one cannot be sure what lies are told in the journey air (or soul) makes through the substance of the body, becoming in the process language, motion, expression, tick, slip of tongue, quirk of gait, or inappropriate wander of the eye. The body, generally a poor expressive mechanism, is exceptionally well suited to subterfuge. Or to quote a familiar phrase, it makes a far better wall than a window.

I may have difficulties telling you for certain what *is* inside the body, besides the now commonly agreed upon glomeration of vessels and associated metabolisms (revealed in chapter 5). But Dolar is more certain: there is nothing there at all—a nothing that the voice, "the subtlest and the most perfidious form of the flesh" (48), obscures with every emotive note.

> The voice comes from some unfathomable invisible interior and brings it out, lays it bare, discloses, uncovers, reveals that interior. By so doing it produces an effect which has both an obscene side (disclosing something hidden, intimate, revealing too much, *structurally* too much) and an uncanny side . . . . One could indeed say that there is an effect—or, rather, an affect—of shame that accompanies voice: one is ashamed of using one's voice because it exposes some hidden intimacy to the Other, *there is a shame which pertains not to psychology but to structure.* (80; emphasis added)

Dolar continues: "What is exposed, of course, is not some interior nature, an interior treasure too precious to be disclosed, or some true self, or a primordial inner life; rather it is an interior which is the result of the

---

7. The internal quote is from Aristotle, *De Anima*, 1.2, 420b6.

signifying cut, its product, its cumbersome remainder, an interior created by the intervention of the structure" (80).

There is, thus, something "essential" to the discomfort Slovenes display in moments of public self-presentation, for they are in fact exposing themselves. According to Dolar, it is correct that they feel, or at least affect the feeling of, shame—as he himself does—when so exposed. He takes pains, however, to make clear that the discomfort that clings to the speaker in moments of "self-presentation" is pointedly a structural (a word three times repeated in this passage) and not an individual one. That is to say, the speaker is rightly disturbed by the self-exposures of emitting their own voice but this is not, according to Dolar, because the voice bears traces of an inner being. Rather, what is exposed is something far more intimate: that there is no such thing as a subject conterminous with itself. No *one* is in there. What is revealed instead is a sort of structural flaw, a "cumbersome remainder," or formal accident that one can (mistakenly) become attached to.

The secret of the subject, here revealed, is that, far from being unified-but-concealed or invisible-yet-true, it is manifestly *not* self-contained and *not* self-determined (see also Žižek 2013, 715–37). It is not even singular. Indeed, it may not even be there. By this measure we are, in our most preciously held moments of singularity, little more than epiphenomena of a structural intervention of otherness. This self as by-product is what Dolar (here quoting Freud) claims "ought to have remained . . . secret and hidden but [which, with the voice] has come to light" (80).

More, however, than simply discomforting the speaker by exposing his or her quintessence to be little more than a structural side effect, Dolar with this argument takes aim at the heart of metaphysics, that branch of philosophy most reliant upon the concept of pure essences:

> If a notion of metaphysics is carried by the propensity to disavow the part of alterity, the trace of the other [in order] to hold onto some ultimate signified against the disruptive play of differences, to maintain the purity of the origin against supplementarity, then it can do so only by clinging to the voice as a source of an originary self-presence. The divide between the interior and the exterior, the model of all other metaphysical divides, derives from here. (38)

Dolar's complaint is that the strange bit—the structural flaw—that is most essential to the constitution of the subject is precisely the bit that metaphysics is most inclined to ignore in order to postulate a subject's integrity. Dolar illustrates his frustration by recapitulating a fundamental disagreement with Derrida, for whom "the voice heard" *is* a mechanism for producing a "pure" sort of innerness, one that is not only "real" (i.e., extant) but also unadulterated. For Derrida, the voice heard is a signifier that "does not borrow from outside itself, in the world or in 'reality,' any accessory signifier, any substance of expression foreign to its own spontaneity. It is the unique experience of the signified producing itself spontaneously from within the self" (1976, 20). For Dolar, that the sound of air pushed through flesh might serve to ground a generative metaphysics is more than folly—it is false. The relation of cause and effect taken to be "constitutive of interiority and ultimately of consciousness, the self, and autonomy" (Dolar 2006, 38–39) does not exist.

Thus do the implications of speaking for and as oneself multiply. Showing one's mouth moving as sound exits lungs, diaphragm, and gullet has the unfortunate effect of exposing one's actual vacuity. Heterogeneity, contamination, or the impurity of the subject, not self-consistency, is what is confirmed in this moment of "self-expression."[8] What is exposed is first "the Other," the traces of which constitute the newly observable flaw at the very core of the subject, and second the false heart of some choice bits of the European philosophical tradition. For Dolar, the speaking voice "trembles," it "plea[ds] for mercy." Nor is one left to wonder why: as he tells it, there is hardly a more vulnerable position for the subject than standing tall, with mouth openly visible, before a room of attentive listeners—their eyes focused, their ears attuned—and being seen speaking of oneself, for oneself, and *as* oneself. *"One is too exposed to the voice and the voice exposes too much*, one incorporates and one expels too much" (81).[9]

8. Or to put Žižek's words to the process: "When our innermost self is directly externalized the result is disgusting" (2006, 60).

9. Michelle Rosaldo (1982), in making an argument against Austin's (1962) notions of performativity (principally as explicated by Searle [1969]), understands "promise" in much the same way that Dolar explains the sound of a word exiting the body. For Rosaldo, a promise is a projection of internal intentionality. She writes, "To think of promising is, I would claim, to focus on the sincerity and integrity of the one who speaks ... a promise would

In such situations there is however always the promise of subterfuge and illusion. One can, in other words, hedge ones' bets. One can cloak oneself in darkness or hide oneself behind tightly packed techno-clutter; one can ventriloquize oneself from speakers mounted in the corner of the room or through headphones placed upon the ears of listeners. The language of one's voice can be changed (indeed the "personality-full" individuality of the voice itself erased) via simultaneous translation. Or, alternately, one's body can be displaced in time, recorded on video, and rebroadcast later. And even then, returning for a moment to the untitled work of Maja Licul (in chapter 1), the voice can be braided so that clarity of "self" and of "source" are at so many degrees of remove that these are reduced to little more than the aesthetics of presence. One can even, like Benjamin, make of oneself a work of art. Or, barring all this, one can simply hide one's mouth, as Dolar does by looking down, as Šušteršič did by turning out the light, as Peljhan did (on another occasion), turning and turning in the smallest of spaces while giving a tour of his *Makrolab* facility such that his back was always facing his audience. By hiding "the orifice, the bodily aperture from which the voice is coming, the mouth . . . the gap, the crack, the hole, the cavity, the void, the very absence of phallus"

---

appear to come authentically from inside. It is a public testimony to commitments we sincerely undertake, born of a human need to 'contract' social bonds, an altruism that makes us want to publicize our plans. Thus the promise leads us to think of meaning as a thing derived from inner life" (211). For the Ilongot with whom she did research, however, such internal intentionality was not the principal way of getting things done; rather a person just demanded in the here and now (and with many rules and hierarchies attached) that others move themselves on one's own behalf. Phrases amounting to "Get up and get me some water" (204), far from being rude, were the standard way of structuring subjectivity and community, as the illocutionary force of such commands literally picked people up and shuffled them around. We do this too, and with some similar rules: children and women are more often pushed into motion than men. In a world structured by such commandments there is little need for interiority, or its expression, as social relations are practiced in the moment. Promising (like keeping appointments) was thus largely absent among the Ilongot because it was necessary neither to social life nor to individual self-concept. Rosaldo writes: "Ways of thinking about language and about human agency and personhood are intimately linked: our theoretical attempts to understand how language works are like the far less explicated thoughts of people elsewhere in the world, in that both inevitably tend to reflect locally prevalent views about the given nature of those human persons by whom language is used" (203). Similarly, Dolar here is trying to make "locally prevalent views about the given nature of those human persons" graspable to nonlocals. His book was published in English by MIT Press; it was made for those not from Slovenia who read and practice philosophy.

(68), one can create the illusion of voice without a source and, thus, one hopes, and Dolar posits, cede less of one's(empty)self to another.

This is how the Christian God (and the Wizard of Oz) speaks: acousmaticly.[10] Theirs are voices "whose source one cannot see, . . . whose origin cannot be identified" (60). When given flesh—in both cases—the authoritative quality of the voice is changed. The Wizard is but a small man with no divinity in him, though he maintains a certain mastery over the technologies of illusion. God made flesh, in the form of his only begotten son, is a man whose divinity is always in doubt. His words when spoken from his embodied mouth hold far less weight than those of his disembodied father. Listeners, simply put, ignore Christ or think him loony more often than they believe in him for what he is: spirit made flesh.

Miracles, a necessity for all gods, are of particular importance to those in human form, while the voices of those who have no bodies, or who hold their bodies apart, have greater affective power for coming from nowhere (everywhere?) or being nowhere (everywhere?) (Auerbach 1991 [1946]). When embodied, the words of a wizard unmasked and of God made flesh are both less enigmatic and less powerful. This degradation of authoritative spirit when voiced by a human might easily be read in terms of the inevitable, unenviable weakness of the flesh, that is, that being embodied means being *seen* for one's imperfections. The spirit when made flesh is often a shocking departure from the ideal, a deception that online dating makes particularly acute.

That such a revelation is simultaneously a serious diminution of the power of the voice is nowhere more solidly apparent than in the person of Wizard of Oz; he is grandiose when hidden behind a screen and represented by a booming voice and head-shaped pyrotechnics. The ruler of a land overfull with remarkable "people" and magical objects of every sort, the Wizard is transformed, when revealed, into a bumbling little man with awkward shoes and little magical power beyond the pomp and circumstance of his well-tooled illusions. Not a god, but (at best) an engineer, a humbug. His voice, most notably, changes from that of stately, indeed mystical, power to that of a man who is, in effect, no one at all. Visibility diminishes him in every dimension.

10. Both examples, the Wizard of Oz and the Christian God, are Dolar's.

Dolar suggests that what looses the authoritative impact of the divine (or the otherwise powerful) is not, however, being *seen* as flesh and blood, but rather being seen to be *speaking*: "It [i]s the voice which itself acquired authority and surplus meaning by virtue of the fact that its source [i]s concealed; it seemed to become omnipresent and omnipotent. The beauty of this mechanism is the simplest possible—it works automatically: the Master, 'by the very cunning of the scene' (Hamlet, II / 2.586), as it were, turns into spirit without a body" (61–62).

The "cunning of the scene" in the Wizard's case is that of a screen. In Pythagoras's it is a curtain hung between himself and his pupils—the original "Acousmatics"—so that over a period of years they heard only the sound of his voice, aurally transmitting his mastery to them, while never laying their eyes upon his speaking body (see also Božovič 2000). In Šušteršič's case, the cunning abided in darkness; in Licul's, it is a TV screen and the production of acousmatic distance through technological remove, while in Peljhan's lecture it was that dense field of mechanical clutter, and in his tour of *Makrolab* the equally opaque back of his head. Regardless of the means, in each case a simple barrier to vision promoted the splitting of the voice from the body; present without a body the voice becomes, according to Dolar, more than itself, while the presumed speaker is aggrandized even to the "God point" of omnipresence and omnipotence by structural means alone. Bodily shirking of the gaze, read thus, is most essentially an embodied pretense at disembodiment. It both shields the speaker from being seen for the flaw (the untoward presence of the Other) that he or she in essence *is* while simultaneously distracting the listeners from the acousmatic process in effect.

Be all of this as it may, it also stands in radical contrast to the public speaking behaviors outsiders both exhibited and expected Slovenes to manifest in situations of public presentation. One simply did not see equal levels of structurally indexed awkwardness (shirking, shrinking, mumbling) among visiting academics, artists, theorists, and curators, who kept rather than cancelled interview appointments, were more likely to present their work without technological accompaniment or with a limited number of slides, to stand rather than sit, to use their own voices rather than microphones and speaker systems (even when these were provided), and to leave their faces visible to, rather than obscuring them from, their audiences. On one notable occasion, when the Serbian art historian Miško Šuvaković gave a public lecture in Ljubljana on the history of the (retro)-avant-garde—a lecture held in darkness with a great many slides—he actually stood in front of the projector's beam while he talked, illuminating himself while inserting his enormous shadow into the midst of the images he'd brought along ostensibly to illustrate his point.

The behavioral contrast should be clear. What remains less clear is that the "thoughtless" ease of outsiders (Šuvaković et al.) if read symptomatically could easily be taken as evidence of self-confidence. In contrast, the public slumping in their seats of Slovenes might likewise be seen as (at best) representative of individuals hugely unsure of themselves, and as (at worst) symptomatic of an incompetence bordering at times on impotence.

Though it may well be that Serbs are unafraid of the spotlight, Brits easily erect, Danes convincingly preachy, Americans utterly sure of the hipness of their interpretive moves, and Slovenes hopelessly immersed in self-doubt, this is not the analysis Dolar, a Slovene, provides. Indeed, not only does he not read such external behaviors as symptomatic of inner states, but his entire treatise on the voice is an implicit argument against such symptomatic readings. To look from surface-level phenomena inward is, in other words, a cultural bias reproduced as much in analytic maneuvers as in commonsensical judgments.

There is another option, Dolar tells us both overtly and between the lines, and that is to move from surface-level phenomena outwards. To ask, rather: To what does the perceptible link us? How does it implicate us in the social and object worlds beyond the limits of our bodies? Rather than probing inward in search of an answer to the question, Who am I? and by extrapolation: Who are we?, one might just as well take the body as physical mass—meat with air in it, shit in it, piss in it, a body that eats and excretes—and ask what proceeds from this physicality? Psychically? Philosophically? And socially?

What Dolar provides us here and what Žižek will provide a bit later is a window into analytic processes that are themselves reflective of a distinctive cultural logic. That such analyses might be particularly well suited to reading everyday behaviors of Slovenes should not come as a surprise. The cultural milieu within which Mladen Dolar thinks and writes is the same as that within which Peljhan (and Šušteršič, Licul, Kariž, et al.) create and speak about creation. With each endeavor one sees a redoubling of effort toward a single point, that (to bring Žižek's voice into the mix) "the 'secret' to be unveiled through analysis is not the content hidden by the form . . . but, on the contrary, *the 'secret' of the form itself*" (Žižek 1989, 11).

Portraits of a Three-Headed Mountain
(1968, 2004, 2007)

Figure 10. Mount Triglav (three-headed mountain), by the artists' collective OHO (Miljenko Matanović, David Nez, and Drago Dellabernardina), Kongresni trg, Ljubljana, 1968. Courtesy of Moderna Galerija, Ljubljana.

Figure 11. *Like to Like / Mount Triglav,* IRWIN, Ljubljana, 2004. Remake, on the basis of a photograph, of *Mount Triglav,* the action of the group OHO. Production by Cornerhouse. Courtesy of Gregor Podnar Gallery. Photo by Tomaž Gregorič.

Figure 12. *Mount Triglav on Mount Triglav,* Janez Janša, Janez Janša, and Janez Janša, Mount Triglav, 2007. Courtesy of Aksioma. Photo by Gaja Repe.

Chapter 3

I. TWO IN THE SAME: JANEZ JANŠA, JANEZ JANŠA, JANEZ JANŠA, AND JANEZ JANŠA

> A proper name [is] a word that answers the purpose of showing what a thing is that we are talking about but not telling anything about it.
>
> John Stuart Mill, *A System of Logic*, 1843

In 2013 one of the Janez Janšas was invited by the Department of Art History and Communication at McGill University in Montréal to present the project *Name Readymade* (2007) to an audience comprised of faculty, students, and interested others.[1] The talk proceeded as most do. Scheduled for 5:30 p.m., it began late as we shuffled into seats, coats sloughed off around us like so many other autumn things. Janša, once introduced, stood to the left of a large white screen, and as the lights dimmed he began to explain.

The section epigraph is John Stuart Mill, *A System of Logic* (I.ii.5), quoted in *Jaz sem Janez Janša* [My name is Janez Janša] (Janša 2012).

1. The event was blurbed here: https://www.mcgill.ca/ahcs/channels/event/speaker-series-janez-jansa-229986.

In 2007, this Janša and two other artists working and living in Slovenia changed their names to Janez Janša—a "loaded" name borrowed from Janez Janša, at that time Slovenia's prime minster, though his renown extended far beyond this temporary (and oft repeated) role. "When the three artists changed their names to Janez Janša," wrote curator Zdenka Badovinac of *Name Readymade*, "they adopted a critical stance toward the Slovenian government, in which—until recently—it seemed that all posts were occupied by a single person: Janez Janša" (Badovinac 2008, 60).

While Janša (the artist) spoke that northern autumn evening, a series of PowerPoint slides played behind him on the screen. Most displayed images of official documents (identity cards, birth certificates, marriage certificates, voter ID cards, &c.) that in the early years just after the name change, before the Janšas began doing art-like things, served as the project's primary material evidence. *Name Readymade*, which does travel as an "artwork," consists mostly of these identity cards, reissued birth certificates, bank cards, passports, and the like, effectively stranding the Janšas without these documents for the run of any show. Many of the documents also contain the Janšas' home addresses, making the artists accessible in an unusually intimate sort of way. One can mail them something or just stop in and ask for a cup of tea.

While the talk held true to form, everything playing out in a correct and recognizable "artist's talk" sort of way, it all broke down in the Q&A. Primarily because the audience manifested no particular interest in the "art" part of the project. Rather, what they wanted to know about was Janša's tattered subjectivity. Did he feel "torn" by having taken on someone else's name? Or did he feel "more himself" beneath the "mask" of a false name? (To which Janša wrinkled his brow and said simply, "No.") The name change, as a performance that smudged into real life, bothered them. Who was this Janez Janša, the man who stood before them? They suspected that something was wrong with his integrity, with his person, that he had broken himself by means of this legal act. They pushed hard to get him to admit, or to show, or at the very least to confirm in some small way that his doubling made him less himself. Whereas, the opposite was more likely the case. Doubled he was denser. The complex play between the two—the Emil Hrvatin (for that is what this Janša was once called) of the past and the Janez Janša of the present—allowed for a resonance of being in time. Like the play of oil with water, the surface scum of identity grew resplendent in the rainbowed mixing of the two. This effect was produced in part by his redoubling twice over: as Janez Janša née Emil Hrvatin; as a Croatian now also a Slovene.

Even I, over dinner, contrived never to say: "Janez, please could you pass me the mustard, or the salt, or, how do you find the weather, how are things in Slovenia these days, it's been so long since I visited?" I did, of course, ask him these things, but I too sidestepped calling him by his taken name: Janez Janša. This was not a personal failing (my own), but rather an extension of what the artwork was meant to do: it made every mundane act of addressing him or calling for his attention ("Hey, Janez—salt?") heavy on the lips and hard on the tongue. It felt too much like thinking.

My assumption, at the time, however, was that my reticence to use his new name was because I had known Janez years earlier, when he had been named otherwise. I had worked for him in 2001 at *Maska* [*The Mask*], a Slovene glossy for the performing arts, its offices in Metelkova, an old Yugoslav army garrison in downtown Ljubljana. Metelkova was then in the process of becoming a vibrant arts center, but was still largely run down and squatted, its protean dance clubs small enough that they rotated through audiences by days of the week (Monday heavy metal; Tuesday punk; Wednesday gay bar; Thursday rave, &c.).[2] *Maska* was an early inhabitant of the ruin and suffered a bit from infrastructure-in-collapse (the water undrinkable, the doors unlockable, the plaster crumbling). I liked it there.

For my few months at *Maska*, I did the odd job of reading through legal contracts in English to divine their terms, then translating them into an English that a nonnative speaker might hope to understand. Janez (not called that then) was my boss, the magazine's editor, and a performance artist. I liked him too. And even after my unsanctioned departure by gradual attrition, we often ran into each other around town. "*Zdravo, zdravo*" (Hi, hi). And so it went. When I left Slovenia two years later, I did not seek him out to say goodbye.

---

2. Metelkova mesto (www.metelkovamesto.org/) is today an alternative living, working, and arts space that has drawn the city into itself. The contemporary arts museum (+MSUM) is there and the old prison has become a youth hostel, each cell redesigned by a practicing local architect and artist. Events today (Tuesday, February 14, 2017) include a cooking workshop with the tagline "friendship through food," a public screening of the sci-fi film *Death Race 2050* (Echternkamp 2017), and a rock concert by an experimental "cabaret punk" band from LA.

I knew the other two artists who would become known as Janez Janša less well. One I'd met after climbing over the red velvet rope meant to delimit the private space in a Venice gallery from the public, only to find the artist in residence (i.e., he appeared to be living there, much to the curator's dismay, as I would later learn). The third Janez Janša I'd seen perform several times, most notably in *Brainscore* (2003), a curious piece that melded digital frenetics with bodily immobility (Bakke 2017). I knew the most famous Janez Janša (the politician) not at all. Nor did I know any of the eight other men who went by the name Janez Janša, who were living in Slovenia when the three soon-to-be Janez Janšas filed the paperwork to change their names in the summer of 2007. It's a common enough name. Parents give it to sons.[3]

Name Readymade's project of finding and then appropriating a name was an explicit play on Marcel Duchamp's famous work of putting everyday "found" objects, or "readymades," into galleries, giving them a title, and thus making them Art. A wood and galvanized iron snow shovel, in pristine condition, became *In Advance of a Broken Arm* (1915). Thrice lost and replaced, its specificity remains linked to its aesthetics (its "look"), and its status as a work of art confirmed by its displacement from a hardware store to a contemplative art space. No longer for digging, it became a thing of catalog essays and MOMA retrospectives—"an ordinary object elevated to the dignity of a work of art by the mere choice of an artist" (Breton and Éluard 1938).[4] However, despite the common perception that Duchamp picked up anything that came to hand (in part due to his own casual claims in this regard),[5] he was, to the contrary, quite careful in his selections, at times joining two found objects into the sort of thing one would never happen

3. In July 2019, Slovenia had 11 Janez Janšas, 20,955 Janezes, and 327 Janšas; https://www.stat.si/ImenaRojstva/FirstNames/SearchFirstNames?Ime = Janez&Priimek= Janša&Spol = M.

4. The first definition of a readymade (quoted everywhere) is from André Breton and Paul Éluard's *Dictionnaire abrégé du surréalisme* (1938). About readymades, Duchamp himself said, "It's not the visual aspect of the Readymade that matters, it's simply the fact that it exists. . . . Visuality is no longer a question: the Readymade is no longer visible, so to speak. It is completely gray matter. It is no longer retinal" (quoted in Girst 2003).

5. See especially, Duchamp as quoted in proceedings from The Art of Assemblage: A Symposium, The Museum of Modern Art, New York, October 19, 1961 (Seitz 1961); found at https://www.moma.org/documents/moma_catalogue_1880_300062228.pdf. See especially p. 46.

upon in a street, bar, gutter, or home—a stool topped with a bicycle wheel, for example (Girst 2003). The same was true of *Name Readymade*. The name was not selected by happenstance. Far from having been "found," it was known, and was as evocative, and provocative, a choice for reattribution as a urinal might have been when Duchamp called one *Fountain* and placed it, in 1917, into an art gallery (a gesture copied, of course, by Malevich in "The International Exhibition of Modern Art" described in chapter 1).

In 2007, when *Name Readymade* launched, Janez Janša was the prime minister of Slovenia and the head of the Slovenian Democratic Party (SDS) which he had led since 1993.. He was due, the following year to rotate into the presidency of the Council of the European Union. He would be elected prime minister again in 2012, then go to prison, and then be exonerated, in a boom-and-bust cycle that characterized the whole of his professional political life. A writer, a dissident, a xenophobe, and a pacifist, Janša was the minister of defense during Slovenia's nearly bloodless departure from Yugoslavia in 1991. All of this mythos and ethos has added up to Janša having one of the most recognizable names in Slovenia. His life is not only interwoven into the fabric of the nation's contemporary history, but he has, in significant ways, been determinant of that history. He has done wise and honorable things; he has also been a total schmuck. Everybody knows his name.

A less all-encompassing, but still substantial, "everyone" also knew the given names of the three artists—Emil Hrvatin, Žiga Kariž, and Davide Grassi—who would become Janez Janša, Janez Janša, and Janez Janša. This "being known" in the register of fame, which is to say one's name, one's face, one's work, but not one's person, was a critical element of the project, and one that is often overlooked by non-Slovenes to whom the name Janez Janša means nothing more or less than Žiga Kariž or Ivo Saliger or Gretchen Bakke.

The point—that both the name taken and the names erased meant something within a local context—was brought home at the same dinner in Montréal at which I so vigorously avoided asking Janez (by name) for the salt. As we contemplated a trio of sea urchin mousses, each to be spooned from its own spiny shell, one of the others at the table said off-handedly that such a project—artists coming to matter for having chosen to legally change their names to the name of somebody else—would have been impossible in America. Her meaning, I think, was that no one would care or notice, given all the oddities that regularly happen with names in that country—like when twenty-three-year-old Tyler Gold legally changed his name to "Tyrannosaurus Rex" or when a white guy went to court to become "Mister Radical Fuckcensorship Supernigger" or when one Andrew Wilson changed his name to "They," or when Kristin Sue Lucas went through the complicated procedure of legally "renewing" her name, formally changing it to Kristin Sue Lucas.[6] The sky is the limit and weirdnesses run the gamut. Janša's answer to this critique was both quick and stony. "Of course it would be," he said, "but one would need a famous man, a man with a name familiar to all, to take the name of another famous man. Johnny Depp," he said, "could change his name to Barack Obama."[7] That would be an intervention of the same sort, or at the same scale. People would most certainly notice. The news would pick it up. It would be *as* radical, and weird-feeling to media-consuming regular Americans as Emil Hrvatin becoming Janez Janša. To which she replied, "but then wouldn't he [Depp] wear blackface?"

It was a joke, but one that stabs straight at the heart of *Name Readymade* and misses that heart entirely. The Janez Janšas, like the Slovene Benjamin, have taken on a name, not an identity. They have also each given up a name, but not an identity. The equivalent would be Johnny Depp continuing to be Johnny Depp, doing all his recognizable Johnny Depp stuff—pirate movies, model dating, funny tiny beard, possible spouse beating, underground tunnel?—but always, every day insisting on being called Barack Obama, by friends, family, lovers, lawyers, coworkers, bosses, and rivals. His name, Barack Obama, would with every utterance also evoke another man, with another history, and with his own strength of story threatening to interrupt and overwhelm the banal practice of simply being oneself under different cover (Arns and Sasse 2006, 6). The project thus is designed to create an awkward excess of signification. Or, as Janez put it that Montréal evening, it is supposed to overcrowd the signifier, making it

6. The case of Kristin Sue Lucas is from Janša 2012; the others were found by googling around on the Interweb.

7. Quotations are from notes taken after the dinner in question. They are not, as such, direct quotes, but were remembered and written in the near aftermath of the happening.

too dense with meaning. This would already be true with just the one once-Depp and the always-Obama occupying the same name-space; now do it two more times. This was what Hrvatin, Kariž, and Grassi did to Janez Janša, playing in point of fact on the slogan of Janša's Slovenian Democratic Party: "The more we are, the faster we will reach the goal!" (*"več nas bo, prej bomo na cilju"*).

Name Readymade is, as Badinovac pointed out, a political intervention under guise of an artwork. It is a play with words on two fronts: first, by taking a party slogan at its word, it literalizes it in a sort of gleefully boneheaded way; second, in the doubling and redoubling of the number of inhabitants of a name, it "overexposes" (in Janša's words) the place of power. "It is as if this space is booked by someone, and yet you can occupy that spot. You can bring too much light on that place where the light was fixed—you bring yourself into the place which was not meant for you."[8]

The fact that this undertaking is local politics first is part of why a North American audience missed the point of *Name Readymade*. In one register, it was never made for them—the intricacies of the Slovene political scene remain far from any center stage (even in the era of Melania trumping Žižek as Slovenia most famous export). And yet, because *Name Readymade* also operates as, and under the guise, of art, it is meant to travel beyond politics and beyond Slovenia. A doubled thing, it is misunderstood by design.

Curiously, how it is misunderstood, the lines of concern it evokes, changes from one audience to the next. American professors at dinner ask different things of the project and assume different things about it than do Canadian students at a public presentation, than do Slovene theorists when asked to wax intelligent about it in an exhibit catalogue. An American, in this case, saw banality in the shift of name, but caught herself (like Velcro to its own hook) on the question of race. The university students couldn't turn their eyes away from the problem of a split, unknown, or confused self to dwell a moment in the substance of the artwork. And Slovene commentators saw "a conscious and carefully planned

8. Quotation from the Q&A of Janša's 2013 presentation at McGill with which this chapter opened.

overidentification" designed to reach into "the traumatic core of the Slovenian state and its transition" (Lukan 2008, 16).[9]

Speaking of the Association for the Advancement of Creative Musicians (AACM), a very different, jazzy, sort of arts organization, philosopher Eric Lewis calls this process of tempting varied misunderstandings "aesthetic thickening." As he writes,

> Thickening is a result of the multiple aesthetic perspectives one should take when considering the music of the AACM .... Yes, [it] is critiquing race relations and making universalist comments about music and culture *and* contributing to ongoing debates about art music *and* commenting on the history of jazz *and* exploring aspects of black identity. It is simply not doing just one of these or any of these at the expense of the others. (Lewis 2017, 157; italics in original)

Along the same lines, one might say that the Janšas court an easy critique of one or more facets of their work while nevertheless providing all the material for a broad set of often contradictory alternate readings. *Name Readymade* is a complex, culturally nuanced commentary on local politics *and* an art historical, art theoretical engagement within a genre (or two). Simultaneously it is a politics of action *and* playful, joyful fun-making.[10]

Despite the andandpersand, appearing here at last in its full glory, and despite the aesthetic density it enables, the project's stickiness arises from one move in particular: the misalignment of the thing with itself. In *Name Readymade*, as in case after case presented in this small book, efficacy rests with a sort of cleaved twoness—each Janus-faced Janez is simultaneously himself and other-unto-himself. Each is one made from two, though not in an exact, additive way. The distinctive features of each do not

9. This refrain, "the traumatic core of the Slovenian state and its transition," is a common one, used to explain a surprisingly broad array of phenomena. It is also, I have found, usually pretty right on. This one is from the *NAME: Readymade* exhibit catalogue (Janša, Janša, and Janša 2008).

10. Lewis (2017) writes: "Works may be fascinating precisely because of shifts between equally permissible ways of perceiving them. And the enormous richness of some works is due in part to the variety of permissible, and worthwhile ways of perceiving them" (Walton 1970, 362). . . . what we have here is the recognition that what I call aesthetic denseness is itself an aesthetic value" (144–45). Where, "by aesthetic we understand the ways that music-as-culture produces both meaning and pleasure" (143).

disappear when combined with the other (1+1 = 2). Rather, the singular is never lost, never absorbed, never resolved into the other, which is nevertheless also there in the same place. It's this with that. Each one (1) disrupted by the presence of another one (1) remains right there with the first one (1) to create a persona which is difficult (in this the students were right) because it's overcrowded (in this Janez was clear).[11] The project was designed to maximize this sense of crowding, such that in each case the constituent elements (e.g., Emil & Janez) remained a distinct feature of this Frankensteinean new man. He is (and is made of) two-in-one.[12]

This doubling was also done in a way that denies purchase to notions of stereoscopic resolution (the two as a "deeper" appearing version of the one). Depth, even its illusion, is disrupted by the noncoincidence, yet undeniable co-presence, of the two-at-once: Emil Hrvatin & Janez Janša; Davide Grassi & Janez Janša; Žiga Kariž & Janez Janša; Croatian & Slovenian; Italian & Slovenian. And the places where it didn't work: Kariž, for example, is Slovenian by birth and thus did not double with the change, remaining Slovenian & Slovenian. This awkward coincidence of the one with itself was solved, however, when in 2012 this Janša changed his name back to Kariž. Then, in 2017, Kariž changed his name again to Janša and later in the same year this Janez Janša once again changed his name to Žiga Kariž. Today, Žiga Kariž is known as the artist formally known as Janez Janša (twice over). The two-in-one is now more firmly bound to him than could ever have been afforded by the first change alone. This leaves two new Janezes (a good number) and the politician. But even *that* Janez Janša would play his part, coming to double himself as means of coping with the others, who had redoubled him first.

11. When somebody at the McGill talk asked Janez why there were three of them, he replied: "It is much simpler and much easier when you are not alone in this situation."

12. One may have noticed that footnotes in this text play an interesting role; they serve as a sort of imperfect parallel narrative. They are evocative, personal, and citational, allowing depth of reference to emerge without burial (in endnotes or in the "wink wink" of citational practice that assumes a consonance of knowledge and interest between reader and writer). The two texts—notes and the manuscript they supposedly modify—are not the same, though they are alike. Intertwined, they amount to more than one but less than two. And since, as a theorist, I am seduced by form (and attempt to use it seductively), such notes, and sections such as this, exist to break the desire for slick grace, to give in to the story and to the mess that is the spirit of cultural life that ethnography attempts to capture.

In 2008, *Janez Janša: A Biography* [*Janez Janša: Biografija*] (Štefančič 2008) was published—a book that many assumed, before the joke was made awkwardly public, would be a biography of *the* Janez Janša Not so.

> This richly illustrated biography narrates, as most biographies do, the story of the life of Janez Janša. However, in this case the story does not involve the life of one single person. Instead the biography is a merging of biographical data and images of the life of the three artists, a fact cunningly commented on in the [sub]subtitle: *The Life of Janez Janša Is the Life of Us All*. All information is presented chronologically without making any distinction between the three, as a result of which Janez Janša emerges from these pages as a highly discontinuous subject. (Bleeker 2013, 152)

Sixteen years earlier, in 1992, the politician Janša had also published something like an biography. Written as a recent history of Slovenia, his book: *The Making of the Slovenian State, 1988–1992: The Collapse of Yugoslavia* [*Premiki: Nastajanje in obramba slovenske države 1988–1992*] featured his own life and activities so prominently as to effectively function as autobiography. It was as if from Janša's point of view the nation, in its current form, could not exist without the part he played and equally as if he had no story outside his intertwining with the history of his home country. Geopolitics and biography twinned into an impenetrable snarl called by a single name: Janša.

If *Name Readymade* made little impression on the politician (he has never offered official comment on the project), Štefančič's biography seems to have wounded his pride.[13] This is a supposition with a single piece of

---

13. Unofficially however, "his first public reaction came on February 2, 2011, during a radio interview on Radio Slovenia, Channel One. In her final question, journalist Darja Groznik asked him: 'Do you, for example, follow the work of the three artists, intermedia artist Janez Janša, performer and author Janez Janša, and visual artist Janez Janša?' To which Janez Janša replied, 'I don't know if these people are artists; I haven't seen any of their creations yet. But I do think that if someone is a good artist, he doesn't need to change his name into the name of someone famous to be noticed by the people. I have been encountering these names lately, especially because I have been receiving various appeals when postmen make mistakes and deliver to me various summons or court orders to pay fines for offences committed by these guys. Not long ago, I was even subpoenaed by a Paris district court because one of these people supposedly failed to pay some rent for 15,000 euros, and quite a lot of talking to the post had to be done to come to an agreement that this wasn't me'" (Janez Janša, personal communication, July 2019).

evidence. After its publication, Janša began to sign official documents with his given name, Ivan Janša, rather than with the name he'd been known by for the whole of his life, Janez Janša.[14] Like Kariz (if in a minor scale), Ivan Janša thus became the politician formally known as Janez Janša. His name-space had grown so crowded that he took a small step out of it, and he did this by enacting precisely the same move as his nominal interlopers—he doubled himself, without complaint and without comment. Just as the new Janšas had, as the Slovene Benjamin did, as Laibach and IRWIN and Luther Blisset do, he just took another name and used it, giving himself some breathing room by making himself two.

II. THIS IS GOING TO HURT A LITTLE

Ich bin ein doppelgänger (I am double).

Nietzsche, quoted (doubled) in Župančič, *The Shortest Shadow*, 2003

A person, a man or a woman, a child when alone, anyone when single and singular, is, in Slovene, *človek* (pronounced "chloh-vehk"). They are a person, a human, one. When two such singular entities meet and become a

---

To these accusations a Janša replied, "I strongly reject any criminalization of this sort. I have never been subpoenaed by a court, let alone for failing to pay rent in Paris, where I have never lived. As regards changing my name into the name of a famous person, let me just mention that numerous organizers of presentations of my work abroad often ask if they may use my former name, because overseas nobody knows who Janez Janša is." Another Janša wrote: "I hereby state that I am no guy, but a person with a name and a surname, Janez Janša, which I use as in accordance with the law. In contrast to the politician, whose official name, as far as I know, is Ivan Janša and who, by using another name, is in fact breaking the Law on Personal Names, Article 2, which was passed while Janša was in power: 'Personal name is the citizen's right and it is used for distinction and identification of natural persons. The citizen is obliged to use his/her personal name'" (Janez Janša, personal communication, July 2019). A third response can be found in the *"Odgovor"* section of the daily newspaper *Delo*, February 3, 2011, p. 2.

14. The new Janšas met this change gleefully. One of their constant needlings (there were many) of the prime minister was the claim that when they signed documents with Janez Janša they were signing with their real name, whereas when Janez Janša—whose given name is Ivan—did it, he was using a pseudonym. Even now (2017), the Wikipedia page for Janez Janša begins "Ivan Janša, baptized and best known as Janez Janša, . . . " The citation given on Wikipedia for this "technical note" is entitled *"P.S. Janez ni moj vzdevek"* [PS: Janez is not my nickname] and was published online in 2010. Since it is Wikipedia, it is possible that the other Janezes put this insistence in place. The Slovene page for "Janez Janša" echoes, but does not replicate, this point.

Figure 13. "Old Name, New Faces," campaign poster, 2018, on the occasion of Janez Janša's run for parliament, in Janez Janša's home town, Grosuplje. Photo by Janez Janša.

pair—friends, lovers, handball partners, as the case may be—the singular is transformed into the dual. These two, in Slovene, are called *človeka* (pronounced "chloh-vehka"). They are a doubled form of the singular, never less nor more than two. The term is both additive and precise. *Človeka* is a double made of two of the same type: one person plus one person become two persons together. These are not yet "people," not yet a mass noun of a collective type, not yet humanity. That comes only when three people, or four, or five people, or three million or six billion people are uttered as a collective mass: *ljudje* (pronounced "luhd-yeh").

Slovene is thus very different from the other spoken languages in its Indo-European family, in which "people," the collective plural of "person," like the plural forms of all nouns, comes into use as soon as there is more than one of anything or anyone.[15] Whether doctors, lawyers, policemen,

15. There is, of course, always an exception to blanket statements of this sort. In this case it is approximately fifty thousand remaining speakers of Sorbian who live in pretty, forested area of what was once the east of a divided Germany.

bananas, Chihuahuas, cummerbunds, buckets, bottle-rockets, low riders, or snap pea pods, all we know from the words themselves is that none of these things is lone. Each is doubled, at least twice and perhaps ten thousandfold. When it comes to questions of number, neither subtlety nor precision are Indo-European strong suits, and very little space is left for the middle ground between the one and the many, or the individual and the mass.

In Slovene, and not only when speaking of persons or of people, the two, the dual, or the double is marked both lexically and grammatically. In spoken language and in written language, at church and in the vilest of slang, for female things and for male ones, both speaker and audience are well aware of ones, *twos*, and manys. And, whereas the singular is used far less often than the plural in those languages that bifurcate the world into monads and masses, in Slovene all three grammatical forms of number balance out. One speaks in the dual, of twos and pairs and couples, about as often as one speaks of individuals, singulars and ones, and likewise, with about the same frequency that one uses the plural for collectives and masses of three or more. Two is not a secondary category; it is as common as its numeric (singular, plural) brethren. The dual eats away at the mass of the plural, reducing its frequency by half, and it bring the singular into sharper relief by giving it a complement. Two cups of coffee please. Two sugars with that. We (two) love the snow. They (two) went to London. It's been raining for the last two weeks. Where are your (two) children? The eyes (both) that one has upon the world know it differently, see it differently, because everywhere at every moment there is an awareness of what is two, where is two, who is two, in precisely the same way that speakers of all Indo-European languages (Slovene included) are absolutely, easily, ignorantly aware, grammatically and actually, of singulars and of plurals.[16]

16. If you have seen the movie *Arrival* (Villeneuve 2016), it's not like that. Nevertheless, Benjamin Lee Whorf's claims regarding the effects on thought of grammatical and lexical categories underlie this analysis. In brief one can express or think anything in any language, but some languages make certain modes of expression or thought easier than others. The specificities of ease or difficulty matter, Whorf argues, to how the world is perceived and interacted with. His classic example is that New Englanders will behave cautiously with fire around gasoline drums but less cautiously around "empty gasoline drums, because empty things are not recognized as being explosive in English." See especially Whorf 1956, 135. For a more punchy popular version of the same, see Deutscher 2010.

Thus, do the three genders of nouns (female, male, neuter) decline through all six cases (nominative, genitive, dative, accusative, locative, instrumental) in the singular, dual, and plural. Adjectives decline in agreement with the nouns they modify, and so have gendered singular, dual, and plural forms. Number is likewise marked in the verb. Thus, in Slovene, when the voice (*glas*) of God (or, with equal magnificence, that of the Wizard of Oz) booms, acousmatically, through the noontime air, do I tremble (*tresem*), you tremble (*treš*), and she trembles (*trese*) to hear it.[17] We-two also tremble (*treseva*), as do you-two (*treseta*), and they-two (*treseta*). We-all, in fact, tremble (*tresemo*); just as you-all tremble (*tresete*), indeed, the very leaves upon the trees tremble (*tresejo*) at the sound. And, just in case one needs extra precision, there are the lexical indicators more familiar to speakers of Indo-European languages: both (*obe/obedva*), both sorts of (*oboj*), and two (*dva*). All also decline and are inflected for gender.

Such grammatical exactitude concerning twoness is lacking only in situations where the naturalness of pairs is given. Ears, for example, or twins, parents or legs, gloves or kidneys, crutches or wings, skis or nostrils. These things are two by their nature and Slovenes take no care to mark them specially.

The term *humans*, people in the plural, thus has a resonance in Slovene that is distinct from that of in English (or French, Polish, Punjabi, Tajik, &c.), and in two different ways. The first is simply that *people*, understood

---

17. The full declension of the monosyllabic, inanimate, masculine noun *glas* (voice) is as follows. Note that it gains the infix -*ov* in the dual and plural and has a Ø ending in the genitive dual/plural. This is characteristic of most monosyllabic nouns that do not end in -c, -č, -š -ž, or j, but is not used for polysyllabic nouns (with one exception). Thus, *glas* is not a perfectly "representative" declension so much as a contextually apt one.

		singular	dual	plural
Nominative		glas	glasova	glasovi
Genitive		glasú	glasov*	glasov*
Dative		glásu	glasovoma	glasovom
Accusative		glas	glasova	glasove
Locative	pri**	glásu	glasovih*	glasovih*
Instrumental	z**	glasom	glasovoma	glasovi

* The dual and plural forms in the genitive and accusative cases are almost always identical.
** The locative and instrumental cases are only used with prepositions. Here, as in all grammars of Slovene, they have been included.

collectively and abstractly, begins with a glomerate of three persons rather than of two. The second is that the word for person as it changes to reflect number also shifts between the singular/dual root *človek-* and the plural root *ljud-*.[18] The technical term for this replacement of the root forms of words with new root forms, as individual things become plural ones, is called nominative suppletion and it is familiar to speakers of Slavic languages (Russian, for example, has three, including *chelovek/ljudi*). Verbal suppletion, its counterpart, is downright common across the Indo-European language tree (e.g., go/went). In Slovene, however, the transformation of one person or two persons into people is a lone case.[19] There is no other instance of nominative suppletion in the language.[20]

What is interesting in Slovene, then, is not so much the fact of nominative suppletion but its retention. Like the dual itself, the uniqueness of *človek/človeka/ljudje* alone marks it as meaningful. This is not to say that in Slovenia the complexities of personhood can be reduced to one, or per-

18. Arguments have been made that this shift echoes that of *Mann/Leute* (person/people) in German, with *Leute* serving as an arguable cognate of *ljudje*—though in German *Mann* also has the nonsuppletive plural form *Männer* (man/men) and the gender neutral *Person*, which might serve as a more accurate singular to *Leute* than does *Mann*. Regardless of the suppletive peculiarities of German, there seems to be some agreement that Proto-Slavic and Proto-Germanic shared a suppletive idea regarding person/people and that these two were more similar to each other than to the other Indo-European languages, Baltic languages excluded (Tom Preistly and Marko Snoj, personal correspondence, July 2009).

19. As in Slovene, it is true across languages that though suppletion in nouns is rare, "nouns referring to humans are most often suppletive, that number is the most common grammatical feature involved in nominal suppletion and that 'child' is by far the most common noun to be suppletive cross-linguistically" (Vafaeian 2010, 2). It should be noted that child (*otrok*) in Slovene is not suppletive; its dual is *otroka* and its plural, *otroci*.

20. There is a wavering of roots within the dual that depends upon case. So that while *človek-* clearly governs the singular and *ljud-* just as clearly governs the plural, the dual is formed in all cases save the genitive and locative with *človek-* while these later two use *ljud-*. As was seen above this is likely because throughout the language the genitive and locative forms are identical in the dual and plural; it is only because *človek/ljudje* is the sole exemplar of nominative suppletion that a general governance of the dual by the plural in these two cases becomes clear.

		dual	*plural*
N		človeka	ljudje
G		ljudi	ljudi
D		človekoma	ljudem
A		človeka	ljudi
L	pri	ljudeh	ljudeh
I	z	človekoma	ljudmi

haps two, grammatical peculiarities (or even three, if we are to include the "vocative gap").[21] However, the ways in which these linguistic structures map on to and duplicate certain intransigencies and habitudes also in evidence in macro-social phenomena tempt me to say that they are not external, nor even of secondary importance, to local practices of being an individual person (*človek*), a couple (*človeka*), or a part of a larger familial, national, or human group (*ljudje*). There is even an explicitly normative saying (*pregovor*) in Slovene that urges dallying and pleasure-happy couples toward reproduction, to get a move on and make their two (*človeka*) into a three-plus (*ljudje*), becoming in this way not just a family (as would happen in English) but a part of humanity more generally conceived.

My argument is not that categories of language shape human minds, nor even that the unconscious is structured like a language, but rather that these categories are materials by means of which social realities might be approached and tweaked. They give room for play. In Slovene, just such a playful place is located in the dual—where two of the same can be articulated, noted, and counted, where the transubstantiation of human substance from individuals into a mass is not yet affected, though it looms. Plus, as Alenka Župančič (2003) pointed out in her discussion of the false Hitler in chapter 1, the double is, almost by its nature, funny: it destabilizes the sense of reality, truth, sincerity, and authenticity while beckoning the mind that can recognize it and duping that which can't.[22]

---

21. It is not so much that Slovene is missing the vocative case, though it is, but that it is missing situations in which the vocative might be used, thus rendering the case irrelevant. Practically (and to this ethnographer's pleasure), this means that proper names in Slovenia are almost never used when the person being named is present. I likely heard my own name uttered in my presence less than five times during the three years I lived in country, and I rarely used anyone else's name in their presence. Nicknames and generalizations, however, abound.

22. Erving Goffman, in speaking about the performance of self, writes: "At one extreme one finds that the performer can be fully taken in by his own act; he can be sincerely convinced that the impression of reality he stages is the real reality. When his audience is also convinced in this way about the show he has put on—and this seems the typical case—then for the moment at least only the sociologist [or anthropologist, I add] or the socially disgruntled will have any doubts about the 'realness' of what is presented. At the other extreme; we find that the performer may not be taken in at all by his own routine" (1990 [1959], 28). Of course, there are many in-betweens to be found on this continuum, but the Janez Janšas are doing a remarkable job of positing themselves toward the first extreme and then making doubting sociologists of us all.

This is the first layer and the second: one can accept what is given, the two *as if* truly one ("Janez, would you be so good as to pass the salt"). Or one can delight in the fact that what is given both is and isn't conterminous with itself ("That's it! That is what Hitler looks like!" "But sir," replies the actor, "that is a picture of me!"). This book, like Slovenia itself, overflows with the second. The delight in the noncoincidence of an object or person with itself is everywhere at play: the Slovene Benjamin, Laibach, Luther Blisset, Janez Janša, Jevgenij Skavčenko, the masquerading catalog essay, the impossible Mondrians, &c. &c. So much so that at times living in Slovenia felt like circulating through the center of a giant inside joke. A friend said, referring to somebody I did not yet know, "She is one of IRWIN's girlfriends." Yet IRWIN is not some*one* who could have a girlfriend. It is the collective eponym of a group of five painters. An appellative oddity that left me wondering which of IRWIN's girlfriends she was. Even after having met her, I would continue to wonder this. He had a name of course, the boyfriend—I even knew his name, but as IRWIN tended to appear in clumps of two to five, and because the vocative gap meant that people's given names were almost never used when they were present, I was on friendly terms with three of IRWIN (one of whom *would* turn out to be the boyfriend) well before I had the foggiest idea what each was called.

Similarly silly: shortly after the name change (though before the project had been made public), one of the Janezes got married, the other two serving as groomsmen and legal witnesses to the nuptials. With the gravity befitting the moment, as the officiant came to the part of the ceremony devoted to the filling in of forms—still the central act of weddings in many formerly communist countries—he simply couldn't keep a straight face. First the groom was asked to sign, Janez Janša. And then the bride, Marcela Okretič. The first witness, Janez Janša. But, by the second witness, and third Janez Janša, the officiant was wiping his mirthful eyes as state ceremony slid over into performance art. It was a real wedding, conducted with love and also with something else, something goofy. Indeed, the new Janezes have spent a great deal of time in the years since the name change enjoying themselves. Whether or not these renamed selves are the selfsame selves as those who came before is less important than the sheer and obvious delight taken at life made over into a preeminently gleeful masquerade.[23]

This second interpretive mode, what Žižek calls "the noncoincidence of the One with itself" (2006, 11), is also where contemporary Slovene philosophy fights many of its battles. The whole of Župančič's short treatise in which the false Hitler makes his appearance—*The Shortest Shadow: Nietzsche's Philosophy of the Two*—is a plea for a broad recognition that the two is the appropriate category with which to think. As she moves through Nietzsche's oeuvre, Župančič finds in him a strong bias for moments and moves that bring two into noncoincident singularity. What is lovely about the book, in addition to her intensity of care for this issue, is that the two-in-ones that she finds in Nietzsche (the seam, the edge, midday, and the doppelgänger) are quite different from those commonly circulating in Slovenia, such that her own understanding of the double's forms and how these might operate analytically in the world was evidently expanded by her encounters with Nietzsche.

In each case, however, whether speaking of Nietzsche, the Janez Janšas, or a bunch of impossible Mondrians, the two is never simply additive. Nor is it a metaphysical opposition (à la Hegel), made to serve as a theoretical starting point for combinatory processes. Nor is it stereoscopic, whereby two perspectives are conjoined to grant a "deeper" impression of a thing. Nor is it redolent of a productive capacity that might emerge from multiple perspectives combined into a fuller sense of a whole. Rather, Župančič wants to see the two become eerie, uncanny, and discomforting; here, in the gap between the one and same, is where disjuncture has the potential to become formative, such that one can use the nonidenticality of the one with itself to approach so-called social reality with less surety about what it all adds up to, what makes it tick, what indeed, it even is.

---

23. "Laughter has the remarkable power of making an object come up close, of drawing it into a zone of crude contact where one can finger it familiarly on all sides, turn it upside down, inside out, peer at it from above and below, break open its external shell, look into its center, doubt it, take it apart, dismember it, lay it bare and expose it, examine it freely and experiment with it. Laughter demolishes fear and piety before an object, before a world, making of it an object of familiar contact and thus clearing the ground for an absolutely free investigation of it. Laughter is a vital factor in laying down that prerequisite for fearlessness without which it would be impossible to approach the world realistically" (Bakhtin 1981, 328).

Žižek hoes a similar row, for what is the parallax view but an insistence upon seeing the same thing from two inconsistent and irresolvable vantage points? "The first critical move," Žižek writes, "is to replace this topic of the polarity of opposites with the concept of the inherent 'tension' gap, noncoincidence" (2006, 7). "Take a step further," he continues, "and reach beneath this dualism itself, into a 'minimal difference' (the noncoincidence of the One with itself) that generates it" (11). "For it is minimal difference [that] . . . divides one and the same object from itself . . . a 'pure' difference which cannot be grounded in positive substantial properties" (19). "What emerges via distortions of the accurate representations of reality," he says, paraphrasing Lacan, "is the real—that is, the trauma around which social reality is structured" (1994, 25).

Rather than resolving the discordance of two vantage points by finding something stable upon which to focus, Žižek's suggestion is that it is the conflict *between* them that should trap our attention. The irresolvability of the two, he intimates, tells us more about a social world grounded in misaligned perceptions than does the so-called objective truth (what he would call a symbolic fiction) of an excavated singular.

To explain, Žižek (twice) tells the same story, about an "aboriginal village" in South America (in *Mapping Ideology*) or a Winnebago tribe near the Great Lakes (in *The Parallax View*). In both cases the story is credited to Claude Lévi-Strauss, who did write something similar in a chapter of *Structural Anthropology* called "Do Dual Organizations Exist?" (1963).[24] Here, at some length is the former (*Mapping Ideology*) version of the tale. I have chosen this rather than the other version, which is roughly the same, because its half-invented, half-misremembered character is very much in keeping (thematically) with the fruitful going-wrongs of things that come in irresolvable twos and of copies that seem to callously disregard most of the particulars of their originals.

> In order to clarify this uncanny logic of antagonism qua real let us recall . . . .
> Lévi-Strauss's exemplary analysis of the spatial arrangement of buildings in
> an aboriginal South American village . . . . The inhabitants are divided into
> two subgroups; when we ask an individual to draw the ground plan of his or

24. One wonders if Žižek's initial attraction to the worries of the Winnebago can be simplistically reduced to the title of Lévi-Strauss's essay.

her village (the spatial arrangement of cottages) on a piece of paper or on sand, we obtain two quite different answers, depending on which subgroup he or she belongs to: a member of the first subgroup (let us call it "conservative-corporatist") perceives the ground-plan of the village as circular—a ring of houses more or less symmetrically arranged around the central temple; whereas a member of the second ("revolutionary-antagonist") subgroup perceives his or her village as two distinct clusters of houses separated by an invisible frontier.... Lévi-Strauss's central point is that this example should in no way entice us into a cultural relativism according to which the perception of space depends on the observer's group membership: the very splitting into the two "relative" perceptions implies the hidden reference of a constant—not the objective "actual" arrangement of buildings but a traumatic kernel, a fundamental antagonism the inhabitants of the village were not able to symbolize, to account for, to "internalize," to come to terms with: an imbalance in social relations that prevented the community from stabilizing itself into a harmonic whole. The two perceptions of the ground-plan are simply two mutually exclusive endeavors to cope with this traumatic antagonism, to heal its wound via the imposition of a balanced symbolic structure.

Common sense tells us that it is easy to rectify the bias of subjective perceptions and ascertain the "true state of things": we have only to hire a helicopter and photograph the village directly from above .... In this way we can obtain an undistorted view of reality, yet we completely miss the real of social antagonism, the non-symbolizable traumatic kernel that found expression in the very distortion of reality, in the fantasized displacements of the "actual" arrangement of houses. (1994, 25-26)[25]

One of the oddities of Žižek's work is that he tends to stop here, as if an awareness of a hidden discord or the crack of a broken circuit were enough. In book after book, he pushes at this singular point of understanding: namely, that disparate viewpoints matter inordinately and that rather than resolving these, the fruitful, correct move is to crank open the gap between the one and itself.[26] His point is not merely that two different

25. The same story is told in slightly different terms in Žižek 2006, 25-26. And then there is this funny reference about an entirely different case, the procedure he's employed: "Perhaps we must risk a different approach and read Plato's [allegory of the cave] as a myth in Levi-Strauss's sense, and to search for the meaning of significance, not by direct interpretation, but by ... comparing it with other versions of the same story" (Žižek 2005, 8).

26. Althusser, following Lenin, famously described ideology as "the imaginary relationship of individuals to their real conditions of existence." Continuing the thought, he writes: "the ideology of ideology thus recognizes, despite its imaginary distortion, that the 'ideas' of

ways of saying (seeing) the same thing are indicative of a disturbance or a discord, but that the *disavowal* of this discord is the fundamental social glue. Dissonance, for Žižek, is pointedly not the result of a lack of accord between an impression (of a thing) and its hidden depths. Rather it is a discord between a thing and itself. The human capacity to miss *this* point, to pretend at the integrity of a deeply flawed thing, or to locate dissonance between a clean surface and an unknowable interior, or to retreat to the objective truth (of the scientific method or of the helicopter) frankly seems to drive Žižek a little nuts.[27] But he also understands well enough that the effort involved in trying to paper over the permanent, irritating, irresolvable fact of "minimal difference" is what holds together human individuals *as selves*, as much as it does human societies as markedly patterned, rendered thusly both recognizable and typifiable.[28]

In other words, one can imagine that what makes the South American Winnebago recognizable as such is the very particular mode by which they contrive to *not* be bothered by the inconstancies in their midst. Similarly, the ways Americans produce their constant entreaties for openness and self-exposure, as if the surface were some sort of hardened, featureless falsehood, are part of what makes them recognizable *as* Americans. Likewise, the Western European obsession with authenticity, as if anything other than being true to (read: self-consistent with) oneself were criminally suspicious. Call it ideology, or minimal difference, or desire, or the *objet petit a*, or the parallax gap; call it what you will. But the pat-

---

a human subject exist in his actions, or ought to exist in his actions, and if that is not the case, it lends him other ideas corresponding to the actions (however perverse) that he does perform" (2014, 260). Undoing ideology then would seem to involve, for Žižek, not so much the pretense of being able to step outside of these relations and assumptions but rather the recognition of these imaginary ways as *imagined*.

27. Thomas Kuhn, speaking of the duck/rabbit, resolves the problem of the flicker (of duck to rabbit to duck to rabbit to duck) by suggesting that viewer back away from what is pictured toward the realization "that it is the lines that [one] really sees," even while recognizing that one "alternately sees them as a duck and as a rabbit" (Kuhn 1962, 114).

28. We know this largely because Lacan says it quite clearly in the "The Mirror Stage" (2006, 75–81). Here *méconnaissance* or "misrecognition" is a fundamental early stage of human development that continues onward through life as an individual struggles (wrongly) to create an integrated integral "self," a process grounded in misrecognition, because he or she is always a social product.

terned, labor-intensive *failure* to recognize the noncoincidence of the one with itself is what makes us who we are, as cultures and as individuals.

I suspect that for Žižek, Župančič, Janez Janša (all of them), IRWIN, and many other Slovene speakers poking at notions of unified or singular identity, this discord between the one and itself is blindingly obvious; they have a tool at their disposal that we do not: twos are easy for them to notice and impossible for them to ignore. The Canadian college students were thus on the right track. All they could see of Janez was the nonconcurrence of himself with himself, and all they could do with it was prod with anxious fingers at the gap and ask if it hurt. Janez seemed to find this a bit dull, but Žižek would have been proud.

Name Readymade is not, however, any object, nor any everyday, casual misunderstanding. It is a crafted affront to the idea of a singular consistent persona. In this way, the project takes a decided step beyond Žižek's claims to a ubiquitous misalignment between a thing and itself. *Name Readymade* is aggressive in a way that the general social phenomena of which Žižek speaks are not; it forces the parallax gap down your throat, until you choke and cough and sputter out an ellipse " . . . please pass the salt." It contrives to write a gap into the text of an ongoing conversation. With *Name Readymade*, there was no avoiding the irresolvable cut between the thing and itself; the man and himself. And it is this purposefulness that forces a layer of analysis beyond the generic claim that neither singularity nor consonance are ever really qualities of persons.

A jump cut. I remember a letter written to the popular American newspaper sex advice columnist Dan Savage in 2009. In it a woman who serves as master to her husband-as-slave is preparing for the arrival of his mother. The mother is in the midst of a rough divorce and needs a place to stay for a while, a month, perhaps more. What the master-wife wants to know from Savage is if it would be ok, during the mother's stay, for them to continue to perform their relationship, with its distinct pleasures (dog collar, leash, and harness on the husband at breakfast, or better yet, a public flogging/pegging just when the mother is wandering in for her morning coffee). Clearly, this is titillating to the couple, though more the wife than the husband. It is, after all, his mother who would be walking into the kitchen at the wrong moment (or "right" one, depending). She the fly, right into a trap expertly strung.

My suspicion is that the letter writer expected Savage to say, "Sure." He is that kind of sex-positive guy. Instead, he reacted with a surprising vehemence in the other direction. His NO was unequivocal, and his reasoning was this: "The idea of your husband's mother knowing that her son is your bitch may turn you on, and it may turn your husband on intermittently, but when someone witnesses your husband's submission that person is *participating in his erotic humiliation,* that person is playing *an active role in the sex you're having with your husband.*"[29] At best, it would be gauche and pornographic; at worst, a kind of sexual assault. It's rapey to recruit others into a role—even just that of audience—within a sexual relationship that they neither chose nor agreed to.[30] Take off the collar, he says, and keep the sex in the bedroom. Close the door. Unlay the trap and let the mother-in-law be.

If this story were not about sex, but about a work of identity politics into which numbers of people are recruited (as audiences) and trapped (as flies in webs), it would be the story of *Name Readymade*—an artwork premised upon the constant recruitment of people into a relationship they neither chose nor agreed to. As such, the work is more mean-spirited than it might at first appear and more complexly political—in that its politics extend far beyond explicit commentary launched at a specific individual (Mr. Janša, the first). All of this may be couched in a genteel playfulness but *Name Readymade* is also a deliberate praxis—a praxis with teeth—foisted by the artists upon the unexpecting in a way that necessitates a response, whether in the form of an officiant's mirth, a politician's shifted signature, a biographer's labor, a theorist's postulate, a student body's worries, or a colleague's slipped-tongued stumblings. Doubleness here is the

29. Dan Savage, "SL Letter of the Day: Don't Tell Mama," *The Stranger*, December 8, 2009, www.thestranger.com/slog/archives/2009/12/08/sl-letter-of-the-day-dont-tell-mama&view=comments; italics in original.

30. If this seems an overly strong parallel, it stems from a Spanish friend of mine breaking down in a rage after having been forcibly incorporated into a theatrical piece in Slovenia in which the audience was ordered to bring their chairs into the midst of the play, and then throughout the piece to move occasionally and according to script. It seemed a funny idea (to me) and sort of lowbrow creative to the students in the theater camp who came up with the idea. To my friend it was not funny. It was an assault, whereby her subjectivity and role (as audience member) was not simply broached but wrenched, without her permission, from her control. *Name Readymade* works in a similar way, but more radically, having disbanded the theater. Life, the whole of it, becoming the stage (see Goffman 1959 here again of course).

delivery system for an assault, not Trojan horse-style (nothing is hidden) but thick and deliberate, against the desire to merge inconstant perceptions into whole entities.

Slovene theorist and curator Igor Zabel, speaking of a different project, figures this holding of completeness of "closed structures" at bay as an artistic move against ideology: "Through an 'unserious' and 'irresponsible' approach to [established narratives, activism, art, and professional and scholarly discourses]," he writes, "an artist can break such closed structures and throw light on the repressed contradictions, heterogeneities, and discontinuities inherent in them. 'The whole is the untrue,' Adorno declares in his *Minima Moralia*, indicating that the effect of completeness and wholeness is essentially ideological. If this is so, then that which is incomplete, unordered, and heterogeneous might, in fact, point a way to the truth" (Zabel n.d.). With *Name Readymade*, this "pointing a way" is not just an index finger waved casually in the direction of something like truth. It is rather more like the parallax gap on crack because it allows its summoned audience no rest. It is not enough to know, and then paper over, the minimal difference between a thing and itself. With *Name Readymade* one takes this difference to dinner, greets it on the street, gets angry with it or hurt by it, shares in its glee, and knows it for what it is— the dual made flesh. Four times over, a Janez charts his own path through the two-in-one, *as* the two-in-one, as comfortable to him as it is ever so slightly vertiginous to everyone else.

Chapter 4

I. IS SLAVOJ ŽIŽEK FULL OF SHIT?

Man is like divine shit, he fell out of God's anus.

Slavoj Žižek, with credit to Martin Luther, *The Parallax View*, 2006

It is not unusual to hear it said that Žižek is full of shit. For example, "I like Zizek. He might be full of shit 99 percent of the time, but it's very entertaining shit"; or "I don't want to assert that 'the rock star of cultural theory' is full of shit, but y'know, Slavoj Žižek seems to me to be kind of full of shit"; or, this in a more academic vein (though the sentiment is certainly the same), "Žižek is a big fake, but one that typifies today's celebrated (read: celebrity) scholar."[1] And on it goes: it's "just all posturing verbi-

---

1. The first quote is from "In Defense of Lost Causes by Slavoj Zizek," Radical Ebook Archive, posted September 8, 2009, http://radicalebooks.blogspot.com/2009/09/in-defence-of-lost-causes-by-slavoj.html, accessed July 2019; the second, a comment by "Imogen," who recommends one of Žižek's more recent books to "hipster assholes": "Violence: Six Sideways Reflections," GoodReads, comment posted August 4, 2008, http://www.goodreads.com/book/show/2638701.violence, accessed January 2011; the last, from savage-minds.org, an anthropology blog, speaking of Lindsey Waters's article "A Call for Slow Writing," "The Slow Writing Movement," Savage Minds, posted March 17, 2008, savageminds.org/2008/03/17/the-slow-writing-movement/, accessed March 2008.

age"; "he's pretty charismatic and pretty nonsensical"; "the language is needlessly complex"; "Zizek's article . . . can be described as 'random thoughts about a few movies with a bit of psychoanalysis thrown in'"; "I'm sure many people here have seen philosophers' tendency to abusively use scientific lingo to make their writings sound more profound. Some philosophers do this more than others, and I think Zizek is a prime example of it."[2] Or this, which makes an on-again, off-again appearance on Wikipedia: "Harpham calls Žižek's style 'a stream of nonconsecutive units arranged in arbitrary sequences that solicit a sporadic and discontinuous attention.' O'Neill concurs: 'a dizzying array of wildly entertaining and often quite maddening rhetorical strategies are deployed in order to beguile, browbeat, dumbfound, dazzle, confuse, mislead, overwhelm, and generally subdue the reader into acceptance.'"[3] And then there is this, from philosoraptor.com:

> So what does Zizek mean by all this? Are we suppose to take him literally? Well, if we were to take him literally, he's simply wrong, dead wrong about so many things. He said "I mean it quite literally" but let's not take him literally because he's just wrong.
>
> So are we supposed to take him metaphorically? I mean many philosophers in the past have used metaphors to describe things, right? Quine for example really likes "web" to explain naturalized epistemology. Neurath used "a boat" to explain gradual reconstruction of scientific knowledge.
>
> These metaphors are meaningful because Quine and Neurath makes their claims meaningful and explicit.
>
> Zizek does not do this. His claims are not meaningful. His claims also are not literal and explicit, so there is no way for metaphors to refer to something. It's all nonsense.[4]

---

2. "Slavoj Zizek - any good?" Urban 75, comment 23, posted by "TruXta," November 14, 2010, http://www.urban75.net/vbulletin/threads/323897-Slavoj-Zizek-any-good; http://forums.philosophyforums.com/threads/a-human-example-zizek-31504-2.html, comment 8, comment 11, and comment 19. All accessed January 2011; site no longer available.

3. Wikipedia entry for Slavoj Žižek. The quotes here listed seem to appear and disappear as various editors weigh in and weigh out. As of March 2017 they were there, in January 2011 they could be found only here: http://forums.philosophyforums.com/threads/a-human-example-zizek-31504-2.html, comment 11, and as this book goes to press in July 2019, they are gone again.

4. Winston Smith, "Bullshit Litmus Test: Slavoj Zizek," *Philosoraptor* [blog], April 30, 2012, http://philosoraptor.blogspot.ca/2012/04/bullshit-litmus-test-slavoj-zizek.html, accessed June 2017; page no longer available.

Similarly, when Noam Chomsky pens an offended critique of Žižek, it is headlined "Noam Chomsky Thinks Slavoj Žižek Is Full of Shit" (Emanuele 2012). Though the former never says so much, he does delineate the problem:

> I'm not interested in posturing—using fancy terms like polysyllables and pretending you have a theory when you have no theory whatsoever. So there's no theory in any of this stuff, not in the sense of theory that anyone is familiar with in the sciences or any other serious field. Try to find in all of the work you mentioned some principles from which you can deduce conclusions, empirically testable propositions where it all goes beyond the level of something you can explain in five minutes to a twelve-year-old. *See if you can find that when the fancy words are decoded.* I can't. So I'm not interested in that kind of posturing. Žižek is an extreme example of it. *I don't see anything to what he's saying.* (emphasis added)

From there Chomsky pulls a classic move of one-upmanship: "Jacques Lacan I actually knew. I kind of liked him. We had meetings every once in awhile. But quite frankly I thought he was a total charlatan" (Emanuele 2012).[5] On and on it goes in this vein. On and on.

It is easy to be cruel with the Internet as your filter. Within its shelter, meanness as practice has become something like the final volley of a snowball fight: it doesn't matter which claim hits home, what matters is that quantity assures that sooner or later the object of attack will be struck, hurt even, perhaps (is this the dream?) cowed into shutting the fuck up. Formally, taken en masse, what the above quotations intimate is that there is something not quite right, not quite believable *to a certain sort of audience* in what (or rather how) Žižek writes, speaks, or generally plies his trade as a philosopher. Or, to put it another way, just as there are genre

---

5. In Tom Wolfe's excoriation of Noam Chomsky (and, curiously also Charles Darwin [2016]) he points out that Chomsky played fast and loose with the insults, thus making the swing of the bat at Žižek (full-of-shit) and Lacan (charlatan) part of a career-long bullish and bullying pattern of dismissal-by-epithet. "Any random figure of note who persisted in challenging his authority," writes Wolfe, "Chomsky would summarily dismiss . . . as a 'fraud,' a 'liar,' or a 'charlatan.' He called B.F. Skinner, Elie Wiesel, Jacques Derrida, and the 'American intellectual community' frauds. He called Alan Dershowitz, Christopher Hitchens, and Werner Cohn liars; he pinned the charlatan tag on the famous French psychiatrist Jacques Lacan . . ." (97). "A charlatan," he continues fifty pages later, is "a fraud who specializes in showing off knowledge he doesn't have. The epithets ('fraud,' 'liar,' 'charlatan') were Chomsky's way of sentencing opponents to Oblivion" (143).

conventions to the "art historical lecture," "the exhibit-catalog essay," and acts of self-representation, each of which vary to greater and lesser degrees between cultures and persons, so too are there genre conventions to philosophy. And these are treated with a similar playfulness and pointed disregard by Slavoj Žižek as by the Slovene Benjamin.

If you have made it this far into this small book you already know that the reason for the easy designation of Žižek's full-of-shitness subtends the very artful way in which he balances between a serious "real" instantiation of a "philosopher" and, equally, a sort of spoof of that thing—the balancing act (not the judgment rendered) being the interesting thing. Žižek's trick is in being X *and* not-X *and* recognizable as such (one, its inverse, and the two at once). He argues as if Quine, as if not-Quine, and as if Quine-not-Quine, with unabashed simultaneity.[6] So assiduous, so consistent, so concerted is Žižek in this—the "all at onceness"—that only a fool would think he is just another continental philosopher. And though he offers readers ample opportunity to read him according to a single valence, one might even say he tempts his readers, and other audiences, to easy judgment ("charlatan," "fake," "celebrity scholar," "nonsensical," "nonserious," &c.) in rather the same way that a certain serpent tempted Eve in the garden with an apple. He is also always giving everyone the opportunity to read him differently. All one really has to do is watch his rather serious and insightful musings on different national toilet structures and the way that they allow for the contemplation, or not, of the shit in the bowl to understand that he would be somewhat stunned if you compared him in all earnestness to Quine.[7] That joke's on you.

6. Of the Slovene Benjamin (see chapter 1), we could say he was pretending to be Benjamin, not-pretending to be Benjamin, and pretending to be Benjamin not-pretending to be Benjamin. The third term names the copy that speaks for itself. Of the Janez Janšas (see chapter 3) we could say each was Janez Janša, not-Janez Janša, and Janez Janša-not-Janez Janša, where again the third term—in which the embodied simultaneity of contradiction holds the performative clout—is where the project breaches both art and politics, becoming something else.

7. "In a traditional German toilet, the hole into which shit disappears after we flush is right at the front, so that shit is first laid out for us to sniff and inspect for traces of illness. In the typical French toilet, on the contrary, the hole is at the back, i.e., shit is supposed to disappear as quickly as possible. Finally, the American (Anglo-Saxon) toilet presents a synthesis, a mediation between these opposites: the toilet basin is full of water, so that the shit floats in it, visible, but not to be inspected. . . . It is clear that none of these versions can be accounted for in purely utilitarian terms: each involves a certain ideological perception of how the subject should relate to excrement. Hegel was among the first to see in the geographical triad of

Equally however, Žižek's a bit too bright and well read to disregard as "not philosophical at all." Hence the problem for the serious critic. One can pull him into a role (philosopher), but it is constantly, irritatingly impossible—he makes it impossible—to do this with any perduring sense of purity. The nonphilosopher, the man at play, is always also there, a counterpunctual beat that strikes at nearly the same moment as the main rhythm, to jangle the nerves. And, and, ampersand all over again.

Once, years ago, I saw Žižek give a talk at some sort of scholarly conference, a big room filled with fans and tourists drawn to a name of repute (before us the room had served as stage to Cornel West, also of repute, also doing his thing; it was that kind of conference). Unlike West, when Žižek's time was up he just kept talking. He stayed at the podium, he kept taking questions. After a while the cautious waving of the timekeeper became more and more exaggerated, until she came out on the stage and said to him, still with the polite bow of deference a bureaucrat reserves for a star, that it was time to go. Yes, yes, he said into the microphone, in one minute, and continued to talk. One minute doubled to two, two quintupled to ten, and the timekeeper was out again: "You really must go!" And yes, yes he said and took another question, the room now doubly full, as the people there to see the next speaker had come in, leaked out into the aisles, and filled up every spare cranny barely there before. Now nobody could get out if they wanted to. It was like a nightclub fire waiting for the spark of ignition. The organizers begin to mass at the side of the stage; you could see them wishing they had that kind of hook on a very long stick that belonged to the early days of vaudeville, when one could reach out and grab a performer by the waist and physically pull him off into the wings. But this is Žižek, the celebrity philosopher one can no more yank from his podium

---

Germany, France, and England an expression of three different existential attitudes: reflective thoroughness (German), revolutionary hastiness (French), utilitarian pragmatism (English). In political terms, this triad can be read as German conservatism, French revolutionary radicalism, and English liberalism. . . . The point about toilets is that they enable us not only to discern this triad in the most intimate domain, but also to identify its underlying mechanism in the three different attitudes towards excremental excess: an ambiguous contemplative fascination; a wish to get rid of it as fast as possible; a pragmatic decision to treat it as ordinary and dispose of it in an appropriate way. It is easy for an academic at a round table to claim that we live in a post-ideological universe, but the moment he visits the lavatory after the heated discussion, he is again knee-deep in ideology" (Žižek 1997, 5; 2006, 257–58).

than one could Cornel West. These men brook no interruption. The room grows fuller, the minutes pass, the questions keep coming, Žižek talks and wipes his brows and plucks at his shirt, his nose, his hair, his accent thick and lisped and foreign. Do I remember anything that he said from that stage? Not a word.[8]

In the end, for it does end, a man comes out and takes the microphone, twisting it away from Žižek and toward his own mouth. He says, "This session is done." The audience had been a part of something, inside something, that was not "conference" and also not "nightclub." It didn't smell of philosophy, it smelled of man. The man is soaked with sweat and doesn't care. The crowd surges forward, too many of them moving toward him rather than away toward the doors and on to the next thing bound to be of a different order than this one. The organizers now have a new problem: some minor portion of the audience, but still too large, has become a nimbus floating six deep around Žižek, whom the timekeepers have finally gotten off the stage and onto the robustly carpeted floor. I am there too, in the turbulent bubble. I have something to say about a book I might write one day about Slovenia, I want to warn him that it's coming. Before I get the chance, he looks me in the eye and tells a dirty joke, he points to his pantsed dick, to our chests, laughing heartily (and all around him, we laugh too) at the punch line.

It makes me feel at home, like a blister of Slovenia has come to rest here in this awkward conference venue. There (here), I am always pushed off guard, so much so that there is no balance, only off-balance and wildly insufficient sea legs. It's a hominess of vertigo, of falling down, of constant resplendent failure. I laugh because it's funny—not the joke necessarily (though it might have been), but the whole remarkable genius horror of the thing.

The nimbus slowly rotates as the men and women in charge (they seem to have called in reinforcements now, there are rather a lot of them) push

8. My notes have a better grasp of the situation than my memory. It was a panel on the death of God, and Google fills in the rest. Sunday, November 8, 2009, American Academy of Religion Annual Meeting, Montréal, Québec. There was even another speaker, though he got so few words in edgewise that one can be forgiven for having forgotten he was there. His name was Thomas Altizer. One can watch much of this on YouTube but it is there divided up into concise fifteen-minute bites, effectively erasing all of the Wagnarian torture of the audience by lagtime alone.

the whole constellation toward the doors. But it's a big room, and the doors are far away. It takes another twenty minutes to disgorge the speaking thing and its aureole out into the hallway.

It's been *three hours* since Žižek took the stage, and those devoted to the smooth functioning of conferences in conference centers (technically centres, since it's Canada) will likely remember him forever as the worst speaker in conference centre history. "What a piece of shit." It was performance art. No more or less than it was anything else. Žižek doing Žižek, being part of what Žižek does best.

It's perhaps in his nature, whatever that means. There are other things I remember. I remember how he showed a filmmaker, in a documentary she was making about him, that he keeps his clothes folded neatly in the kitchen cabinets. I've had friends like this, but none of them are famous, nobody is putting their questionable sock drawer on camera. And this difference between doing or being someone deeply quirky and showing that you are such a someone is more important than it might seem, because there is something wrong about how Žižek does Žižek. This wrongness links the fact that it seems to be "in his nature" and the ease with which he is called "full of shit."

The man is irritating and the irritant is specific—Slavoj Žižek always feels more like a show than like a person.[9] He feels this way live; he feels this way on film; he feels this way on the typeset page. It is as if he cannot simply be Žižek, but must always perform Žižek as if he himself were a role not a person—albeit a role that gives every impression of endlessly delighting its performer. So assiduous is Žižek in this performance, so unwavering, that it becomes impossible to imagine a moment of repose when he stops playing at Žižek and simply is himself. Perhaps one is given to wonder: Is the show all there is? Perhaps there is no self under there for him to be—perhaps it's just surface, bluster, and then nothing at all.[10]

9. As P. David Marshall neatly puts it, celebrities might be seen as a "production locale for an elaborate discourse on the individual and individuality" (1997, 4).

10. In an interview on the Swiss television program *SFR Kulture*, the interviewer Barbara Bleisch's first question to Žižek is, *"Wer sind sie?"* (Who are you?) to which he replies, *"Das weiss ich es nicht und ich will das nicht wissen!"* (I don't know and I don't want to know). The question, thus deflected, comes back much later, around minute forty-five of the interview, when Bleisch asks again, *"Gibt es trodzdem so was wie das Wahre ich?"* (Is there not

Figure 14. Slavoj Žižek: a scene of repose. IRWIN, *Portrait of Slavoj Zizek at the Occasion of the Anniversary of 100 Years of Jacques Lacan's Birth in Sigmund Freud's Working Room,* 2001. Photo by Michael Schuster.

In this way, one might argue that Žižek does what the new Janšas play at and that he is what the Slovene Benjamin merely flirts with—namely a dreamily splendid, complicated, and confusing shell, a superadequate husk, the carapace of a man scrawled with the word *philosopher.* And if he is all surface, all performance, if there is no there in there, it is easy to imagine

---

then such a thing as a true I?) to which he replies in polyglot, "No, but *es gibt den wahren Abgrund*" (No, but there is a real abyss). The full interview, "Slavoj Žižek: Down with Ideology! SRF Sternstunde Philosophie," can be found here: SRF Kultur, January 18, 2019, video, 55:47, https://www.youtube.com/watch?v=Zm5tpQp6sT4&feature=youtu.be, accessed December 2019.

that the trouble with Žižek for folks more used to a determinant, trustworthy innerness might come with the question: What is he full of? What is inside the body when the normal soulful or authentic self is recognized to be missing? A question to which those comfortable with a surface/depth model of subjectivity and with expectations concerning its earnest performance might easily answer: "Shit." After all, everyone is full of something.

My proposition, thus, is to take Žižek's being full of shit literally.[11] For it is not only his critics who imagine him thusly. Žižek is also wont to treat inner being—the essence of oneself—as a dark, elemental, excremental mass. Quoting Hegel, for example, he writes that "inner being is, in the first instance, 'still simple darkness, the unmoved, the black formless stone'" (2001, 59). And, just in case the analogy is too subtle, he continues, "The anal association here is fully justified: the immediate appearance of the Inner is formless shit" (2001, 59).

Two important aspects of shit are here highlighted in the least metaphoric of ways: first, it is substantive—shit is a mass, a material, a thing in its own right; second, it is formless, which isn't the same as saying it is amorphous, but rather that it is not easily wrought or crafted. He has left out the stinky factor, but we'll come back to that.

II. MORE ON THE SAME SUBJECT

Speaking of "bullshit" (the stuff that flows from the mouths of assholes [James 2012]), philosopher Harry Frankfurt makes the point of shit's *résistance* to artistry rather plainly: "Is the bullshitter by his nature a mindless slob? Is his product necessarily messy or unrefined? The word shit does, to be sure, suggest this. Excrement is not designed or crafted at all; it is merely emitted, or dumped. It may have a more or less coherent shape, or it may not, but it is in any case certainly not wrought" (2005, 21–22).

11. Dolar writes, "Is the external voice literal and the internal metaphorical? . . . Perhaps [it] is the metaphor which constitutes internality and consciousness, so that the very notion of the literal/external depends on taking the metaphor literally" (2006, 83). And Laporte (2000 [1978]) writes, "To touch, even lightly, on the relationship of a subject to his shit, is to modify not only that subject's relationship to the totality of his body but his very relationship to the world and to those representations that he constructs of his situation in society" (29).

There is, in other words, no artisanal asshole. Everyone may make shit but no one makes it nicely. And bullshitters, it seems make bullshit with the same disregard for the artistry of the stuff as shitters who make shit.[12]

Frankfurt, who sees bullshit as among the most salient features of our time, heartily bemoans our lack of a theory of it. "We lack," he says, "a conscientiously developed appreciation of what it means to us . . . . we have no clear understanding of what bullshit is, why there is so much of it, or what functions it serves" (2005, 1). And though Frankfurt spends much of his timely tome attending to the "bull" part of this compound, leaving the "shit" to molder (as a substance, it does seem to repulse analytic attention), he nevertheless provides a way into understanding just what exactly the complaint is against Žižek. Žižek doesn't take enough care (by his critics' measure) of the crap he spews. Rather than crafting an argument that we can take literally, or take metaphorically, or take for its inspiration and insight, we are left with "a stream of nonconsecutive units arranged in arbitrary sequences." What could this describe really, except shit?

Frankfurt's argument regarding bullshit and bullshitters matters here not simply because he is bold enough to take this particular bull by its horns, nor because it does appear to describe what Žižek is doing, but because at its heart it assumes a particular formation of the subject—one premised upon a difference between what is hidden from public view, inside the bullshitter's mind, and the self-aggrandizing, often buffoonable self made publicly available through word and deed. The primary intention of a humbug (a parallel term that Frankfurt also favors) is "to give [his] audience a false impression concerning what is going on in the mind of the speaker. Insofar as it is humbug, the creation of this impression is its main point" (2005, 14).[13] And though Frankfurt takes care to differentiate between the bullshitter and the liar as distinct types, there is never-

---

12. Georges Bataille would say that this is precisely what makes shit shit. There is nothing innate in it that causes it to disgust; rather, its uselessness, its resistance to recuperation matters because this resistance defines the "productive" system as such. As Allan Stoekl writes, of Bataille, "There is nothing inherently . . . repulsive, nonappropriable—in shit or in anything else. It is the relation of that element, that object, to a system in which it cannot be given a stable position that makes it 'rotten.' Its excluded rottenness is *necessary* to the coherence of the system" (2007, 21; emphasis mine).

13. Frankfurt himself points out that the vast majority of bullshitters are male; he is hard put to name more than one female bullshitter in the whole of his modest book.

theless a genealogy of mind he considers worth tracing out (and worth recapitulating here).

> Whenever a person deliberately misrepresents anything, he must inevitably be misrepresenting his own state of mind . . . . Thus, someone who lies about how much money he has in his pocket both gives an account of the amount of money in his pocket and conveys that he believes this account. If the lie works, then its victim is twice deceived, having one false belief about what is in the liar's pocket and another false belief about what is in the liar's mind. (2005, 12–13)

Truth (regarding the amount of money in a pocket, for example) is not what the humbug principally hopes to distort. Rather his aim is to convince others that the state of his mind is other than what it is. It is, in other words, a deliberate misrepresentation of an inner fact—a fact that cannot but be known through its earnest expression. In this way, humbug is the opposite of sincerity, another concept that relies heavily on the notion of a divided subject.

According to anthropologist Webb Keane (2002) (relying on Lionel Trilling's earlier work [1972]), sincerity is yet another "way of characterizing a relationship between words and interior states. To be sincere . . . is to utter words that can be taken primarily to express underlying beliefs or intentions." As such, sincerity "makes that interior state transparent." In sharp contrast to lies, humbug, *and* bullshit, sincere speech aims to convincingly and truthfully represent innerness. Sincerity, Keane continues, "adds and subtracts nothing in *words* that was not already there in *thought*" (74).[14] More specifically sincerity effects this sense of transparency to an audience primed to understand this mode of communication and its implications: both the speaker and those with whom he or she is speaking understand themselves to have inner selves and they share the presumption that these can be known and that they can be earnestly, honestly, and purely communicated.

Leaving aside for the moment that the theory of communication underlying this structure of the self has been well and thoroughly debunked

---

14. Keane continues: "we can call sincerity a metadiscursive term. As such, it is a component of linguistic ideology, that is, of local assumptions about how language functions. This ideology posits a specific sort of relationship between speech and its imputed sources in the speaker's self" (2002, 74).

(that, for example, that the words "money in my pocket" exit my mouth and burrow their way into your mind via your ear, and once in there create the exact *same* money-in-my-pocket notion I'd had in *my* mind before having said the words [Saussure 2011]), what remains is the idea of a split self capable of sincere expression and of the deliberate lie.[15] Whether one is truly or falsely representing what is "known" to be inside one's mind is a quibble in a larger debate of the nature of that mind as such.

In contrast, the humbug or bullshitter cares little for transparency (sincerity) or opacity (misdirection). He is interested in neither the truth nor the lies; what he is principally interested in is himself. For him the facts of matter become aesthetic accoutrement to a different project—the aggrandizement of self. Here is a long quotation from Frankfurt by way of example.

> Consider a Fourth of July orator, who goes on bombastically about "our great and blessed country, whose Founding Fathers under divine guidance created a new beginning for mankind." This is surely humbug . . . . The orator is not lying. He would be lying only if it were his intention to bring about in his audience beliefs that he himself regards as false, concerning such matters as whether our country is great, whether it is blessed, whether the Founders had divine guidance, and whether what they did was in fact to create a new beginning for mankind. But the orator does not really care what his audience thinks about the Founding Fathers, or about the role of the deity in our country's history, or the like. At least, it is not an interest in what anybody thinks about these things that motivates his speech.
>
> It is clear that what makes Fourth of July oration humbug is not fundamentally that the speaker regards his statements as false. Rather . . . the orator intends these statements to convey a certain impression of himself. He is not trying to deceive anyone concerning American history. What he cares about is what people think of *him*. (2005, 16–18)

<hr/>

15. Bakhtin debunks it best in his essay on speech genres (1986): "Courses in general linguistics (even serious ones like Saussure's) frequently present graphic schematic descriptions of two partners in speech communication—the speaker and the listener (who perceives the speech) . . . one cannot say that these diagrams are false or that they do not correspond to certain aspects of reality. But when they are put forth as the actual whole of speech communication, they become scientific fiction. The fact is that when the listener perceives and understands the meaning . . . of speech, he simultaneously takes an active responsive attitude toward it. He either agrees or disagrees with it (completely or partially), augments it, applies it, prepares for its execution and so on" (68). Just as important is "that the speaker himself is oriented precisely toward such an active responsive understanding. He does not expect passive understanding that, so to speak, only duplicates his ideas in someone else's mind. Rather he expects response, agreement, sympathy, objection, execution and forth" (69).

In other words, the bullshitter is a different *sort* of person. Instead of truth (of self or of anything else), the bullshitter principally cares for the nuances of self-aggrandizing performance. He reads audiences and plays them to make himself from their cheers (or jeers, as the case may be). More than just courting "likes," to use Facebook terminology for a common approach to crowd appeal, the bullshitter according to Frankfurt is, both literally and figuratively, full of shit. A fact that he doesn't hide but rather flaunts. As shit is dumped from his mouth, rather than flushing it away, the bulls-hitter holds it to himself and calls it "me." This is not craft work, but the work of impression by accumulation or coalescence. The bullshitter is a common grotesque. We make presidents of them.

It is easy enough, I think, to read Žižek through Frankfurt, and to see relatively little difference between the bullshitter, with his perverse self-constitution, and the Slovene philosopher who also seems to play the part of himself like a some happy vaudevillian at long last granted his moment upon the stage. What matters, however, about Frankfurt's typology and the judgments renderable from it, is that he is principally describing a normative social field, not a man. There is a proper way to do subjectivity, he suggests, which the bullshitter ignores to the detriment not so much of himself as the larger community.

It may well be that rather than manifesting an interest in truth, rather than caring about sincerity, rather even than lying (which at least recognizes the truth, if only to diverge intentionally from it), the bullshitter uses his subjectivity to wrong effect—his innerness seems empty and his words and deeds just for show. He feels wrong, his words "hot air . . . mere vapor. His speech . . . empty, without substance or content. His use of language, accord-ingly does not contribute to the purpose it purports to serve" (Dolar, quoted in Frankfurt 2005, 43).[16] However true this may be, what is interesting is the capacity to pass judgment, to know a form of subjectivity is "wrong" and to call it by a name: "full of shit" or "humbug" or (dare I say it) "Trump."

In other words, a normative field has been articulated, if between the lines. From Frankfurt's careful delineation of the bullshitter it is possible

16. Dolar continues: "There are similarities between hot air and excrement, incidentally, which make hot air seem an especially suitable equivalent for bullshit. Just as hot air is speech that has been emptied of all informative content, so excrement is matter from which everything nutritive has been removed" (quoted in Frankfurt 2005, 43–44).

to back-form his version of the proper subject. The language of a right man should not be "needlessly complex"; it should not ring as "posturing verbiage"; it should not principally be "charismatic," especially when this charisma is built upon "nonsensical" grounds.[17] Language should be content-full, informative, transparent, and (ideally) honest. As such, language is asked to carry something nutritive, a sort of innerness-of-orator that can be known, and ideally, trusted. It should function as a gift of self—that old idea that the speaker invests himself in his utterances, granting, at the very least, the knowledge of his own constitution to his audience. Such a subject knows and cares to know who he really is. He may lie, but at least in the pure act of lying he gives evidence of an inner self that recognizes the difference between right and wrong.

Not to poke too many pointed sticks into the body of the bullshitter—he is too easy a pincushion for those concerned with the rampant rise of fake news and alternative facts—but one feels in Frankfurt's work a sense of moral affront. It is not just the fact that the bullshitter is bullshitting us that marks him as offensive: it is that he does his selfhood wrong. For him, the production of the self as a spectacle-of-the-outer is just another way of being. It is, of course. But ignoring the garden of the inner, leaving its secrets and psychologies unplumbed and untended, means sidestepping an intimate, longstanding procedure of self-formation—what Keith Hoskin (1996) has called the "self-examining" self (267). Far from the "natural" feel one gets from Frankfurt (and in a moment also from the magnificent Cornel West, who is about to come strolling back into the conversation), the "self-examining" self is historically and culturally particular, having arisen in the late 1700s in Europe to become the normative mode of modern subjectivity. To twist toward hegemony for a moment: it is not that one *can* know oneself, it's that one must.

How one does self-knowledge the right way is as simple as it is ubiquitous; it is as much a social procedure as an intimate one. One knows oneself the same way that one knows anything: one conducts an examination. Or, as Adam Smith explained with surprising aplomb in 1749: "When I endeavour to examine my own conduct . . . it is evident, that in all such cases, I divide myself, as it were, into two persons and that I, the examiner

---

17. Complaints leveled against Žižek are from the beginning of this chapter.

and Judge, represent a different character from the other I, the person whose conduct is examined into and judged of" (quoted in Hoskin 1996, 270). In effect, this splitting of the self internalized procedures of examination, marking, ranking, and placement within a statistical field that were becoming ubiquitous in late-eighteenth-century Europe (Foucault 1995 et al.). What was happening institutionally, in the governing of society, was also happening internally, in the governing of selves. The procedures were parallel and of a kind.[18]

A long half century later, in the mid-1800s, there was another shift, whereby self-examination conduced to self-knowledge (and rather a lot of anxiety, it turns out) and became an initial step toward self-improvement.[19] What began as a mode of measurement within a standardized field (what *is*) slipped explicitly over into marking a goal or a target (what *ought* to be). It is this confusion of *is* with *ought* that Hoskin (following Hume) claims constitutes the "modern self" every bit as much as it constitutes modern bureaucracy. One doesn't examine (or audit) systems or persons to gain static knowledge about them. Rather, one conducts such examinations to determine how and in what domain improvements might best be made.

Or, to quote Cornel West, who says it best: "The unexamined life is not worth living, Plato says in line 38a of *The Apology:* How do you examine yourself? What happens when you interrogate yourself ? What happens when you begin to call into question your tacit assumptions and unarticulated presuppositions and begin then *to become a different kind of person?"* (quoted in Taylor 2008). To this he adds, speaking now of himself: "I'm a

18. Hoskin identifies this process as having begun with the strange project of examining students (who would later become bosses of factories and leaders of government) by having them sit in chairs and write about what they know. "Prisons, schools, hospitals, factories, universities, state bureaucracies, and corporate oligopolies most resemble each other, as both social world and the self become more and more subject to a writing, grading, and examining which together ensure the meticulous and continual circulation of plans, examinations, reports, feedback and feedforward evaluations—knowing me, knowing you, in our respective truths" (Hoskin 1996, 268). These exams, he points out, emerged in Germany, England, and Scotland in the 1760s and in France in the 1770s, seemingly without cross-fertilization. See also Hoskin 1993, 280–95.

19. An interesting side effect, Hoskin points out, was that as these exams were standardized, anxiety entered education in a way previously foreign to it. It was not only that one had to pass written examinations (already *de rigueur* in the mid-1700s) but that one had to be demonstrably *better than* the others subjected to the same examination and, ideally, perform best among all examined (see also Buckshot 2017).

bluesman in the life of the mind; I am a jazzman in the world of ideas." This improvisational flexibility marks a self so well known that it can be shifted and altered. He who self-examines is primed for self improvement. He who knows himself can change himself. Cornel West's internal jazzman and bluesman already know so much; they are masters of their genre; they can shift and groove selfhood adaptively. If self-examination leads to change, self-jazzification takes us to next-level interiority, as the self itself is played— the "true I" a constant and demanding work of skilled improvisation.[20]

The bullshitter is thus something of a rebel, characterized not just by his amorphous, uncrafted, and uncultivated innerness, but also by his lack of self-examination. It is not just that he is full of shit; it's that he is shame-lessly, obviously full of it. He is ok with being full of it. Nothing is hidden, further examination yields nothing of surprise, nothing more needs to be known beyond what is given, and there is thus no room for self-improvement—the very material of the self is wrong in its resistance not so much to being known but to being finely crafted.

I suspect that, for those who believe in the Delphic imperative, improper self-constitution is railed against so strongly from fear not of the bullshit-ter *per se,* but of all those regular people who are enraptured when pre-sented with an empty, bullshitty performance. It would seem (feel the hor-ror) that some measure of the crowd, the mass, the electorate, the kids-these-days (and so on) likes the bullshit and likes eschewing the self-examining, self-constituting, "self-clairvoyant and self-understanding" self as a normative imposition (Mahmood, quoted in Buckshot 2017, 183).[21] Which is precisely what it is.[22]

20. Improvisation, across genres, while always about expressivity and innerness, has very different connotations for African Americans than for white ones. See especially Dumit 2017, with its robust bibliography on this subject.

21. Speaking of a lecture given by Žižek at the University of Vermont in 2016 an anony-mous professor (personal communication) writes: "[Žižek] is certainly a spectacle both in the sense of enrapturing the audience, drawing them in, but also in terms of putting on a visual performance. It isn't enough to hear him; you must see him or, at least, his gyrating gesticula-tions and snarling, spitting visage seem to command your gaze. I think this part of his perfor-mance is crucial because he is not only one of our most preeminent dialectical thinkers, but he actually embodies the tensions/tortures of that mode of thinking, literally showing the audience what it's like to have two opposing ideas in your mind at the same time."

22. That this stinks of liberal elitism is obvious, but there is a deeper history to the notion that care of the self and care of shit are not only linked but also socially engineered. Laporte argues that for the modern subject, the rise of anxiety about the self coincides rather

West's and Frankfurt's right ways of doing subjectivity should feel vaguely creepy and ideological even if you are one of those people for whom they also feel mostly right. For, as the necessity to proselytize, even browbeat, for a self-examining self demonstrates, other modes of subjectivity are already everywhere in evidence and should (between the lines) be rejected.

There would be no need to warn against the charms of the man-full-of-shit if that mode of self didn't have significant appeal. The worry is not that Žižek is a bad philosopher, but that people might take him seriously. The worry is that people like those at Frankfurt's fictional Fourth of July picnic (in the long quotation above) might well vote for that humbug. And, for his part, Žižek could only have earned the moniker "celebrity scholar" because (some) people adore him.

I adore him.

He does do subjectivity wrong if you are looking for evidence of self-examination, self-clairvoyance, and self-care (as such, "full of shit" is a fair critique).[23] But in of all his blather and buffoonery he does something else very right: he makes the normative social field, which structures every argument against him, explicit. One technique is to take the shit inside of him (inside of us all) and incorporate it into his philosophical apparatus. A second is to write about it. A third is to perform it.

---

precisely in time and in space with a concomitant rise in worries over the proper disposal of shit *and* a shift to shit being considered one's own refuse rather than something public and belonging to the community: "This little pile of shit, heaped before my door, is mine, and I challenge any to malign its form . . . . What happens in my home, in my family, my dirty laundry, and all the rest is no affair of yours. This little heap in front of my door is my business, it is mine to tend. Mine to see to; mine to mind. Thus it was that the politics of waste branded the subject to his body, and prefigured, not so insignificantly perhaps, the Cartesian ideology of the *I*" (Laporte 2000, 30–31; italics in original).

23. Žižek being Žižek it would be wrong to assume that I have discovered something about him about which he is not already entirely aware. In the same interview with Swiss television cited in note 9, the interviewer closes the conversation by mentioning that she knows that Žižek doesn't really like doing interviews, and she asks him if it was terrible. To which he responds in a mix of English and German "I am afraid of interviews; you know, uh, I put it like this, this will maybe surprise. You know why I talk so much? Because I know, *ein wie sagt man das . . . Minderwertigkeitskomplex* [how do you say . . . inferiority complex]. I am afraid that if I stop, if I stop talking for a second you will get a breathing space to really listen to what I am saying and you will see that it is bullshit. So that to prevent you this distance I have to talk all the time, to distract you, so that you will not step back and say 'Oh my God, this is bullshit.' I have a great distrust into myself."

Žižek may not give a damn about the depth model of the self—split into examiner and examinee with self-knowledge all mixed in with self-improvement—but he cares a great deal about the constitutive power of the immediate environment. He is always making the normative social field evident, collapsing the figure and the ground so that figure (in Žižek's case, always himself) is very shiney but the ground is equally intrusive. The timekeeper at the conference, invisible in every other presentation, is forced to take center stage, to take the microphone and make the entire normative temporal order explicit. Time, here, is not some natural element of modern life, but rather made and enforced, agreed upon and shatterable. It is not the self that needs knowing; it is the normative social field that produces the *sensation* that the self needs knowing that matters. To this end, the minions of time's regimented order were given life, embodied, made visible and brought into play. Even audience members participated, we looked at watches and phones whispering among ourselves about the time and the man who seemed not to care a whit about it. We became witnesses and examiners of social structure, as the *ought* was made explicit in its distinction from the *is*.

One can say the same for the shape of the conference room, with its retractable walls and grand doors only at the back. Venues like that are made to be neutral, flexible spaces, places devoid of personality by design, colored all in beige as a mode of signaled neutrality. Yet as that "ballroom" filled up, it slid toward nightclub or tent revival. The dimensions of the space became evident as one wondered (I wondered) how to get out of there with so many people blocking the aisles? The specter of fire, the trampling rush of bodies hurtling toward too few ill-placed doors. And then, the same space shifted in the absurd effort to get the speaking Žižek off the podium and out of there. A room for a man such as that would have to be designed differently if one's aim were to keep spatial and temporal orders out of public view.

Even as I write this book, I wonder if I can use the word *shit* so liberally in an academic publication. And what of all the *fucks* and *damns* and *assholes* that follow in its wake? Will the academic publishing apparatus allow that portrait of Žižek with its obvious vagina (so what if it's a work of art) to go to press? The ground, which is to say, the larger context of capitalism (essential to the production and sale of books for profit or loss), of the contemporary university (essential for the consumption of said books), and of moral norms (which vary by country and thus by market) comes to life around Žižek. He, as the figure, calls the ground into evidence. He is always directing one's attention to himself *and* to something outside of himself which constitutes the field of operations. Nor is this an accidental side effect of hubris. He does it on purpose.

In a 2008 film called (nonironically) *Examined Life*, filmmaker Astra Taylor interviews eight so-called celebrity philosophers as they wander around the city (Judith Butler, Avital Ronell, Peter Singer, and Martha Nussbaum) or around an airport (Kwame Anthony Appiah), or sit in a cab (Cornel West) or in a rowboat (Michael Hardt), or in Žižek's case, explore a dump. The dump is loud, it stinks, and rats scurry through piles of trash. Taylor explains, in the introduction to the extended transcript of the interview: "A dozen relatively tidy recycling stations provided the depot's public face. Inside we found mounds of used building materials, forlorn household appliances, and assorted junk, as well as enormous mountains of fetid refuse. As an army of trucks and tractors moved the piles around with no discernable logic, some strange spray filtered down on us, a futile attempt to mitigate the stench. Meanwhile, it was a beautiful day: blue skies, birds singing. The contrast couldn't have been more appropriate" (Taylor 2009). And Žižek basks in it. His nose never wrinkles, he barely stops talking when dump trucks and bulldozers heave and tumble piles of trash around them; this is where he wants to be. It is where he wants all of us to be, not flushing our shit down toilets and imagining it is gone; not tossing our water bottles in the trash and imagining the seas are not full of them; not living our perfumed lives unconscious of the fetidness of dumps.

> When we are standing where I am standing now, with a lot of trash behind me, this is where we should start feeling at home. I think in our daily attitude—not only with trash like this but with more literal trash like excrement—in our daily perception, the reality is that this disappears from our world. When you go to the toilet, shit disappears. You flush it, and while, of course, rationally you know that it is there in canalization, at a certain level of your most elementary experience it disappears from your world. The same happens with trash. But the problem is that trash doesn't disappear. (quoted in Taylor 2009)

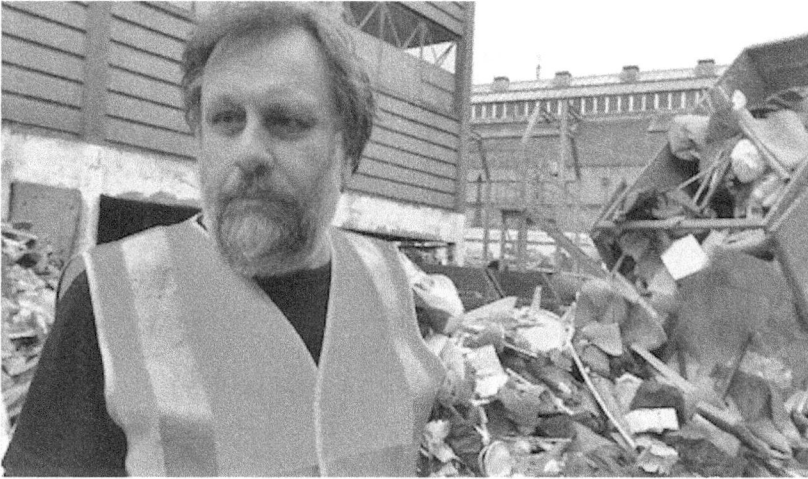

Figure 15. Žižek happy (with trash), from Taylor 2008.

Just as time doesn't disappear, shit doesn't disappear. Just as vaginas and penises don't disappear, capitalism doesn't disappear.[24] We have designed spaces, systems, regimes that, like toilets, swallow up contexts and remnants. With Žižek, though, these spaces, systems, and regimes are brought back. He thinks about the sewers that whisk our shit away and he points to them—with words, an index finger, a story—and they come back to us for an instant. "Why should an ecologist love trash? I would like to turn around the perspective. I think that what is truly threatening is not trash as such, it is separating trash, it is throwing trash out. I think that the ultimate horror is, again, a nice green pasture or whatever where trash

---

24. A case in point (from the robust transcript):

TAYLOR: Let's change topics a bit. What about ecology's relationship to economy? I'm sure you have something to say about this. But first [gesturing to the ground], don't step on the porn!

ŽIŽEK: Porn! Where? My God. This is serious now. [Picks it up.] No, you call this porn? My God, I want real porn. Is there any here?

TAYLOR: Obviously porn shouldn't be trashed.

ŽIŽEK: Why do they always get these guys with the tattoos, as if they have to get some poor sailors or something?

TAYLOR: You mean they should hire professors? [Laughs.]

ŽIŽEK: Like professors of philosophy?

TAYLOR: Exactly. [Laughs.] OK, economy . . .

disappears. I think that an ideally balanced (environmentalists use this term) ecological society would have to be a totally chaotic space where trash is simply part of our environs, not discriminated against" (180).

So yes, Žižek is a bullshitter. But that doesn't mean he is not entirely in earnest. Embracing the bullshit, living with it, using it as an ethical mode is how he constitutes himself via the world, not via plumbing the depths but through an aggressive relationship to what is exterior. "I am not an inside," he seems to say, "all of this is me too, though you might prefer it flushed away, it's there, here, all around: under your pants is a vagina; in this conference is a temporal regime; in this room is a structured space of movement; in that toilet is a cultural ideology of the good relationship to shit." The ground is always present, even more so because there doesn't seem to be any true thing inside Žižek at all. He both is very densely and uniquely himself (like Cornel West) while failing to be either artful or crafted. He is a sweaty, twitchy train wreck, full of shit and happily so.

In this, Frankfurt (and all Žižek's detractors) are right: Žižek makes himself not by attending to inner truths or by splitting into self-examining, self-improving subjectivity, but rather by maintaining a distastefully intimate relationship with the world. He is of it, he makes himself of it, and then he forces this subjective blending, as a sort of human-environmental chimera, upon the rest of us. His mode of being a subject is aggressive: he wants us too to live in a world not of the self, but of and with the intensity of context.

Chapter 5

I. INSIDE THE BODY IS BLOOD AND BONE

In 1999 Ive Tabar, a nurse and a medical performance artist, ate fifteen paper stars, each a bright shade of goldenrod. As a chaser he ingested a significant amount of blue liquid. This rested in his belly, each element mixing with his own acids, each slowly digesting, intermingling, degrading. His audience saw none of this; all of it (stars, blue juice, digestion) was inside of him. But before the digestive process was complete, before it all turned to shit, Tabar inserted the tube of a gastric lavage (stomach pump) through his nose, pushed it down through his esophagus and into his swollen belly, and then switched on the machine. And up it all came, spilling out into the lavage tank positioned on a thin plinth at the center of Kapelica Galerija's small exhibition space—golden stars in a sea of blue. The flag of the European Union mixed with the stuff of Tabar's body; a supranational symbol aswim in a sea of Slovene bile. There Tabar left it, and left the gallery, without further comment, save perhaps the title.

This fit of spleen was called *Evropa I* and it was the first, and arguably most genteel, of a series of four projects Tabar would craft over the next eight years, each called by the same title, *Evropa*, each a wordless play on the theme of Slovenia's integration into the European Union.

Evropa I, though devoid of spoken language, drew upon a local turn of phrase. To have someone or something in (one's) stomach (*"Imeti nekoga ali nekaj v želodcu"*) expresses a sentiment similar to the English "to be unable to stomach something or someone." It is, in Slovene, to feel something so distasteful, so ill making, that to vomit it up or otherwise eject it from one's life is preferable to patiently bearing it (thanks to Krpič 2010, 94 for this insight). What was clear in 1999, five years before Slovenia's entry into the European Union, was that despite widespread popular support for membership, Tabar simply couldn't stomach the thought—so much so that he made this thought flesh and then forcibly, mechanically, sucked it from his belly. He left that thing, an idea plus his own bile, behind; he left the gallery without it. Thus, though Tabar did not speak his distaste—there is no voice here—his choice of medium allowed for certain visceral qualities to enter into what was a very public, indeed performed, political commentary.

In the second of the *Evropa* series—*Evropa II: Luknja v sistemu, buža v kolenu* [Europe II: Hole in the system, drill in the knee] (2001)—the central allegory of the work shifted from that of "expulsion" of the symbol of a united Europe from the Slovene body to the effective "penetration" of this body by the European Union. But Tabar's take on penetration is one in which genteel absorption of foreign elements into one another pointedly does not occur. Integration is not to be confused with homogenization. One thing (drill/Europe) might be inside of another (knee/Slovenia) but its being there hurts like hell.

This piece, which was performed in Obalne Galerije in the coastal town of Koper, consisted almost entirely of the artist drilling through his knee. The performance itself was fairly stark. The only props were a chair and the drill, while the performers (all of whom, Tabar included, were medical professionals), were dressed in the practical aqua and blue scrubs of an operating theater. Tabar sat in the chair, his pant leg rolled up, and injected a bubble of anesthesia just under the skin. The audience then waited, along with Tabar, for this to take effect. After some minutes he picked up a drill with a ten-inch bit and meticulously ran it through the shinbone, just under his kneecap (Novak 2001). He then wrapped the entire apparatus (knee plus drill) in gauze and was loaded onto a gurney and wheeled to a waiting ambulance which sped away, presumably—but not explicitly—to a hospital, where an antiseptic drill-removal procedure might be performed. The actual drilling portion of the performance was extremely short, about five minutes, though the videotaped version, which is how most people have seen it, myself included, extends this slightly by documenting all of the preparation procedures for the knee, which were hidden from the live audience's view by a green scrub curtain.

As in *Evropa I*, Tabar's second piece in this series addressed itself to the project of European integration, though more through its title and subtext than by anything explicit in the content of the work itself. Like the first, it is also a play on a common Slovene phrase, in this case, "*Rajši si zvrtam luknjo v koleno, kot . . .*" (I'd rather drill a hole in my knee than . . .); here the English equivalent is "I'd rather have a hole in my head than . . ."[1] Tabar's two subsequent performances in this series followed this pattern: an explicitly evocative title, a subtle "in the know" reference to an idiomatic phrase likely recognizable only to fluent speakers of Slovene, a common and easily recognizable symbol of a geopolitical entity (usually a flag of some sort), and physical violence enacted by the artist upon his own body.

In brief, and without unnecessary gore, in *Evropa III* (2004), which accompanied Slovenia's accession to the European Union, Tabar slowly separated his fingernail, with a Slovene flag painted upon it, from the flesh of his finger. He then affixed the nail to a plastic *Proteus anguinus*—a local, pale-skinned newt often used in Slovenia as a national totem (see introduction, note 24). In *Evropa IV* (2008), he sliced open his abdomen with a scalpel, inserted a catheter, and then released a stream of dyed blue urine straight from his bladder into a fish tank containing a goldfish and a number of test tubes, each of which stood in for a member nation of the European Union.

There is something both dense and figurative about this series of performances. It quiets audiences. In *Evrope II* (the drill in the knee one), there was an extended silence in the gallery after Tabar was wheeled to the ambulance and driven away. I have never seen a gallery so quiet after a performance or an audience so slow to recover its chattiness. Even the

---

1. Tomaž Krpič in his exceptional article on the work of Ive Tabar (including the *Evropa* series) suggests that the implied phrase after the ellipse is: " . . . than become, at least willingly, a citizen of the European Union" (2010, 94).

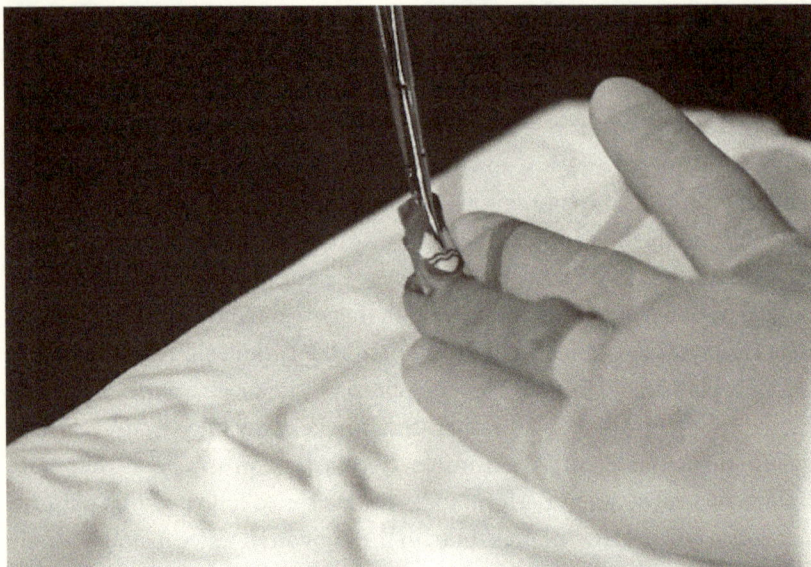

Figure 16. Ok, a little unnecessary gore. (Note the image of Mount Triglav painted on the nail removed.) Ive Tabar, Ljubljana, 2003. *Mladina,* no. 51, December 22, 2003. Photo by Miha Fras.

operator of the video camera forgot to turn it off, such that for about five minutes after Tabar's departure the guests at the event slowly wander in and out of the frame. Wine in hands, solitary and silent.

In the end, speech does reemerge as audience members clump in pairs and plurals, falling into the sorts of conversation that tend to follow performances; conversations in which the art is not discussed. Gallery events are like church socials in this regard, filled with circulating folks chatting about life rather than about God or art, as the case may be. Such conversations about who is doing what with whom after Tabar's performance fade in and out of the microphone's reach; snippets are rendered only partially intelligible by the limits of technology. At some point the videographer remembers him (or her) self and the feed goes dead.

Tabar's work on and with the body—which extends well beyond the *Evropa* series—was not unusual in Slovenia in the late 1990s and early 2000s. During that period a steady stream of body artists, many of international renown, performed in this small country: Orlan, Franko B., Ron

Athey, Kira O'Reily, Havve Fjell, Oleg Kulik, and no less than ten performances by Australian body artist Stelarc between 1995 and 2003 (for more on this subject, see Jones 1998). Many but certainly not all of these performers were hosted by Galerija Kapelica in Ljubljana.

What binds these artists and the curators who arranged their visits in the production of something roughly definable as Slovene art and culture (ca. 1995–2005) was that they produced and performed their work within a distinctly local matrix of economic policies, bureaucratic organizations, moral imperatives, aesthetic concerns, artistic communities, and public interest. In other words, their shows were locally organized and funded; they were attended, supported, and reported upon.

There was thus nothing entirely outrageous within this context about Tabar's choice of his body as the medium for his art (see Bakke 2017). Slovenes had a regularly available diet of performances in gallery spaces across the country in which artists pierced and punctured themselves, to bleed, to stretch, to hang, to sew flesh to flesh. It was as if a constant reminder were necessary, at this particular historical moment, that what the body was, was resplendently full of, was living meat and necessary liquids—blood, bile, urine, pus, tears, mucus. In these performances some obvious ways into the body were shut; lips for example were sewn to lips. Others were stretched open until they were big enough to see into, men's assholes (of the nonfigurative type) most especially.

There was a kind of flatfooted materialism to all of this. Explorations were pointedly of what bodies had on the inside—not a soul, not the ineffable wisp of an inner self, but rather goo of different sorts, viscosities, smells, and colors. All of these substances, which leak or pour forth from flesh when it is cut or punctured, worked as proof of a sort of visceral innerness. This body, the body Slovene audiences came to watch, in performance after performance, year after year, was substantive, all the way in.

These performances did other things as well, metaphoric, cultural, and expressive things (which I will turn to in a moment), but at their base was an unceasing almost rhythmic insistence that one can know the inner self, one can see it, and it is palpable, fleshy, incarnate. One is reminded of Mladen Dolar's ferocity in insisting that the voice is but air pushed through meat and should not be mistaken for "a sound of what has a soul in it" (2006, 24). Just because a thing, a sound, a formed gust of air comes from within the body does not give it magical soul-like qualities. In fact, just the opposite. For Dolar, the voice's origin point inside the body should have a demystifying effect. These performances also hammered that note home. There is no romance here, just a reminder, and again another reminder and another, that inside the body is blood and bone.

As Tabar's *Evropa* series makes abundantly clear, the literalists' approach to the inner self was not the only thing going on in these works. Many also included the same mimetic play with geopolitics that colored Slovene artworks of all sorts during this period. In the words of the impossible Luther Blisset, "slovenian artist likes to copy."[2] What was copied were not only things like paintings (à la Mondrian) but also personages (Walter Benjamin, Janez Janša, Luther Blisset) and institutional forms (the NSK state-in-time, the Parasite Museum, RISGURS, the Slovene Space Agency, and on and on [Bakke 2017]). In works of body art, however, and especially those by Slovenes, the focus was more singular. Geopolitical complexities were enacted on a small scale by artists upon themselves. They made politics flesh and used one technique in particular to accomplish this: the conjoining, interpenetrating, and incorporating of a diversity of elements naturally unfriendly to one another (like drill-bit and leg) into a singular functional entity of short *durée*. In the final years before Slovenia's integration into the European Union, exemplified here by Tabar's series, artworks of this type were ubiquitous.

The local world in which all of this incorporative art was happening was during this same period defined by rapid geopolitical and socioeconomic change. Yugoslavia, of which Slovenia had been a part, was quite violently gone, and union with Europe loomed large on the horizon. Nearly all of this change was both glossed as and actually good for Slovenia. The Slovenes had extracted themselves from Yugoslavia well,

2. There were twenty-five items on this list, most of which I found to be relatively speaking accurate. Here is a taste: "slovenian artist is terribly late / slovenian artist likes comfort / slovenian artist likes money / slovenian artist takes no risks / slovenian artist travels / slovenian artist likes to copy / slovenian artist is very clever / slovenian artist knows everybody / slovenian artist lives up to the expectations . . . " (Blisset 1995/96). The full text can be found at www.ljudmila.org/~vuk/rigusrs/lb.htm. Blisset and his weird subjectivity are an absolute pleasure to read about and into. The interested student can start with Wikipedia or with Bakke 2007, section 7.1.

and by the early 2000s, when Tabar was crafting and performing his *Evropa* series, Slovenia was exiting a decade of increased prosperity, political stability, access to technology, and even substantial money for the arts; the future looked brighter still.

All of this breathless progress also meant that many Slovenes were living in a world of constant unknowns over which individuals had little say and even less control. A generation raised with socialism had been rendered almost instantaneously superfluous, as jobs, skill-sets, and ideologies changed with the swiftness of a bird in flight. Among certain demographics, most notably middle-aged and university-aged men, suicide rates grew to be among the highest in the world (Marušič 1999, Marušič and Brecelj 2000). In Slovenia in the 1990s and early 2000s, there was both peace and great sorrow, prosperity and horrific loss, hopefulness and national dismemberment. Yet in public, only one of these stories was told—that of progress toward ever greater goods. In art, and body art most especially, the soft fleshy underbelly of this progress was laid bare; here weakness, hardship, suffering, isolation, and loss were made palpable. Here, the "work" of maintaining functionality was exposed in ways that were often difficult for artists to endure and for audiences to absorb. Much of this was, however, done without anybody ever saying as much. What was difficult to articulate in daily life may have maintained a forcefulness in contemporary artworks, but both realms were equally characterized by the avoidance of clearly articulated, oppositional messages. As with Tabar's work, you had to be able to "get" the reference embedded in the work. That, or you missed the point.

Despite this quiet, physically invasive artworks were clearly providing an outlet for the other side of the story: art was being used as a visceral and extremely expressive space to articulate things for which there were neither adequate words nor suitable fora for complaint—beyond those offered by galleries. In this way, Slovene artists were laying a certain claim, on the micro level, to what was happening on the macro. In their art, whether they were consuming it or doing it, Slovenes were making shifts in geopolitics immensely local and intimately felt. They were making the nation of their bodies and practicing "integration" on themselves as politics and politicians plied their own integrations on the body politic. By these means, they were finding ways to make the more abstract and vertiginous experiences of transition their own.[3]

It is something of a universal truth to say that, in the era of extractive capitalism on a global scale, bodies politic are full of nonnative objects and persons (exemplary smatterings include: Matsutake Worlds Research Group, n.d.; Gilroy 1993, Hahn and Soentgen 2011). The same can be said of physical bodies, whether via medical devices (like pacemakers or artificial limbs) or ornamentation (like a ring through the nose or silicone in the lips). What was startling about the treatment of these intrusions within contemporary Slovene performance art, however, was that tropes of functional assimilation or absorption were actively eschewed. What was forced upon audiences (and into artists) instead was the undeniable, unalterable fact of difference in the intimate spaces of home and flesh. There was no aesthetic slippage, no beauty, and arguably no sublimity. Material differences of kind were rather allowed to remain unwieldy, uncomfortable, and alien to what they are stuck into—a drill-bit left in the knee, a French hypermart left at the edge of town, an EU law granting foreigners the right to buy property left on the books, an anthropologist sitting down to lunch in your kitchen left in her chair, there. The discomfort is the same across scales, though reactions differed largely from one case to the next. Not everyone was drilling through their knees, but having been that anthropologist at the kitchen table, I'd say that the intimate fact of foreignness hurt just about as much.

In each case, the fit is awkward and the assimilation of such foreign materials arguably impossible. In Slovenia, where things are most often made to work, the task of remarking upon this awkwardness was left to the artists, who "spoke" mimetically with their bodies of things that didn't belong and how it felt to live with them. Their performances worked, therefore, more as a visceral metonym of opinion than as a suggested plan of action. In Slovenia's case, the sensation to be expressed—in art as in

3. Of this feeling of finding ways to make a geopolitical transition intimate, Tadej Pogačar, the artist and curator of the fictitious (though functioning) P.A.R.A.S.I.T.E. Museum, says "Here [in Slovenia], there is push from everyday life, because when you build a new space [independent Slovenia] and you build all the new institutions from post to money, you have a certain feeling that you also need an institution of your own" (personal conversation, June 2002).

life—was primarily of being, experiencing, and coming to understand oneself and one's nation as nonhomogeneous, inconsistent, in flux, in pain yet nevertheless viable (Bakke 2017).

The fleshiness of the body is not secondary to this task, in part because the body is particularly notable in its resistance to these kinds of material incorporations. It's hard to keep those stars down; it's hard to pull that fingernail off. There is pain, but also a physical attachment of the body to its own integrity that must be overcome in order for these performances to work. More than this, however, the viscerality of the flesh (including its resistances) leads, in a decidedly non-Žižekian way, to an understanding of the forcefulness of context. Here, it is not so much that the figure acts to highlight the invisible constraints of the ground but that a broader context is *literalized* in the actual stuff of the body; shit is but one of these things. Here, geopolitical machinations and individual selves get all gummed up, one with another. It's a collapsing of scales that doesn't quite work, which is the point. Readying a state to join an international political body is not the same as readying a body for surgery. The procedure, the sites of labor, the work, the expertise involved, and the thing operated upon are all different. The only similarity is the fact (the act) of preparation itself, behind closed curtains or closed doors as the case may be.

With Tabar, we might ask then, how it feels to be a nation in transition *not* because he is plying his body as a national stand-in (though he is), but because in his work geopolitical change trickles all the way down and into the flesh of him. It hurts. It hurts more (or that hurt is easier to express) when what is being changed is not an inner self—a process we would call "conversion"—but a body, solid and lively and full of its own rhythms and systems and ways of being. Vomit up that European Union. For in refusing the location of resistance (an inner self), Tabar is also refusing a colonial attitude that has held sway for centuries. To make him European you would have to change his body, not his mind, not his essence, not his soul, but his body, because the flesh is all there is. And conversions plied upon flesh tend to come off far more obviously as punishment, or torture, or the immoderate destructions of war. Here, Tabar works these flesh-conversions upon himself (tearing his own fingernails off his own hands) as a means of making obvious the national, cultural, and self-transformations firmly underway. Context is thus literally embodied, and the ideological piece of such transitions—that they do *not* hurt; that they do *no* harm—is resoundingly, viscerally refuted, to be left alone, in a gallery, in a tank filled with bile.

II. ". . . OR AT LEAST FAIL WHILE TRYING"

Timothy Mitchell (1990), in a stunning essay on "our" insistence that all persons be considered as autonomous actors (a bias that itself forms the very core of human rights doctrines), writes the following:

> "*We* tend to think of persons as unique self-constituted consciousnesses living inside physically manufactured bodies. As something self-formed, this consciousness is the site of an original autonomy. This notion of an internal autonomy of consciousness defines the way *we* think of coercion. It obliges *us* to imagine the exercise of power as an external process that can coerce the behavior of the body without necessarily penetrating and controlling the mind" (1990, 545; *emphasis added*).

Though Mitchell never says as much, his use of *we* and *our* and *us*, scattered throughout this quote as throughout the larger text, refers principally to Western-educated social scientists. His critique, in other words, is of an emancipatory politics firmly grounded in the self-conception of formerly colonizing peoples "gifted" to formally colonized ones. Mitchell then proceeds to illustrate this point through a lengthy critique of James C. Scott's *Weapons of the Weak* (1985), an extremely popular book at the time that Mitchell was writing. That book, based upon Scott's research in Malaysia, argues, in sum, that economically as well as politically colonized people have resistance "on the inside." They are autonomous and aware of

---

This section title comes from a poetic catastrophe of a text (I say this in admiration) called "Repetitions of a Text—a Text on Repetition," written by Katja Čičigo (2018) almost as if she were Gertrude Stein. To give a flavor for the whole, the extended quote reads: "This performance worked with what is absent and so does the present text; what they present us with is precisely what they do not present us with; their presence resides in an (always unsuccessful) attempt at a radical absence of each other. This performance worked by producing what is absent and making us experience what is not; the present text will try to repeat the functioning of this performance, repeating the production of what is absent and hopefully making you experience what is not—or at least fail while trying." (102)

their circumstances and they can use their "minds," their "innate" human ability to understand situations, as a means of resisting hegemonic incursions by things like paper money, or new forms of agriculture, or the concentration of wealth in the hands of fewer and often more physically distant people. Equally, this inner fortitude provides a buffer against emissaries of the state, like the police, tax collectors, and in some cases, even armies.

This "internal" ability to distance oneself from material or structural coercion is, Mitchell argues, a misreading of the fact that power, in situations of social change, works by constituting the terms by which these situations (and reactions to them) are understood. Notably what these new things, systems, and emissaries of state do is delocalize and fix patterns of domination. Domination was always there, but before states, and tractors, and paper money, and extractive capitalism really got a hold on village life, the patterns by means of which domination was realized "had to be continuously established and reestablished." Whereas "now," he says, "these are built into the functions of economic and social practices." The idea of a "pure," incorruptible inner self is thus coming into play at the same moment that political and economic changes are shifting experiences of power in daily life from a "tangible and material realm" to one that is more "abstract and enduring" (570).

The hardening of the structures of daily life into coercive architectures is echoed, Mitchell claims, by Scott's optimistic claims about the abilities of the "weak" to understand, reject, and resist ideological persuasion. On the inside they are aware, active, ironic, and arguably even pure, while on the outside (that is, in the material functions of their everyday lives) they are subjected, constrained, coerced, and, though Scott doesn't say it quite like this, pretty much screwed.[4] Thus, though this is a greatly attenuated version of Mitchell's argument, which is in turn much shorter than Scott's book, the argument is clear: material processes of subjugation are not totalizing because humans possess an inner fortitude. Even under the

4. Just to nail the point home, Mitchell continues "*Weapons of the Weak* approaches the question of domination in terms of an essential distinction between physical coercion and ideological persuasion. This approach is inevitably blind to the possibility ... that power now works through novel methods of creating and recreating a world that seems reduced to this simple two-dimensional reality" (1990, 570).

worst conditions, individuals have the capacity to retreat inside their (individual) bodies and brew their resistance there.[5]

Slovenia is not Malaysia (Scott's case). In Slovenia every last village has known, since before Napoleon, about abstracted, distantly administrated, fixed modes of power, about political manipulation, and about the failures and successes of nations (and even empires) on many fronts. Slovenia exports serious refrigerators, cars, and contemporary performance art, not tin and rubber. They make rather than extract.[6] Nevertheless, the feeling of having oneself, not just one's nation and its political allegiances, reformed has been part of Slovenia's transition to a more thorough capitalism, just as it was in Scott's Malaysia. This is likely a universal truth (see esp. Li 2014), but even without such grandiose claims, it is undeniable that converting to capitalism is a serious undertaking whether it is opted for, as across the Eastern Bloc, or imposed, as in much of the global south.

Despite a wave of scholars and activists in the 1990s pushing forward the term "neocolonialism" as the right way to consider the great rush of capital into the former Soviet spaces after communism's collapse, the term and its sentiment of rampant exploitation were always an awkward fit for the economic and political reintegration of Europe into Europe (Chari and Verdery 2009).[7] The people of the central European communist states had been organizing for decades for an expanded market, freer speech, and the freedom of movement. Capitalism was no monster set to devour the region (as it could be rightly figured in the global south). Rather, it was welcomed with open arms by a population who had been struggling to enact just the sorts of economic reforms capitalism effected with such ease. Democracy too was a part of the package. As such, freedom soared into communism's wake upon two wings: the freedom of markets to regulate supply and demand and the freedom of representative

5. A powerful counterargument can be found in the autobiography of Frederick Douglass, (2004 [1845]). See also Weber (1967 [1905]) and Rosaldo (1989).

6. In the early 1980s, the period in which Scott was writing, Malaysia's main exports were rubber and tin; see John H. Drabble, "Economic History of Malaysia," EH.net Encyclopedia, edited by Robert Whaples, July 31, 2004, https://eh.net/encyclopedia /economic-history-of-malaysia/, accessed April 2018.

7. See also the 2012 special issue "On Colonialism, Communism and East-Central Europe" of the *Journal of Postcolonial Writing* 48, no. 2.

democracy to govern the people according to their uncoerced will. This, anyway, was the argument at the time.

History, of course, proved to be more complicated. Specifically, the ideas about what free markets and democratic governance actually meant were translated over into how they felt, as revolutionary days turned to months and then years and now decades of real existing capitalism. Despite how much the details of any particular case matter one can still claim that it is easier to dream a revolution, perhaps even easier to bring one to pass, than it is to preserve in an enduring institutional form the values that drove the uprising. Be this as it may, the idea of 'neocolonialism' sweeping across the east of Europe never gained much steam, and the sorts of critiques that are easier to make about capitalist expansion in Africa or Asia or Latin America (anywhere with villages really) didn't stick well to a welcome shift of central European focus from the Soviet East to the democratic West.

That the transition was by and large welcome, and that its seeds fell upon well-tilled ground, does not mean it was easy. Socialism, in all its various forms (Yugoslavia was not Romania was not Belorussia and so on) had a functionalish institutional culture in place (Ferhérváry 2013; Verdery 1996). There was an economy, if not one that sparkled and charmed; it kept most people well fed, well employed, well educated, and in reasonable health. The roads were paved, the electricity system universal if buggy, and the mail for the most part delivered. Women worked and children were cared for by state-provided daycares, developments that would take decades for Western capitalist countries to mimic (Borneman 1992). In other words, much of what was "replaced" in the former socialist world were extant modes of doing things reasonably well. More often than not, an institution's culture—its ways of working and of commanding and auditing that work, its procedures and hierarchies, its official and unofficial modes of accounting—were reoriented after 1989 around a new set of priorities, rather than scuttled entirely (Berdahl, Bunzl, and Lampland 2000). These priorities were, following Mitchell, less local, in that they were not reflective of the communist value systems that had structured daily life across central and eastern Europe for decades.

In her 2004 book *Privatizing Poland*, Elizabeth Dunn chronicles this process of capitalist conversion as a Polish baby food factory is remade into a Polish baby food factory (the first was owned by the state, the second and same, for the most part run by Gerber, a giant in the American baby food scene). Dunn's study of an ostensibly economic transition is very much in keeping with Tabar's bodily protest about an ostensibly political one. The modes of expression (academic treatise, contemporary body art) are as different as night is from day, but the felt point is the same: there is no such thing as a neutral organizational shift; to say otherwise is to misunderstand the gravity of transition; to pretend otherwise is to perpetrate a lie. People will be remade. Or, in Dunn's words, in order for an American company in eastern Europe to "make the kinds of products it knows, the company first has to make the kinds of people it knows: shop-floor workers, sales people, and consumers like those in the United States" (5). In this way shifts in economic logics work similarly to shifts in religious ones: a belief system is changed via the transformation of bodily and social practices as much as by the particularities of particular deities (Nash 1993; Taussig 1980).

In Poland, in Dunn's study, one of the things people got as they were made recognizable to American corporate structures were inner selves comprised of measurable, knowable, and improvable qualities. Privatization, thus, replaced a set of labor practices that knit individual workers into networks of reciprocity (structured around the control of scarce materials) with a set of management procedures that taught workers to perform in quantifiably measurable ways, organized around distinctly new values, like flexibility or efficiency. No longer was sociality *and with it* baby food built up from an intricate social network of gifting, receiving, and recirculating favors and food as it had been under communism. Now these were derived from measurable and improvable performance standards that were applied, as Dunn shows with aplomb, equally to carrots, as to workers, as to the organizational structure of factory. Things (people, vegetables, flowcharts) were examined, broken down into measurable qualities, and then subjected to improvement element by element.

What Gerber was affecting, then, was a transformation of selves that adheres to Mitchell's argument far more closely than to Scott's. The mechanisms of social control were standardized and they were enforced from further away. Likewise, these mechanisms were designed to reshape self-conception and thus also the very *terms* by means of which future decisions would be made or debates settled, as foreign corporations slowly gained "control of the signs and practices of everyday life as an exercise in *material* coercion" (Comaroff 1989, 267; emphasis added; see also Jansen 2015).

Polish selves were remade in ways convenient to capital. Quality control as the instrument of this transformation remade how state socialism made baby food; *and* it remade carrots as composite products; *and* it remade workers (as if they were also carrots) as composite beings capable of self-knowledge and thus self-improvement; *and* it attempted to remake consumers as collectors of qualities like flexibility, hipness, and youth. (Note the andandpersand rising resplendent.) These new Poles are almost but not quite Cornel West's "jazzmen in the world of ideas" or "bluesmen in the life of the mind," who can move flexibly through a series of unique-feeling, internal improvisations while always holding on to the shape of the piece, while always maintaining a sense of self as principally constituted by a capacity for innovation and change, without fracture. As the italicized *and*s add up, layer after layer of simultaneous performance in multiple registers starts to look like a serious component of the jazzification of subjectivity. If West preaches an internal capacity to shift between registers—a skill premised upon taking the Delphic imperative to "Know thyself" very seriously indeed—then Swedish jazzish musician Fatima (whose music I would recommend) takes us the rest of the way there.

Just in case you still imagine that the feeling of being an authentic creature of your own making, a man or a woman (or neither, or both, as the case may be) whose most intimately felt essence is something other than cultural; in case you still imagine, as Tabar evidently does *not*, that the process of changing political and economic alliances is neutral, or only coercive on the outside (apropos of Scott), then Fatima should help to put an end to all of that.

Fatima is Swedish born and Swedish educated but her biography is nevertheless narrated in such a way that her mother's "Senagelese/Gambian," "African," "West African," "African," Africanness sticks more strongly to her than her own born and bred Swedishness.[8] (Of her father we are told nothing.)

---

8. "Growing up in Sweden as the child of a **Senagelese/Gambian** mom who owned a boutique in Stockholm that traded in **African** wares, Fatima was exposed to the rich vibrations of **West African** music from an early age, sparking an interest in the many musical styles that **African** rhythms have engendered. Now she's managed to bring all those raw

Katie Hawthorne (n.d.), who writes for the independent music and culture magazine *Crack*, says of the young songstress:

> Fatima always sounds singularly herself. It's precisely this quality—an ability to shift and morph genre and sounds, without diluting her distinct identity—that led to Fatima being earmarked as a face of a high-profile "Me Myself and I" campaign [that] celebrates creatives and individuals who are proudly made up of many components—a trait of multiplicity which Fatima exudes. How does she do it? Fatima answers: "Take a little bit of baking soda, a little bit of cinnamon, mix it up . . . Nah, It's just me. I guess that's the magic! That's the sauce! I can't explain it, can't give it away. Wait, would you come into this restaurant and ask for the recipe?" She lets rip a booming laugh: "NEXT QUESTION!"

Fatima bellows, it seems, in all caps, refusing to reveal her recipe though happy to assure the interviewer that the recipe itself is firmly in place. She continues in a more serious vein: "'I've always been sure of myself. I never let go of that. Everyone should always remember their inner voice . . . It's all in your own mind,' she urges. 'Take a grime track, a house track—you don't have to rap, you could growl if you want to. It's about how open your mind is! What's your style? What's your vibe? What does this beat inspire you to do? I just do me. I just flow.'"

Because Fatima knows herself, her style, her vibe, the way particular beats inspire her, because she can "do herself," she can, like West, transform when needed. The fact of the recipe stays in place, but the ingredients can be swapped out, making a chameleon, "a jazzman" of her. But unlike a chameleon, whose qualities change on the outside and without thought, Fatima's recipe is under her own command and it is all within her: her inner voice is remembered, consulted; her mind is known and yet open for the world to see. Shifting and morphing, she is ever sure of herself. So much so, that no matter the circumstances, stresses, or beats, she can say: "I just do me," and she can say, she can sing: "I could be somebody else" (2018).

Fatima, in her ability to conceptualize herself as comprised of a set of distinct manipulatable qualities, is what Gerber wanted all women to be.

---

styles together"; "Fatima," Last.fm, https://www.last.fm/music/Fatima/+wiki, accessed April 2018. In another article she is called a "nomadic child of the cosmos"; "Fatima," *Scandinavian Soul*, http://scandinaviansoul.com/artists-bio/item/fatima, accessed May 2018.

She is (to jump back a moment to early Christianizing missions) what missionaries wanted all natives to be. She is, like Cornel West, a product of imperialism in Africa, of migration outward and northward in Fatima's case and of the slave trade in West's, which brought his ancestors to North America and remains present for African Americans today, as the weirdness of that history ever present means that whites cannot forget the fear they hold of black independence and power.[9] Henry Louis Gates, an African American Harvard professor (like West), was arrested in 2009 going into his own house, for what could a black man be doing in such a fine neighborhood but breaking and entering? Slavoj Žižek has no comparable story (despite being an all round more suspicious character).

It is possible, indeed likely, that both West and Fatima preach themselves and feel themselves as truly known and truly hybrid—in the multiplication of *and*s sort of way—precisely because of an ill-fittedness to a normative white context. A white Sweden, a white Boston. Regardless, they both propose beautiful models of the self grounded in a known inner, a "true I" not to be questioned, dismissed, or judged, but to be admired for its flexibility, creativity, and initiative.[10] These are all also qualities that Gerber explicitly demanded of Polish workers, who though they may well

9. Temporal folding comes up often in works of (and discussions of) Afrofuturism. See especially Octavia Butler's remarkable *Kindred* (1979) and also the Afrofuturism episode of *This American Life* (Drumming 2017).

10. It is strange to think that even in moments of purest belief in the truth of self (or what Saba Mahmood has so nicely termed the "true I" [2005, 150]), the failure to produce what *should* be essential abides. When looking for the plainest-spoken, least-fraught definition of the self by an American, I found this gem: "You have to have a self before you can accept yourself. Having a self means being clear about your beliefs, emotions, likes, dislikes, values, goals, etc. If a patient does not have a stable self, therapy must focus on developing a self before working on self-acceptance" (Spett 2005). Somehow, under some circumstances, "patients" (which is to say, those needing to be cured) find themselves without selves and thus incapable of culturally valorized acts of self-knowledge, self-direction, self-esteem, and self-acceptance. Mahmood, quoting Charles Taylor (1985), provides a similar definition. "Autonomy," she writes, "consists in achieving 'a certain condition of self-clairvoyance and self-understanding' in order to be able to prioritize and assess conflicting desires, fears, and aspirations *within oneself,* and to be able to sort out what is in one's best interest from what is socially required" (150, emphasis added). Accepting oneself is thus, for Spett, a secondary procedure to first forging oneself. To which Taylor adds the important caveat that this happens inside (oneself) and, once rightly accomplished, allows one to autonomously determine the difference between social requirements and true identity. Such a version of human subjectivity should, I hope, seem as idiosyncratic (i.e., culture bound) as anything Slovenes are up to, up for, or up against.

have possessed these characteristics under communism did not then think of them as disaggregatable; they did not imagine themselves as comprised of qualities that, rather like the ingredients in a recipe, might in proper measure add up to just the right kind of person.[11]

Gerber dreams of such subjects as this. Tabar, Žižek, Dolar, and Janez Janša rage against them. In word and deed, they each posit different solutions to the problem of a self-concept in which Fatima is at home. This resistance is not because there is some evil lurking inside the self thusly composed and practiced, but precisely because this way of being and knowing and expressing oneself is so normative, so intimate, and so sneakily imposed. Gerber can neither make nor sell baby food without it; Western democracies cannot govern without it. Capitalism and its twin, democracy, need a certain mode of subjectivity for their furtherance and good functioning. And where these subjects do not exist, they must be made (Dunn 2004, 127; see also Matza 2009). "If democracy is an idea," Mitchell writes, "then countries become democratic by getting that idea into peoples' heads." Capitalism, too, like "democracy is an engineering project, concerned with the manufacture of new political subjects and with subjecting people to new ways of being governed" (2013, 3).

Given the stakes, one can perhaps understand why Žižek would rage against openness, self-liberation, and any call for more complete self-expression; the cost is indeed great. Tabar answers this call in another way: rather than maligning openness as a form of self-practice, he simply opens himself, in the most literal of ways. There is no need to imagine the inner self with Tabar; it is there to be seen, not as an agglomeration of perfectible qualities, not as a secret recipe to be mastered by an exceptional chef-of-the-self, but as a mass of liquids and attachments (of the sort a fingernail feels to its bed). Tabar literalizes the call for self-examination and self-knowledge; he takes the Delphic imperative to heart. He looks inside himself and shows us what can be found there and, in an elegant twist, he turns all of this into a politics of resistance. It is not only that European Union which he will not let rest in his body, it is the nature of an ephemeral but essential inner self that he will not admit. If democracy and market economy demand this of persons as

---

11. It should be noted that before Gerber, workers were equally flexible about the recipes they used for baby food. So much so that sometimes they just made jam instead.

they sweep from west to east, corporation by corporation and ballot box by ballot box, then he is having nothing of it.

Resistance here is not Scott's inner purity, nor Mitchell's fixing of power in ever more distant, unnavigable locations. Tabar's resistance sticks more truly to the technical sense of the term. In circuitry, resistance is a mode for creating heat by using materials unfriendly to electricity to slow down the passage of a current. Resistance hinders a force but does not stop it. It causes "distant" power to do "local" work. The free market would come to Slovenia, it's there now, a decade after the last of Tabar's *Evropas*. But Tabar and the others in their multifaceted refusal of a particular mode of subjectivity have slowed it down; simmering and at times boiling, they resist this one overwhelming underpinning of a true capitalist conversion.

What, after all, are the new Janšas doing but embracing democracy wrongly as they flit about at events, joyous in their rejection of the notion of individual unique personhood? What is Žižek doing but being a celebrity, while always doing so distastefully, his evident bullshit revealing a wrong approach to the substance of the subject? What is Dolar doing in his strident rejection of the voice as pure evidence of individual particularity, coming as it does from within the body, traveling in breath and vibration to touch the ears, the hearts, and the minds of others? What is Peljhan doing as he crouches behind his nimbus of technology? And the Slovene Benjamin? And Laibach with their single name, borrowed uniforms, and rejection of originality in art? And then there is Tabar, who utters his protest not by raising his voice in outrage, but by giving himself over to hurt, publicly. By being undeniably fleshy, corruptible, invadable, but never cleanly so, he gives the ideological imperative ("open thyself," "know thyself," "transform thyself") a home. He makes it his own. One can, in other words, seek the inner self of a Slovene, as Tabar shows and shows and shows us, but what comes out is blood and bile, piss and pain. Inside the body is just more body. Nothing's jazzy here.

Afterword

MELANIA TRUMP (NÉE MELANIJA KNAVS)

I just know that I used my own words when I wore the dress.

Representative Joyce Beatty, 2016

I was momentarily excited. Before it became clear that Donald Trump would take the conventions of the American presidency as merely conventional and conform to them more or less as he liked, I thought there would be a Slovene supermodel—wife to the American president—in the White House. Given my expertise in the somewhat underappreciated subcategory of Slovene models (Slovene ballroom dancers and Slovene ski jumpers), I thought I might at last be about to say a something. Sadly, for me, Mr. Trump was joined in his new abode (at least initially) not by his wife, but by his children from other, earlier marriages and their spouses, keeping the White House safe for Americans. By the time Melania made the jump from penthouse to White House, America had so many other problems with that president and more generally, that nobody much cared that for the first time in history a foreign woman would be living at 1600 Pennsylvania Avenue.

Even once finally bedding down where a First Lady should, Melania was not effusive about her new position. Many a First Lady has felt the same. Louisa Adams, the only other First Lady in US history to be foreign-born (to an American mother), was renowned during her time in Washington for "binge-eating chocolates, writing poetry and plays about a 'repressed' female character who was supposed to represent herself, and ... raising and harvesting her own silkworms for sewing" (Waxman 2016). Like Mrs. Adams, Mrs. Trump has made her dissatisfaction evident, but she has done so in less obvious ways than chocolate, proto-feminist poetry, and the husbandry of worms. If Louisa Adams sounds rather like a maudlin undergraduate forced off to college, then Melania Trump stands multiply accused of a more subtle crime. She just isn't very enthusiastic about the job. She does not revel in it and, more generally, seems almost insufficiently full of life. She is quite still, and when she does speak, her delivery is wooden, canned, teleprompted. Even her Twitter account—much maligned—is primarily read as evidence of her being locked up tight and pretty happy about it. One essayist proclaims, having looked at Melania's tweeted photographs as a "Body of Work," that "she is Rapunzel with no prince and no hair, locked in a tower of her own volition, and delighted with the predictability and repetition of her own captivity" (Imbach 2017).[1]

I could go on in this vein but since I demonstrated amply in chapter 4 how blithely mean critics can be when the media is their medium, suffice it to say that Melania approaches her role as First Lady with a legible lack of enthusiasm; she does do it, but for the most part, according to minimal expectations and while wearing very large hats. This minimal conformity to role is then read "into" in various ways by American observers and pundits: perhaps she hates her husband, perhaps she is a robot (with articles entitled things like "Malfunction of the Melania-bot"), perhaps she is a happy Rapunzel, perhaps she has a body double.[2]

In all of this, there is one instance—her 2016 "plagiarism" of Michelle Obama's 2008 convention speech—that shines forth among her irritating

1. Entitled "A Deep Analysis of Melania Trump's Social Media Photos Reveals a Woman in Hiding from the World," this essay obviously gets it all wrong from the start. Nevertheless it is a stunningly ideological reading of Melania Trump's psychology, in which we learn a great deal about what an American considers to be a viable/healthy mode of self-expression via exploitation of its negative (Imbach 2017).

2. Among the many critiques of her circulating online there is a wonderful short video, done by Tracey Ullman, of robot replacements for public figures that shows the Melania robot being recalled after she refuses to hold her husband's hand in public; "Tracey Ullman – Melania Trump Robot," video, 2:46, from *Tracey Breaks the News*, June 25, 2017 https://www.youtube.com/watch?v=b6NqscIsidQ.

(to Americans) if obvious failures to do subjectivity right. By right, I mean, like an American; by right I mean a continuous and enthusiastic outpouring of an inner self to any and all who will listen.

Her husband, who exhibits other anomalies of subject performance, at least gets this bit right. We all know Donald Trump's opinion about everything (including himself) all the time. It is, however, his wife standing there in the shadow of his bluster who interests me here, for she has reaped her fair share of shaming in his short time in office. Indeed, mass-mediated critiques of Melania are syncopated, coming at seasonal intervals as the press swings round regularly to the project of reminding the American public that *this* First Lady is not the same as all the others. The genre of this critique is the gossip of the coffee klatch; its mode is the normative horror of suburban wives at the untoward doings of a new neighbor. Thus do we have the flabbergastingly chilly White House Christmas decorations scandal of 2017; the public swatting away of her husband's attempt to hold her hand of May 2017; the wearing of very high heels when touring the wreckage of various hurricanes; the scalding analysis of her Twitter account; and as I write this (in 2018), a new plagiarism scandal has bloomed, this one having to do with a cyber-bullying booklet Melania claimed as her own, but that has proven to be nearly identical to a pamphlet released by the Federal Trade Commission under Barack Obama. I trust that these eruptions of indignity will continue apace, so long as her husband holds office. You should thus feel free to add your own knowledge of future events here, as further after the fact proofs-of-concept.

※

Shortly before not moving into the White House, in 2016 Melania Trump gave a speech in support of her husband's candidacy for president of the United States at the Republican National Convention in Cleveland, Ohio. For this she was widely and resoundingly criticized. It is likely that this would have been true, at least by critics on the left, even without the problem of potential plagiarism compounding (what would become) her trademark wooden delivery. In this case, however, Melania's generalizable lack of effusiveness would be drowned out by another issue: most of her words appear to have belonged to another, and to not just any other but the then-sitting First Lady, Michelle Obama, who had said similar, and in some cases, identical things at her own speech on the same occasion eight years earlier. The degree of resemblance pushed what might, in a subtler form, have appeared as homage over into the gauche and unredeemable category of straight-up plagiarism.

Here are the most egregious liftings (with credit to *Newsweek*), to which I have added emphasis in two ways. Exact borrowings—word-for-word copies—have been **bolded** and rephrasings of the same basic sentiment using slightly different words have been marked with *italics*.

(1) Melania Trump (RNC 2016): "My parents impressed on me the **values** that **you work hard for what you want in life: that your word is your bond and you do what you say** *and keep your promise;* **that you treat people with respect.**"

Michelle Obama (DNC 2008): "And Barack and I were raised with so many of the same **values:** that **you work hard for what you want in life; that your word is your bond and you do what you say** *you're going to do;* **that you treat people with** dignity and **respect,** even if you don't know them, and even if you don't agree with them."

(2) Melania 2016: "[My parents] taught and showed me **values** and morals in their daily life. That is a lesson that I continue *to pass along to* our son, and we need to pass those lessons on *to the many generations to follow.*"

Michelle 2008: "And Barack Obama and I set out to build lives guided by these **values,** *and pass them on to the next generations.*"[3]

(3) Melania 2016: "**Because we want our children in this nation to know that the only limit to your achievements is the** *strength* **of your dreams and your willingness to work for them.**"

Michelle 2008: "**Because we want our children**—and all children **in this nation**—**to know that the only limit to** the height of **your achievements is the** *reach* **of your dreams and your willingness to work for them.**"

Though one could do an analysis of the slight variations between the two First Ladies' two versions of the same sentiments—drawing out, for

3. The full text of both speeches can also be found here: Josh Lowe, "Michelle Obama and Melania Trump: Compare the Speeches," Newsweek, July 19, 2016, http://www.newsweek.com/melania-trump-michelle-obama-plagarism-compare-speeches-full-text-481779..

example, the differences implied by the *strength* rather than the *reach* of dreams—I will allow such musings to hang pregnant in the air, sandwiched between bolded exactitudes. The curious student of language can profitably unpack them as there is much here to say about race and nation, family and community, imagination and the ethics of accord and discord (not to mention the interpenetration of speakers, husbands, speechwriters, staffs of various sorts), all of which I will now proceed to ignore.

The critique of Melania after the speech, which was ubiquitous and heavy handed, hinged not just on whose words she used, but on how she delivered them. Where Mrs. Obama was dynamic and impassioned, her voice and body both expressing a range of heartfelt emotions, Mrs. Trump was stiff and precise, her English unwieldy in her mouth and her dependence on the teleprompter evident. Her arms never moved, her hands were never visible, and nary a wrinkle was formed in the starched white of her dress (or brow). All of which is to say, that even if Melania had *not* used the same words as Michelle she would have made a very different sort of impression than had her precursor. Not a worse impression: in fact before the plagiarism was discovered and reveled in, she received over-all good remarks, from the right, for the performance.[4]

The critique, then, that sprung to gleeful life was not only of her unabashed borrowing of sentiment, but of the fact that her reuse of these words seemed to drain them of life. It didn't feel like imitation was the highest form of flattery, it felt like a copy as an empty version of an original. It felt like stealing. And in the racially charged landscape of contemporary America it stunk of bad faith. Here was a white woman cribbing, stripping of life, and then claiming as her own something that belonged to a black woman. The failure of attribution thus stung; the theft more egregious for the ways in which it mapped onto four hundred years of American racism—a practice which hinges on white people using the liveliness of black people to their own ends without compensation or acknowledgement. This mode of violence, as Melania's plagiarism and reactions to it intimates, has not

---

4. This is even more clear in the videos than in the quotes and they are, for that reason, worth watching. Here is a good place to start: "Trump Campaign Denies Melania Plagiarized Michelle Obama's Speech," video, 2:32, July 19, 2016, https://www.youtube.com /watch?v=Tec-DgpnRbk, accessed May 2018.

ended. America remains a place where race and poverty are twined ever-tightly together around the bottom rungs of the ladder of dreams.[5]

It was within this context of racialized inequality that one of the more stunning and pointed reactions to Melania's speech emerged, not from the media flurry, but in the person of Congresswoman Joyce Beatty. As Beatty, an African American, took the stage at the Democratic National Convention (about a month after the original stink had been made), the tumult began: she wore a crisp, white, puffy-sleeved dress identical to Melania's RNC outfit. The media delighted: "Did Joyce Beatty just plagiarize Melania Trump's outfit?" @mashable asked. "DRESS PLAGIARISM," @NYDailyNews tweeted. For her part, Beatty refused to comment on her choice of gown. She did however pause to make the point that regardless of what she was wearing, she'd at least spoken her own words, thus mapping identity back into the body. Centering the self where it ought to be, not in words and sentiments and persons admired beyond one's tender self, but found within and known, to be communicated in ways understood to be sincere and truly spoken. At least she'd used her own words when wearing the dress. In an artful move, one minor wardrobe decision (credit for which Beatty gave to her husband), the congresswoman cast shade upon the potential First Lady while simultaneously pointing out that she (Beatty) was doing subjectivity right (LeVine 2016).[6] We weren't left to notice this, it was proclaimed. Simultaneously she dismissed the kerfuffle about the dress, and by this means established a hierarchy of plagiarism (identical dresses ok; identical words, sentences, sentiments not so much), while also shifting attention away from herself and away from the fumblings of Mrs. Trump on a "night of extreme historical significance" that she and all the rest of the Democrats were gathered to celebrate (or rather, proclaim).

5. A recent issue of *South Side Weekly*, a neighborhood paper in Chicago, reported the median household income in Chicago as follows: Black $30,303; Latino $41,188; Asian $56,373; White $70,960. On average, then, a black family in the city makes less than half what a white family earns. This is racialized inequality (Powell 2018).

6. See also Fox News: "Who Wore It Better? Dem Rep Wears Melania Trump's RNC Dress to DNC," Fox News Insider, July 28, 2016, http://insider.foxnews.com/2016/07/28/joyce-beatty-wears-melania-trumps-rnc-dress-dnc.

What was lost in the swirl of scandal around the RNC (of which Congresswoman Beatty's dress plagiarism was but a minor if delightful note) was that the multiple punctuations of the speech by **values values values** and the values under discussion belonged to neither Michelle nor to Melania but rather to a long history of American rhetoric funneled in both cases through a staff of political speechwriters working to wrangle that history into a syncopated and believable expression of "right" First-Lady-ness. In practical terms what this meant was that the source of one woman's words (but not the other's) was excavated by no less august an institution than the *New York Times*. What they found, unsurprisingly, was a third woman, Meredith McIver, the in-house staff writer for the Trump campaign. For Melania's values, McIver was willing to both explain and take the fall: "In working with Melania Trump on her recent First Lady speech, we discussed many people who inspired her and messages she wanted to share with the American people. A person she has always liked is Michelle Obama. Over the phone she read me some passages from Mrs. Obama's speech as some examples. I wrote them down and later included some of the phrasing in the draft that ultimately became the final speech."[7]

The source of Melania's words was, in other words, found to have come from outside herself. They were not her words, doubly, trebly, quadruply so. They were the words of a professional writer, who borrowed them from Michelle Obama who we can presume—but, *critically*, do not know—spoke the words of another professional writer. In any case, the words described sentiments of such generic American goodness that neither the particularities of lexicon nor phrasing should have mattered at all. That they do matter, of course, means we are talking about something other than language, and this something—as the "Hi, I'm Michelle" meme makes abundantly clear—is the proper ownership of one's own subjectivity. Oneself really isn't something one should be borrowing, the meme intimates and proclaims. Because Melania spoke words that could be identified as having not come from inside herself, words that had a clear

---

7. She continues: "I did not check Mrs. Obama's speeches. This was my mistake, and I feel terrible for the chaos I have caused Melania and the Trumps as well as to Mrs. Obama. No harm was meant"; Jason Horowitz, "Behind Melania Trump's Cribbed Lines, an Ex-Ballerina Who Loved Writing," *New York Times*, July 20, 2016.

Michelle: Hi, I'm Michelle.
Melania: Hi, I'm Michelle.

Figure 17. Speaks for itself. Found on the World Wide Web everywhere but only for a couple of days in 2016. Photo by Chuck Kennedy.

source in somebody else's mouth, a somebody she admired; and because her words were demonstrably not her own, so that a third somebody (McIver) was also pulled into visibility and made equally and publicly responsible for a speech meant to be from somebody else's heart. Melania was, in other words, doing her subjectivity exactly right, albeit only if you take the Slovene view on things. She had shown herself to subsist in a world beyond, rather than inside, her skin. She had tied herself to an awkward chain of social relations, multiplying and rendering more complex her person by means of the external world that it reflects (and which is reflected in it); she had done this without opening herself and in such a way that there can be no accidental mistaking of her voice as the sound of "what has a soul in it" (yep, Dolar 2006 again). Everything is as it should be, except for the context, which is all wrong and from which misreadings resplendent in their details spring forth and grow tangled if gleeful vines of harsh judgment.

A final moment then. Eighteen months later, Melania set herself to the decoration of a White House she now lived in for the festive season of Christmas. These decorating decisions were probably not as bad as they were made out to be in the Interweb, which focused on a particular few that did indeed render the White House a Gothic castle. Chilly in white and silver, dead branches spiking up from urns, trees so generously flocked as to appear made from (plastic) ice, and all of it lit from below, such that monstrous shadows were projected upward upon walls and human faces were rendered gaunt in the crisp contrast of light and shadow. The president and his wife, their family and staff, transmogrified into the walking dead in the halls of state. And yet, there is a moment where Melania is standing impassive on a staircase, again dressed in white, while in front of her ballerinas twirl through a wonderland of trees and branches all also dressed in white and silver, and though Mrs. Trump doesn't move, her joy is palpable if suspicious as the dancers dance within a world she has created for them.[8] Unmoving, she too dances, with their bodies, twirling through the flocked forest of subjectivity.

❁

8. The least-weird (and surprisingly touching, as the fantastic copyeditor of this book has noted) rendition is here: "'Nutcracker' Comes to the White House," *Washington Post*, November 27, 2017, https://www.washingtonpost.com/video/national/nutcracker-comes-to-the-white-house/2017/11/27/ecd5a5d2-d399-11e7-9ad9-ca0619edfa05_video.html?.

Bibliography

Abu Lughod, Lila. 2004. *Dramas of Nationhood: The Politics of Television in Egypt*. Chicago: University of Chicago Press.

Adorno, Theodore. 1978. *Minima Moralia: Reflections from Damaged Life*. London: Verso.

Althusser, Louis. 2014. *On the Reproduction of Capitalism: Ideology and Ideological State Apparatuses*. London: Verso.

Arns, Inke. 2011a. "The Nigerian Connection: On NSK Passports as Escape and Entry Vehicles." *E-Flux*, no. 34, http://www.e-flux.com/journal/34/68336/the-nigerian-connection-on-nsk-passports-as-escape-and-entry-vehicles/.

———. 2011b. "The Oil Show." HMKV. Revolver: Berlin.

———. 2006. "Tripping into Art (Hi)Stories: Genealogy and/as Fiction on the exhibition "What Is Modern Art? (Group Show)." In *What Is Modern Art? (Group Show)*, edited by I. Arns and W. Benjamin, 712. Archiv für aktuelle Kunst, vol. 2. Frankfurt am Main: Revolver.

———. 2002. *Neue Slowenische Kunst (NSK): Eine Analyse ihrer kuenstlerischen Strategien im Kontext der 1980er Jahre in Jugoslawien*. Regensburg: Museum Ostdeutsche Galerie.

Arns, Inke, ed. 2003. *IRWIN: Retroprincip 1983–2003*. Ljubljana: Tiskarna Ljubljana.

Arns, Inke, and Sylvia Sasse. 2006. "Subversive Affirmation: On Mimesis as a Strategy of Resistance." *Maska* (Ljubljana) 21, no. 3–4 (98–99): 5–21.

Atkinson, Michael. 2002. "Fifty Million Viewers Can't Be Wrong: Professional Wrestling, Sports-Entertainment, and Mimesis." *Sociology of Sport Journal* 19, no. 1: 47–66.

Auerbach, Erich. 1991 [1946]. *Mimesis: The Representation of Reality in Western Literature.* Princeton, NJ: Princeton University Press.

Austin, J. L. 1962. *How to Do Things with Words.* Oxford: Oxford University Press.

Badovinac, Zdenka. 2008. "What Is the Importance of Being Janez?" In *Name Readymade*, edited by J. Janša, J. Janša, and J. Janša, 51–66. Ljubljana: Moderna galerija/Museum of Modern Art.

Badovinac, Zdenka, Eda Čufer, and Anthony Gardner, eds. 2015. *NSK from Kapital to Capital: Neue Slowenische Kunst: An Event of the Final Decade of Yugoslavia.* Cambridge, MA: MIT Press.

Baker, Catherine. 2015. *The Yugoslav Wars of the 1990s.* London: Palgrave Macmillan.

Bakhtin, Mikhail M. 1986. *Speech Genres and Other Late Essays.* Edited by C. Emerson and M. Holquist. Austin: University of Texas Press.

———. 1984. *Problems of Dostoevsky's Poetics.* Minneapolis: University of Minnesota Press.

———. 1981. *The Dialogic Imagination: Four Essays.* Edited by M. Holquist. Austin: University of Texas Press.

Bakke, Gretchen. 2017. "Incorporations: Contemporary Slovene Art and the Body Politic." In *Anthropology of the Arts: A Reader*, edited by G. Bakke and M. Peterson, 213–22. London: Bloomsbury Academic.

———. 2008. "Reframing History." *Slovene Studies* 30, no. 2: 185–217.

———. 2007. Contemporary Slovene Art and Artifice. Ph.D. dissertation, Department of Anthropology, University of Chicago.

———. 2001. "'The Inauthentic Authentically Performed' Professional Wrestling's Awkward Place in American Sport." Presentation at the American Anthropological Association Annual Meeting, Washington, D.C.

Bateson, Gregory. 2000 [1972]. *Steps to an Ecology of Mind.* Chicago: University of Chicago Press.

Baudrillard, Jean. 1995. *Simulacra and Simulation.* Ann Arbor: University of Michigan Press.

———. 1990. Revenge of the Crystal: Selected Writings on the Modern Object and its Destiny, 1968–1983. London: Pluto Press.

———. 1983a. Simulations. New York: Semiotext(e).

———. 1983b. In the Shadow of Silent Majorities, or the End of the Social, and other Essays. New York: Semiotext(e).

———. 1981. For a Critique of the Political Economy of the Sign. St. Louis: Telos Press.

Benderly, Jill, and Evan Kraft, eds. 1996. *Independent Slovenia: Origins, Movements, Prospects.* New York: St. Martin's Press.

Benjamin, Walter. 2006. "On Copy," In *What Is Modern Art? (Group Show)*, edited by I. Arns and W. Benjamin. Archiv für aktuelle Kunst, vol. 1. Frankfurt am Main: Revolver.

———. 1968. "The Work of Art in the Age of Mechanical Reproduction." *Illuminations: Essays and Reflections*, edited by Hannah Arendt, 217–52. New York: Schocken Books.

Benson, Michael, dir. 1995. *Predictions of Fire*.

Berdahl, Daphne. 1999. *Where the World Ended: Re-Unification and Identity in the German Borderland*. Berkeley: University of California Press.

Berdahl, Daphne, Matti Bunzl, and Martha Lampland, eds. 2000. *Altering States: Ethnographies of Transition in Eastern Europe and the Former Soviet Union*. Ann Arbor: University of Michigan Press.

Biehl, João, Byron J. Good, and Arthur Kleinman, eds. 2007. *Subjectivity: Ethnographic Investigations*. Berkeley: University of California Press.

Bleeker, Maaike. 2013. "Being Janez Janša." In *Performance, Identity, and the Neo-Political Subject*, edited by F. Walsh and M.Causey, 138–53. London: Routledge.

Blisset, Luther. 1995/96. "L'artista sloveno." *Luther Blisset: Rivista mondiale di guerra psichologica*, no. 3 (inverno). Found at www.ljudmila.org/~vuk /rigusrs/lb.htm, accessed July 2019. Read this one.

Boas, Franz. 1940. "Decorative Designs of Alaskan Needle Cases: A Study on the History of Conventional Designs, Based on Materials in the U.S National Museum." In *Race, Language, and Culture*, edited by F. Boas, 564–92. Chicago: University of Chicago Press.

Borneman, John. 1992. *Belonging in the Two Berlins: Kinship, Nation, State*. New York: Cambridge University Press.

Boyer, Dominic, and Alexei Yurchak. 2010. "American Stiob: Or, What Late-Socialist Aesthetics of Parody Reveal about Contemporary Political Culture in the West." *Cultural Anthropology* 15, no. 2: 179–221.

Boyer, Pascal. 1988. *Barricades mystérieuses et pièges à pensée: Introduction à l'analyse des épopées Fang*Paris: Société d'Ethnologie.

Božovič, Miran. 2000. *An Utterly Dark Spot: Gaze and Body in Early Modern Philosophy*. Ann Arbor: University of Michigan Press.

Brazeau, Bryan. 2014. "'Emotional Rescue': Heroic Chastity and Devotional Practice in Iacopo Sannazaro's *De partu Virginis*." *California Italian Studies* 5, no. 1: 225–46.

Breton, Andre, and Paul Éluard. 1938. *Dictionnaire abrégé du surréalisme*. Paris: La Galerie Beaux-Arts.

Briggs, Jean. 1970. *Never in Anger: Portrait of an Eskimo Family*. Cambridge, MA: Harvard University Press.

Brubaker, Rogers. 1996. *Nationalism Reframed: Nationhood and the National Question in the New Europe*. Cambridge: Cambridge University Press.

———. 1992. "Citizenship as Social Closure." *Citizenship and Nationhood in France and Germany*, 21–34. Cambridge, MA: Harvard University Press.

Buckshot, Costanzia. 2017. "The Comparative Method: A Novella." In *Between Matter and Method: Encounters in Anthropology and Art*, edited by G. Bakke and M. Peterson, 171–89. London: Bloomsbury Academic.

Butler, Judith. 1993. *Bodies that Matter: On the Discursive Limits of "Sex."* London: Routledge.

Butler, Octavia. 2003 [1979]. *Kindred*. New York: Beacon Press.

Chari, Sharad, and Katherine Verdery. 2009. "Thinking between the Posts: Postcolonialism, Postsocialism, and Ethnography after the Cold War." *Comparative Studies of History and Society* 51, no. 1: 6–34.

Čičigoj, Katja. 2018. "Repetitions of a Text—a Text on Repetition." *Maska, Performing Arts Journal*, special issue on Repetition [*O Ponavljanju*] 33 (191–92): 101–6.

Clark, Katarina, and Michael Holquist. 1984. *Mikhail Bakhtin*. Cambridge, MA: Harvard University Press.

Clifford, James, and George Marcus. 1986. *Writing Culture: The Poetics and Politics of Ethnography*. Berkeley: University of California Press.

Comaroff, Jean, and John Comaroff. 1991. *Of Revelation and Revolution*. Vol. 1, *Christianity, Colonialism, and Consciousness in South Africa*. Chicago: University of Chicago Press.

Comaroff, John. 1989. "The Colonization of Consciousness in South Africa." *Economy and Society* 18, no. 3: 267–96.

Cornea, Christine. 2003. "David Cronenberg's Crash and Performing Cyborgs." *The Velvet Light Trap*, no. 52 (Fall): 4–14.

Cox, John K. 2009. *Slovenia: Evolving Loyalties*. London: Routledge.

Debord, Guy. 1995. *The Society of the Spectacle*. New York: Zone Books.

de Certeau, Michel. 1995. *The Mystic Fable*. Vol. 1, *The Sixteenth and Seventeenth Centuries*. Chicago: University of Chicago Press.

Deleuze, Gilles. 1994. *Difference and Repetition*. New York: Columbia University Press.

Demento, Dr. 1994. "Permanent Record: Al in the Box." Found at http://dmdb .org/al/booklet.html, accessed December 2019.

Derrida, Jacques. 1976. *Of Grammatology*. Baltimore: The Johns Hopkins University Press.

Deutscher, Guy. 2010. "Does Your Language Shape How You Think?" *New York Times Magazine*. August 26. http://www.nytimes.com/2010/08/29/magazine /29language-t.html.

Dolar, Mladen. 2006. *A Voice and Nothing More*. Cambridge, MA: MIT Press.

———. 2003. "Three Voices on the Artists' Group IRWIN: Zdenka Badovinac, Mladen Dolar, and Goran Scmidt." In *IRWIN: Retroprincip 1983-2003*, edited by I. Arns, 154–58. Ljubljana: Tiskarna.Douglass, Frederick. 2004

[1845]. *Narrative of the Life of Frederick Douglass.* Smyrna, DE: Prestwick House.

Drumming, Neil, host. 2017. "We Are in the Future." *This American Life,* August 18. https://www.thisamericanlife.org/623/we-are-in-the-future.

Dumit, Joseph. 2017. "Notes toward Critical Ethnographic Scores: Anthropology and Improvisation Training in a Breached World." In *Between Matter and Method: Encounters in Anthropology and Art,* edited by G. Bakke and M. Peterson, 51–72. London: Bloomsbury Academic.

Dunn, Elizabeth. 2005. "Standards and Person Making in East Central Europe." In *Global Assemblages: Technology, Politics, and Ethics as Anthropological Problems,* edited by A. Ong and S. Collier, 173–93. London: Blackwell.

———. 2004. *Privatizing Poland: Baby Food, Big Business, and the Remaking of Labor.* Ithaca, NY: Cornell University Press.

———. 2003. "Audit, Corruption, and the Problem of Personhood: Scenes from Postsocialist Poland." In *Entangled Histories and Negotiated Universals: Centers and Peripheries in a Changing World,* edited by W. Lepenies, 127–45. Chicago: University of Chicago Press.

Eley, Geoff, and Ronald Grigor Suny, eds. 1996. *Becoming National: A Reader.* New York: Oxford University Press.

Emanuele, Vince. 2012. "Virtual Town Hall: Interview with Noam Chomsky." *Veterans Unplugged.* Podcast audio, http://chomsky.globl.org.

Erjavec, Aleš. 2003. "Neue Slowenische Kunst—New Slovene Art: Slovenia, Yugoslavia, Self Management, and the 1980s." In *Postmodernism and the Postmodern Condition: Politicized Art under Socialism,* edited by A. Erjavec, 135–74 Berkeley: University of California Press.

———. 1994. "Mountain Photography and the Constitution of National Identity." *Filozofski vestnik* 15, no. 2: 211–34.

Erjavec, Aleš, and Marina Gržinić, eds. 1991. *Ljubljana Ljubljana: Osemdeseta leta v umetnosti in kulturi* [Ljubljana Ljubljana: The 1980s in Art and Culture]. Ljubljana: Založba Mladinska knjiga.

Fallon, Steve. 1999. *Lonely Planet Slovenia,* 1st ed. Oakland: Lonely Planet.

Ferhérváry, Krisztina. 2013. *Politics in Color and Concrete: Socialist Immaterialities and the Middle Class in Hungary.* Bloomington: Indiana University Press.

Ferry, Anne. 1983. *The "Inward" Language: Sonnets of Wyatt, Sidney, Shakespeare, Donne.* Chicago: University of Chicago Press.

Foucault, Michel. 1995. *Discipline and Punish: The Birth of the Prison.* Translated by Alan Sheridan. New York: Vintage Books.

Frank, Susi, Renate Lachmann, Sylvia Sasse, Schamma Schahadat, and Caroline Schramm. 2001. "Vorwort." In *Mystifikation—Autorschaft—*

Original, edited by S. Frank, R. Lachmann, S. Sasse, S. Schahadat, and C. Schramm, 7–21. Tu?bingen: Gunter Narr Verlag.

Frankfurt, Harry. 2005. *On Bullshit*. Princeton, NJ: Princeton University Press.

Geertz, Clifford. 1973. "Person, Time, and Conduct in Bali." *The Interpretations of Culture*. New York: Basic.

Gell, Alfred. 1999. *The Art of Anthropology: Essays and Diagrams*. Edited by E. Hirsch. London: Athlone.

Gellner, Ernest. 1983. *Nations and Nationalism*. Ithaca, NY: Cornell University Press.

Gilroy, Paul. 1993. *The Black Atlantic: Modernity and Double Consciousness*. Cambridge, MA: Harvard University Press.

Girst, Thomas. 2003. "(Ab)Using Marcel Duchamp: The Concept of the Readymade in Post-War and Contemporary American Art." *The Marcel Duchamp Studies Online Journal*, April 1. http://toutfait.com/abusing-marcel-duchamp-the-concept-of-the-readymade-in-post-war-and-contemporary-american-art/.

Goffman, Erving. 1990 [1959]. *The Presentation of Self in Everyday Life*. New York: Penguin Books.

Gow, James, and Cathie Carmichael. 2000. *Slovenia and the Slovenes: A Small State and the New Europe*. London: Hurst & Company.

Greenblatt, Stephen. 1980. *Renaissance Self-Fashioning: From More to Shakespeare*. Chicago: University of Chicago Press.

Grow, Kory. 2015. "Cannabis and 'The Sound of Music': What Laibach Learned in North Korea." *The Rolling Stone*, August 25. https://www.rollingstone.com/music/music-features/cannabis-and-the-sound-of-music-what-laibach-learned-in-north-korea-62726/.

Gržinić, Marina. 2000. *Fiction Reconstructed: Eastern Europe, Post-socialism, and the Retro-Avant-Garde*. Vienna: (Hg) Springerin.

Gupta, Akhil. 1992. "The Song of the Nonaligned World: Transnational Identities and the Reinscription of Space in Late Capitalism." *Cultural Anthropology* 7, no. 1: 63–79.

Hahn, Hans Peter, and Jens Soentgen. 2011. "Acknowledging Substances: Looking at the Hidden Side of the Material World." *Philosophy & Technology* 24, no. 1: 19–33.

Hankins, Joseph. 2013. "An Ecology of Sensibility: The Politics of Scents and Stigma in Japan." *Anthropological Theory* 13, no. 1–2: 49–66.

Haugeland, John. 1998. *Having Thought: Essays in the Metaphysics of Mind*. Cambridge, MA: Harvard University Press.

Hawthorne, Katie. n.d. "Fatima: See How Things Grow." https://crackmagazine.net/article/long-reads/fatima-see-how-things-grow/, accessed April 2018.

Heelas, Paul, and Andrew Lock, eds. 1981. *Indigenous Psychologies: The Anthropology of the Self.* New York: Academic Press.

Hegel, G. W. F. 1977 [1807]. *Phenomenology of Spirit.* Translated by A. V. Miller. Oxford: Oxford University Press.

Henderson, Andrea. 1996. *Romantic Identities: Varieties of Subjectivity, 1774–1830.* Cambridge: Cambridge University Press.

Herder, Johann Gottfried von. 2007 [1792]. *Herder: Philosophical Writings.* Translated and edited by Michael Forster. Cambridge: Cambridge University Press.

Hobsbawm, Eric J. 1992. *Nations and Nationalism since 1780: Programme, Myth, Reality.* Cambridge: Cambridge University Press.

Holland, Dorothy, and Kevin Leander. 2004. "Ethnographic Studies of Positioning and Subjectivity: An Introduction." *Ethos* 32, no. 2: 127–39.

Hoskin, Keith. 1996. "The 'Awful Idea of Accountability': Inscribing People into the Measurement of Objects." In *Accountability: Power, Ethos, and the Technologies of Managing*, edited by R. Munro: 265–82. Bloomington, IN: International Thomas Business Press.

———. 1993. "Education and the Genesis of Disciplinarity: The Unexpected Reversal." In *Knowledges: Historical and Critical Studies in Disciplinarity*, edited by E. Messer-Davidow, D. Shumway, and D. Sylvan, 271–305. Charlottesville: University of Virginia Press.

Imbach, Kate. 2017. "A Deep Analysis of Melania Trump's Social Media Photos Reveals a Woman in Hiding from the World." *Quartz*, April 17. https://qz .com/960985/a-deep-analysis-of-melania-trumps-social-media-photos- reveal-a-woman-in-hiding-from-the-world/.

Irvine, Judith, and Susan Gal. 2000. "Language Ideology and Linguistic Differentiation." In *Regimes of Language: Ideologies, policies, and identities*, 35–84. Santa Fe, NM: School of American Research Press.

IRWIN. 2013. "Introduction." Catalog of the Association of American Painters and Sculptures, International Exhibition of Modern Art, New York 1913. Republished by the Museum of Contemporary Art, Belgrade.

James, Aaron. 2012. *Assholes: A Theory.* New York: Anchor Books.

Jansen, Stef. 2015. *Yearnings in the Meantime: "Normal Lives" and the State in a Sarajevo Apartment Complex.* New York: Berghahn Books.

Janša, Janez. 1992. *The Making of the Slovenian State, 1988–1992: The Collapse of Yugoslavia [Premiki: Nastajanje in obramba slovenske države 1988– 1992].* Ljubljana: Mladinska knjiga.

Janša, Janez, dir. 2012. *Jaz sem Janez Janša* [My name is Janez Janša].

Janša, Janez, Janez Janša, and Janez Janša, eds. 2008. *Name Readymade.* Ljubljana: Moderna galerija/Museum of Modern Art.

Jarosinski, Eric. 2002. "Architectural Symbolism and the Rhetoric of Transparency: A Berlin Ghost Story." *Journal of Urban History* 29, no. 1: 62–77.

Johnson, Jim. 1988. "Mixing Humans and Nonhumans Together: The Sociology of a Door-Closer." In "The Sociology of Science and Technology," special issue. *Social Problems* 35, no. 3: 298–310.

Jones, Amelia. 1998. *Body Art/Performing the Subject*. Minneapolis: Minnesota University Press.

Keane, Webb. 2008. "Others, Other Minds, and Others' Theories of Other Minds: An Afterword on the Psychology and Politics of Opacity Statements." *Anthropological Quarterly* 81, no. 2: 473–82.

———. 2002. "Sincerity, 'Modernity,' and the Protestants." *Cultural Anthropology* 17, no. 1: 65–92.

———. 1997. "From Fetishism to Sincerity: On Agency, the Speaking Subject, and their Historicity in the Context of Religious Conversion." *Comparative Studies in Society and History* 39, no. 4: 674–93.

Kingston, Sean. 1999. "The Essential Attitude: Authenticity in Primitive Art, Ethnographic Performances and Museums." *Journal of Material Culture* 4, no. 3: 338–51.

Kirkpatrick, John T. 1983. *The Marquesan Notion of the Person*. Ann Arbor, MI: UMI Research Press.

Kockelman, Paul. 2013. *Agent, Person, Subject, Self: A Theory of Ontology, Interaction, and Infrastructure*. Oxford: Oxford University Press.

Kockelman, Paul, and Nick Enfield, eds. 2017. *Distributed Agency*. Oxford: Oxford University Press.

Kohn, Eduardo. 2013. *How Forests Think: Toward an Anthropology beyond the Human*. Berkeley: University of California Press.

Kondo, Dorinne. 1990. *Crafting Selves: Power, Gender, and Discourses of Identity in a Japanese Workplace*. Chicago: University of Chicago Press.

Krauss, Rosilind. 1986. "Originality as Repetition." *October* 37: 35–41.

Krpič, Tomaž. 2010. "Medical Performance: The Politics of Body-Home." *PAJ: A Journal of Performance and Art* 32 no. 1: 36–43.

Kuhn, Thomas. 1962. *The Structure of Scientific Revolutions*. Chicago: University of Chicago Press.

Lacan, Jacques. 2006. "The Mirror Stage as Formative of the I Function as Revealed in Psychoanalytic Experience." *Ecrits: The First Complete Edition*. Translated by Alan Sheridan, 75–81. New York: W. W. Norton & Co.

———. 1979. *The Four Fundamental Concepts of Psycho-analysis*. Edited by J-A. Miller. New York: Norton.

Laibach. 2017. Lyrics to "WAT." *Genius*. genius.com/Laibach-wat-lyrics, accessed July 2019.

———. 1988. "Laibach." http://www.zona.lt/Sites/zona1/news/laibach.html, accessed December 2019.

———. 1985–90. "Interviews from 1985–1990." Found at www.laibach.org/interviews-from-1985-to-1990/, accessed November 2017.

———. 1983. "10 Items of the Covenant." *Nova Revija*, no. 13/14.Laporte, Dominique. 2000 [1978]. *History of Shit*. Translated by Rodolphe el-Khoury. Cambridge, MA: MIT Press.

LeVine, Lauren. 2016. "Democratic Congresswoman Copied Melania Trump's R.N.C. Dress, but Not Her Speech." *Vanity Fair*, July 29, 2016.

Lévi-Strauss, Claude. 1963. "Do Dual Organizations Exist?" *Structural Anthropology*, 132–66. New York: Basic Books.

Lewis, Eric. 2019. *Intents and Purposes: Philosophy and the Aesthetics of Improvisation*. Ann Arbor: University of Michigan Press.

———. 2017. "What Is 'Great Black Music'? The Social Aesthetics of the AACM in Paris." In *Improvisation and Social Aesthetics*, edited by G. Born, E. Lewis, and W. Straw, 135–59. Durham, NC: Duke University Press.

Li, Tania Murray. 2014. *Land's End: Capitalist Relations on an Indigenous Frontier*. Durham, NC: Duke University Press.

Link, Jürgen. 2004. "The 'Power of the Norm' to 'Flexible Normalism': Considerations after Foucault." *Cultural Critique* 57: 14–32.

———. 1999. *Versuch über den Normalismus: Wie Normalität produziert wird*. Opladen: Westdeutscher Vertlag.

Litts, Daryl. 2004. "Interview: Laibach." *Legends Magazine*, no. 139. www .legendsmagazine.net/139/laibach.htm, accessed July 2007, site discontinued.

Livingston, Jennie, dir. 1990. *Paris Is Burning*.

Luhmann, Niklas. 2002. "Identity: What or How?" *Theories of Distinction: Redescribing the Descriptions of Modernity*, 113–27. Stanford: Stanford University Press.

Luhrmann, Tanya. 2006. "Subjectivity." *Anthropological Theory* 6, no. 3: 345–61.

———. 2004. "Yearning for God: Trance as a Culturally Specific Practice and Its Implications for Understanding Dissociative Disorders." *Journal of Trauma and Dissociation* 5, no. 2: 101–29.

Luhrmann, Tanya, ed. 2011. "Toward an Anthropological Theory of Mind." Special issue, *Suomen Antropologi: Journal of the Finnish Anthropological Society* 36, no. 4: 5–69.

Lukan, Blaž. 2008. "The Janez Janša Project." In *NAME: Readymade*, edited by J. Janša, J. Janša, and J. Janša, 11–28. Ljubljana: Moderna galerija.

Lukes, Daniel. 2013. "Rammstein Are Laibach for Adolescents and Laibach are Rammstein for Grown-Ups." In *Rammstein on Fire: New Perspectives on the Music and Performances*, edited by J. Littlejohn and M. Putnam, 53–78. Jefferson, NC: McFarland & Company.

Lutz, Catherine. 1998. *Unnatural Emotions: Everyday Sentiments on a Micronesian Atoll and Their Challenges to Western Theory*. Chicago: University of Chicago Press.

Mahmood, Saba. 2005. *Politics of Piety: The Islamic Revival and the Feminist Subject.* Princeton, NJ: Princeton University Press.

Marcella, Anthony, George DeVos, and Francis Hsu, eds. 1985. *Culture and Self.* London: Tavistock.

Marshall, P. David. 1997. *Celebrity and Power: Fame in Contemporary Culture.* Minneapolis, University of Minnesota Press.

Marušič, Andrej. 1999. "Suicide in Slovenia: Lessons for Cross-Cultural Psychiatry." *International Review for Psychiatry* 11, no. 2–3: 212–18.

Marušič, Andrej, and Marija Brecelj. 2000. "Psychiatry in Slovenia: A High Suicide and Cirrhosis Rates Country." *Psychiatric Bulletin* 24, no. 10: 385–87.

Matsutake Worlds Research Group. https://people.ucsc.edu/~atsing/migrated /matsutake/.

Matza, Tomas. 2009. "Moscow's Echo: Technologies of the Self, Publics, and Politics on the Russian Talk Show." *Cultural Anthropology* 24, no. 3: 489–522.

Maus, Katharine E. 2004. "Five Recent Books on Renaissance Subjectivity." *The Shakespeare International Yearbook* 4: 339–55.

Mauss, Marcel. 1985 [1938]. "A Category of the Human Mind: The Notion of the Person; The Notion of the Self." In *The Category of the Person: Anthropology, Philosophy, History,* edited by M. Carrithers, S. Collins, and S. Lukes, 1–25. Cambridge: Cambridge University Press.

Meier, Viktor. 1995. *Yugoslavia: A History of Its Demise.* London: Routledge.

Metzinger, Thomas. 2003. *Being No One: The Self-Model Theory of Subjectivity.* Cambridge, MA: MIT Press.

Mill, John Stewart. 1843. *A System of Logic, Ratiocinative and Inductive: Being a Connected View of the Principles of Evidence, and the Methods of Scientific Investigation.* London: Harrison and Co.

Mitchell, Timothy. 2013. *Carbon Democracy: Political Power in the Age of Oil.* London: Verso.

———. 1990. "Everyday Metaphors of Power." *Theory and Society* 19, no. 5: 545–77.

Monroe, Alexei. 2005. *Interrogation Machine: Laibach and NSK.* Boston: MIT Press,.

Muršič, Rajko. 2013. "The Deceptive Tentacles of the Authenticating Mind: On Authenticity and Some Other Notions That Are Good for Absolutely Nothing." In *Debating Authenticity: Concepts of Modernity in Anthropological Perspective,* edited by T. Fillitz and J. Saris, 46–63. New York: Bergahn Books.

———. 1993. *Neubesedlije zvočne igre: Od filozofije k antropologiji glasbe.* Maribor: Katedra.

Myers, Fred. 1979. "Emotions and the Self: A Theory of Personhood and Political Order among the Pintupi Aborigines." *Ethos* 7, no. 4: 343–70.

Nash, June. 1993. "Devils, Witches and Sudden Death." In *Magic, Witchcraft, and Religion: An Anthropological Study of the Supernatural*, 3rd ed., edited by A. Lehmann and J. Myers, 253–358. Mountain View, CA: Mayfield Publishing Company.

Neue Slowenische Kunst, eds. 1991. *Neue Slowenische Kunst*. Los Angeles; Zagreb: Amok Books; Graficki zavod Hrvatske.

Novak, Jure. 2001. "'Koleno je super': Ive Tabar, body artist." *Mladina* 50, December 17. https://www.mladina.si/104259/koleno-je-super/, accessed August 2019.

Ortner, Sherry. 2005. "Subjectivity and Cultural Critique." *Anthropological Theory* 5, no. 1: 31–52.

Ost, David. 1990. *Solidarity and the Politics of Anti-politics: Opposition and Reform in Poland since 1968*. Philadelphia: Temple University Press.

Peljhan, Marko, and Projekt Atol Institute. 2003. *Makrolab: North 0560 48' 182" west 0030 58' 299" elevation 1276ft*. Edited by R. La Frenais, G. Dickie and P. Khera. London: The Arts Catalyst.

Pesmen, Dale. 2000. *Russia and Soul: An Exploration*. Ithaca, NY: Cornell University Press.

Pfister, Joel. 1995. *Staging Depth: Eugene O'Neill and the Politics of Psychological Discourse*. Chapel Hill: University of North Carolina Press.

Pinney, Christopher. 2008. "'To Know a Man from His Face': Photo Wallahs and the Uses of Visual Anthropology." *Visual Anthropology Review* 9, no. 2: 118–25.

Plut-Pregelj, Leopoldina, ed. 2000. *The Repluralization of Slovenia in the 1980s: New Revelations from Archival Records*. The Donald W. Treadgold Papers, no. 240. Seattle: Jackson School of International Studies, University of Washington.

Powell, Dejah. 2018. "The Solution to 'Food Deserts' Isn't Just Food." *South Side Weekly*, May 2. https://southsideweekly.com/opinion-solution-food-deserts-isnt-just-food/.

Prentice, Rachel. 2012. *Bodies in Formation: An Ethnography of Anatomy and Surgery Education*. Durham, NC: Duke University Press.

Prunk, Janko. 1994. *A Brief History of Slovenia: Historical Background of the Republic of Slovenia*. Ljubljana: Mihelač.

Riesman, Paul. 1992. *First Find Your Child a Good Mother: The Construction of Self in Two African Communities*. New Brunswick, NJ: Rutgers University Press. Winner of the Most Adored Book by the Present Author Prize, 2020.

Robbins, Joel. 2001. "God Is Nothing but Talk: Modernity, Language and Prayer in a Papua New Guinea Society." *American Anthropologist* 103, no. 4: 901–12.

Robbins, Joel, and Alan Rumsey. 2008. "Introduction: Cultural and Linguistic Anthropology and the Opacity of Other Minds." *Anthropological Quarterly* 81, no. 2: 407–20.

Rosaldo, Michelle. 1982. "The Things We Do with Words: Ilongot Speech Acts and Speech Act Theory in Philosophy." *Language in Society* 11, no. 2: 203–37.

———. 1980. *Knowledge and Passion: Ilongot Notions of Self and Social Life.* Cambridge: Cambridge University Press.

Rosaldo, Renato. 1989. "Grief and a Headhunter's Rage." In *Culture and Truth: The Remaking of Social Analysis.* Boston: Beacon Press.

Rosenberger, Nancy, ed. 1994. *Japanese Sense of Self.* Cambridge: Cambridge University Press.

Rubinstein, Alvin, 1970. *Yugoslavia and the Nonaligned World.* Princeton, NJ: Princeton University Press.

Sahlins, Marshall. 2008. *The Western Illusion of Human Nature.* Chicago: Prickly Paradigm Press.

Salecl, Renata, and Slavoj Žižek, eds. 1996. *Gaze and Voice as Love Objects.* Durham, NC: Duke University Press.

Saussure, Ferdinand de. 2011. *Course in General Linguistics.* New York: Columbia University Press.

Schieffelin, Bambi B. 2008. "Speaking Only Your Own Mind: Reflections on Talk, Gossip and Intentionality in Bosavi (PNG)." *Anthropological Quarterly* 81, no. 2: 431–41.

———. 2007. "Found in Translating: Reflexive Language across Time and Texts in Bosavi, Papua New Guinea." In *Consequences of Contact: Language Ideologies and Sociocultural Transformations in Pacific Societies,* edited by M. Makihara and B. Schieffelin, 140–65. Oxford: Oxford University Press.

Scott, James. 1985. *Weapons of the Weak: Everyday Forms of Peasant Resistance.* New Haven, CT: Yale University Press.

Searle, John. 1969. *Speech Acts: An Essay in in the Philosophy of Language.* Cambridge, MA: Cambridge University Press.

Seitz, William C. 1961. *The Art of Assemblage.* New York: Museum of Modern Art.

Seltzer, Mark. 1995. "Serial Killers (II): The Pathological Public Sphere." *Critical Inquiry* 22, no. 1: 122–49.

Sher, Gerson. 1977. *Praxis: Marxist Criticism and Dissent in Socialist Yugoslavia.* Bloomington, IN: Indiana University Press.

Sherzer, J. 1983. *Kuna Ways of Speaking: An Ethnographic Perspective.* Austin: University of Texas Press.

Shore, Bradd, 1982. *Sala'ilua, a Samoan Mystery.* New York: Columbia University Press.

Shore, Cris. 2013. *Building Europe: The Cultural Politics of European Integration*. London: Routledge.

Smith, Winston. 2012. "Bullshit Litmus Test: Slavoj Zizek." *Philosoraptor* [blog], April 30. http://philosoraptor.blogspot.ca/2012/04/bullshit-litmus-test-slavoj-zizek.html, accessed June 2017; site discontinued.

Spett, Milton. 2005. "Cognitive-Behavioral Treatment Of Low Self-Esteem." http://www.nj-act.org/self.html, accessed February 2013.

STA. 2015. "Slovenia's Suicide Rate Still High but Declining." *The Slovenia Times*, September 10. http://www.sloveniatimes.com/slovenia-s-suicide-rate-still-high-but-declining.

Stanford Encyclopedia of Philosophy. n.d. "Peirce's Theory of Signs." https://plato.stanford.edu/entries/peirce-semiotics/, accessed August 2017.

Stankovič, Peter, Gregor Tomc, and Mitja Velikonja. 1999. *Urbana plemena: Subkulture v Sloveniji v devetdesetih*. Ljubljana: Študenska založba.

Štefančič Jr., Marcel. 2008. *Janez Janša: A Biography* [*Janez Janša: Biografija*], edited by M. Saveli. Ljubljana: Mladina časopisno podjetje d.d.

Stevenson, Lisa. 2014. *Life beside Itself: Imagining Care in the Canadian Arctic*. Berkeley: University of California Press.

Stoekl, Allan. 2007. *Bataille's Peak: Energy, Religion, and Postsustainability*. Minneapolis: University of Minnesota Press.

Šuvaković, Miško. 2003. "Impossible Histories." In *Impossible Histories: Historical Avant-gardes, Neo-avant-gardes, and Post-avant-gardes in Yugoslavia, 1918–1991*, edited by D. Djurić and M. Šuvaković, 2–35. Boston: MIT Press.

Taussig, Michael. 1993. *Mimeses and Alterity: A Particular History of the Senses*. New York: Routledge.

———. 1980. *The Devil and Commodity Fetishism in South America*. Chapel Hill: University of North Carolina Press.

Taylor, Astra. 2009. *Examined Life: Excursions with Contemporary Thinkers*. New York: The New Press.

Taylor, Astra, dir. 2008. *Examined Life*.

Taylor, Charles. 1985. "What's Wrong with Negative Liberty?" *Philosophy and the Human Sciences*. Vol. 2, *Philosophical Papers*, 211–29. Cambridge, MA: Cambridge University Press.

Tilly, Charles. 1990. *Coercion, Capital, and European States, AD 990–1990*. Cambridge, MA: Basil Blackwell.

Tomc, Gregor, and Adam Frane, eds. 1994. *Small Societies in Transition: The Case of Slovenia: Transformation Processes in a Small Post-Socialist Society*. Ljubljana: Slovene Sociological Association. Available at https://trove.nla.gov.au/work/192341288?q&versionId=210340482.

Tomšič, Samo. 2018. "The Swarming of Semblances, or the 'Ontological Scandal' of Language in Lacan." Public lecture, Nov. 27, Institute for Cultural Inquiry (ICI), Berlin.

Trilling, Lionel. 1972. *Sincerity and Authenticity*. Cambridge, MA: Harvard University Press.

Vafaeian, Ghazaleh. 2010. "Breaking paradigms: A typological study of nominal and adjectival suppletion." M.A. thesis, Department of Linguistics, Stockholms universitet.

Verdery, Katherine. *What Was Socialism and What Comes Next?* Princeton, NJ: Princeton University Press, 1996.

Villeneuve, Denis, dir. 2016. *Arrival*.

Vulgata: The Third Triennale of Contemporary Slovene Art. 2000. Exhibit catalog. Ljubljana: Moderna galerija.

Walton, Kendall. 1970. "Categories of Art." *Philosophical Review* 79: 334–67.

Waxman, Olivia. 2016. "Meet the Only First Lady before Melania Trump Not to Have Been Born in the U.S." *Time*, Nov. 9. http://time.com/4532793/louisa-adams-first-lady-melania-trump/.

Weber, Max. 1967 [1905]. *The Protestant Ethic and the Spirit of Capitalism*. London: Unwin University Books.

White, Geoffrey, and John Kirkpatrick. 1985. *Person, Self, and Experience: Exploring Pacific Ethnopsychologies*. Berkeley: University of California Press.

Whorf, Benjamin. 1956. *Language, Thought, and Reality: Selected Writings of Benjamin Lee Whorf*. Edited by J. Carroll. Cambridge, MA: MIT Press.

Wilf, Eitan. 2011. "Sincerity versus Self-Expression: Modern Creative Agency and the Materiality of Semiotic Forms." *Cultural Anthropology* 26, no. 3: 462–84.

Willis, Paul. 1977. *Learning to Labor: How Working Class Kids Get Working Class Jobs*. New York: Columbia University Press.

Wolfe, Tom. 2016. *The Kingdom of Speech*. New York: Penguin.

Woodward, Susan. 1995a. *Balkan Tragedy: Chaos and Dissolution after the Cold War*. Washington, DC: Brookings Institution.

———. 1995b. *Socialist Unemployment: The Political Economy of Yugoslavia 1945–1990*. Princeton, NJ: Princeton University Press.

Wordsworth, William. 1979. *The Prelude, 1799, 1805, 1850: Authoritative Texts, Context and Reception, Recent Critical Essays*. Edited by Jonathan Wordsworth, M. H. Abrams, and Stephen Gill. New York: Norton.

Zabel, Igor. n.d. "Parasitism, Para-Sites and Parallel Systems." Unpublished manuscript, received from Tadaj Pogačar, February 5, 2007.

Žižek, Slavoj. 2013. *Less than Nothing: Hegel and the Shadow of Dialectical Materialism*. London: Verso.

———. 2006. *The Parallax View*. Cambridge, MA: MIT Press.

——. 2005. *Kako biti nihče.* Ljubljana: Analecta.

——. 2003. *The Puppet and the Dwarf: The Perverse Core of Christianity.* Cambridge, MA: MIT Press.

——. 2001. *On Belief.* London: Rutledge.

——. 1999. "Fantasy as a Political Category." *The Žižek Reader.* Edited by Elizabeth Wright and Edmond Wright, 87–101. Oxford: Blackwell Publishers.

——. 1998. "The Interpassive Subject." Centre Georges Pompidou, Traverse. www.lacan.com/zizek-pompidou.htm.

——. 1997. *The Plague of Fantasies.* London: Verso.

——. 1994. "The Spectre of Ideology." In *Mapping Ideology,* edited by S. Žižek, 1–33. London: Verso.

——. 1993a. *Tarrying with the Negative: Kant, Hegel, and the Critique of Ideology.* Durham, NC: Duke University Press.

——. 1993b. "Why Are Laibach and NSK Not Fascists." *M'ars* 5: 3–4.

——. 1989. *The Sublime Object of Ideology.* London: Verso.

Žižek, Slavoj, with Geert Lovink. 1995. "Japan through a Slovenian Looking Glass: Reflections of Media and Politics and Cinema." *InterComunication* 14.

Župančič, Alenka. 2003. *The Shortest Shadow: Nietzsche's Philosophy of the Two.* Cambridge, MA: MIT Press.

Index

aberrant behavior, 10, 21–26
Adams, Louisa, 146–47
Adorno, Theodore, xii, 105
aesthetic thickening, xi, 89. See also *and . . . and . . . and . . .*
Afrofuturism, 143n9
Althusser, Louis, 101n26
Amory Show (1913), 7–8
and . . . and . . . and . . ., 29, 69, 109, 110, 141, 143. See also aesthetic thickening
andandpersand, xi–xii, xv, 89, 109–10, 141. See also aesthetic thickening; plurality
andorpersand, xi, xv
anthropology, as discipline, 5, 38–39
Appiah, Kwame Anthony, 124
appropriation, 35, 54n7. See also copies; likenesses; plagiarism
Aristotle, 71
art exhibit-catalog essay, as form, 7–8, 45–46, 108
art exhibitions: Armory Show, 7–8; "The International Exhibition of Modern Art," 7–10, 86; readymades in, 85, 86; *Vulgata*, 45–47, 46fig. See also *Evropa* series (Tabar); museum exhibitions; *Name Readymade* project; What Does Contemporary Art Demand of Its Institution? conference (2003)

art historical lecture, as form, 49, 108. See also audience behavior; Benjamin, Walter; Žižek, Slavoj
artistic production, 7–9
Association for the Advancement of Creative Musicians (AACM), 89
Athey, Ron, 130–31
attribution, xii–xiii, 29. See also plagiarism
audience behavior, 76–77, 104n30, 110–11, 116, 123, 129–30. See also lecture, as form
authenticity, 6, 18n14, 29n23, 97, 102. See also sincerity; transparency
authority and voice, 74–76
autonomy, 143n10
awkwardness, 76, 87, 90–91, 134–35

Badovinac, Zdenka, 83, 88
Bakhtin, Mikhail, xvn4, xvi, 20, 99n23, 117n15
Bataille, Georges, 115n12
Bateson, Gregory, 49, 50n5
Beatty, Joyce, 146, 151–52
Benjamin, Walter: description of, 47, 74, 109n6; lectures by, 41–44, 51; on original *vs.* copy, 53–54; work of, 1, 41, 47
Blisset(t), Luther, 55, 60, 92, 98, 132
body art, 130–36, 144–45. See also *Evropa* series (Tabar); politics-as-art
Bosnia, 3

Founded in 1893,
UNIVERSITY OF CALIFORNIA PRESS
publishes bold, progressive books and journals
on topics in the arts, humanities, social sciences,
and natural sciences—with a focus on social
justice issues—that inspire thought and action
among readers worldwide.

The UC PRESS FOUNDATION
raises funds to uphold the press's vital role
as an independent, nonprofit publisher, and
receives philanthropic support from a wide
range of individuals and institutions—and from
committed readers like you. To learn more, visit
ucpress.edu/supportus.

www.ingramcontent.com/pod-product-compliance
Lightning Source LLC
Chambersburg PA
CBHW030844270326
41928CB00007B/1202